Glenna Steinberg

Once They Had a Country

Europe at the outbreak of World War II. Königsberg, then in East Prussia, is now Kaliningrad, Russia; Osterode, then in East Prussia, is now Ostróda, Poland; Stettin, then in Pomerania, is now Szczecin, Poland.

Once They Had a Country

Two Teenage Refugees in the Second World War

Muriel R. Gillick

THE UNIVERSITY OF ALABAMA PRESS
Tuscaloosa

Copyright © 2010
The University of Alabama Press
Tuscaloosa, Alabama 35487-0380

Manufactured in the United States of America

Typeface: Caslon

∞

The paper on which this book is printed meets the minimum requirements of American National Standard for Information Sciences-Permanence of Paper for Printed Library Materials, ANSI Z39.48-1984.

Library of Congress Cataloging-in-Publication Data

Gillick, Muriel R., 1951–
Once they had a country : two teenage refugees in the Second World War / Muriel R. Gillick.
p. cm.
Includes bibliographical references and index.
ISBN 978-0-8173-5620-0 (pbk. : alk. paper) — ISBN 978-0-8173-8399-2 (electronic)
1. Garfunkel, Hans. 2. Wulff, Ilse. 3. Jewish children—Germany—Biography. 4. Jewish refugees—Germany—Biography. 5. World War, 1939-1945—Jews—Biography. I. Title.
DS134.42.G374 2010
940.53′180922—dc22
[B]

2010020151

For the children of La Hille, their children, and their children's children

Once we had a country and we thought it fair, . . .
We cannot go there now, my dear, we cannot go there now.
—"Refugee Blues," W. H. Auden

Contents

Acknowledgments

My greatest debt is to my parents, who spent countless hours being interviewed for this book. Sometimes the memories were painful, but they let me probe nonetheless, in the hope that their story would be recorded for future generations. My research also turned up new facts that were difficult for them to learn—such as where and how my grandmother Paula Lonky Garfunkel died, and what life was like in Shanghai, where my other grandmother, Lotte Berndt Wulff, spent the last six years of her life.

I appreciate having had the opportunity to interview other children of La Hille, including Walter Reed (the former Werner Rindsberg) and two who are now sadly deceased, Addi Nussbaum and Inge Berlin. My thanks to Peter Black, senior historian at the United States Holocaust Memorial Museum, for pointing me to some crucial reference materials.

Several friends read part or all of an earlier version of the manuscript: the comments of Jim Sabin, Bob Levin, Joni Blum, and Angelo Volandes were helpful and encouraging. My sons, Daniel, Jeremy, and Jonathan, also served as valuable and critical readers. I am especially grateful to Jeremy, a future historian, for carefully preparing the index. To my mother goes a second thank-you for having read the entire manuscript through twice, with special attention to accuracy, and also for helping me decipher and translate many of the letters from her parents and from my father's parents.

The staff of the University of Alabama Press believed in the importance not only of telling my parents' story but also of emphasizing the refugee theme. I was fortunate to have Anne R. Gibbons as a copy editor: her perfect pitch repeatedly rescued my language from veering off key.

Finally, I would never have undertaken this project without the strong persuasive powers of my husband, Larry. He thought I should take the plunge and got me started by helping me find an appropriate digital recorder. His confidence remained unshaken as successive agents and publishers assured me there was no market for any more "Holocaust memoirs." And he listened patiently over the years as I told and retold the stories of the various remarkable discoveries that made the end product feasible.

Once They Had a Country

Introduction

January 30, 1939, was bitter cold in Cologne, Germany, but that did not deter thousands from marching in a parade celebrating the sixth anniversary of Adolf Hitler's accession to power. Thousands more lined the streets to cheer on the brown-shirted *Sturmabteilung* (SA) and the black-uniformed *Schutzstaffel* (SS) as they goose-stepped through the streets, playing martial music, carrying banners forecasting glory for Germany, and waving swastika-emblazoned flags. The Garfunkel family—Julius, his wife, Paula, and their fourteen-year-old son Hans—did not watch the parade, though they no doubt heard the ecstatic cheers of the crowds from their hotel room. They assuredly did not listen to Hitler's speech at the Reichstag in Berlin, broadcast on the radio that evening, in which he threatened that "if the international Jewish financiers in and outside Europe should succeed in plunging the nations once more into a world war, then the result will not be the Bolshevization of the earth and the victory of Jewry, but the annihilation of the Jewish race in Europe."[1]

The Garfunkels were in Cologne to bring Hans to the designated meeting place for some fifty children from all over Germany and Austria who had secured passage on a Kindertransport, a children's rescue mission, to Belgium. Julius Garfunkel had obtained permission to accompany his son from Berlin, where the family lived, to Cologne. And though most hotels were off-limits to Jews by that time, Julius Garfunkel had managed to procure two hotel rooms for the night by brazenly clicking his heels, giving the Nazi salute, and demanding accommodations for his family.

The following day was bright and sunny. The Garfunkels brought their son to the Jewish Community Center, where he received a tag to wear with a number that matched a corresponding label on his one small suitcase. They felt confident they were doing the right thing: Hans would travel with the other children to Brussels where he would be safe, safe from the SA with their rubber truncheons and rifle butts, comfortable in the home of a distant cousin of his father's. Maybe it was the Belgian cousin that had led them to choose a Kindertransport to Belgium instead of one to England, where the vast majority of the 10,000 children who escaped from Nazi-controlled Germany, Austria, and Czechoslovakia were sent in the nine months before the outbreak of world war.[2]

That same day, Hermann and Lotte Wulff traveled with their daughter, Ilse, from their home in Stettin, a port city near the mouth of the Oder River on the Baltic Sea, to Berlin. They were joined by a small circle of close relatives: her *Onkel* Erich and *Tante* Trude—her mother's brother and his wife—and her beloved seventy-seven-year-old grandfather. The family gathered to say goodbye to Ilse, who had just turned thirteen on Christmas Day the month before. Like the Garfunkels, the Wulffs had realized after Kristallnacht, the nationwide pogrom on November 9–10, 1938, that Jews had no future in Germany and had made arrangements for their child to leave Germany via a Kindertransport to Belgium.

Ilse's parents handed her over to a woman from the Jewish Refugee Committee who was escorting several children from Berlin to Cologne, the central meeting point. Like Hans and the other children, Ilse was given a placard to wear around her neck bearing the same number as her suitcase. And then she said goodbye, a quiet girl who had not yet reached puberty and who would not have her mother to teach her about menstruation or give her piano lessons or tuck her in to bed at night.

Twelve years later, Hans and Ilse would become my parents.

I grew up with this story and many others from those early tumultuous years of my parents' lives. My parents were not like the many adults who never spoke of their past or the smaller number who made up new identities for themselves, in extreme cases bringing up their children to think of themselves as Christian.[3] By the time I was in preschool, I knew I was Jewish, and by kindergarten I had heard about Hitler and the Nazis. For my mother, one of the most thrilling moments of my childhood occurred when I came home from school at age seven or so and asked her, "What did you say was the name of that bad guy when you lived in Germany?"—proof both that she had told me about her past and that for me, Hitler was history. But the version of my parents' past that became part of me was essentially a children's edition of their biography. And because the outlines of their history were so familiar, I never thought to ask them much about their early years after I myself was an adult.

When my parents turned eighty, I realized that if I was going to find out more of their story and pass it on to my children, I better not delay. With some trepidation—I had been told this could be a stressful, even a painful process—I bought a small digital recorder and a blank notebook and began interviewing my parents. I worried about the accuracy of their recollections so many years after the events. But the prominent Holocaust scholar Lawrence Langer had posed the question I had been concerned about: "How credible can a reawakened memory be that tries to revive events so many decades after they occurred?" and then answered his own question: "There is no need to revive what has never died."[4] Eva Hoffman, another eminent writer about the period, echoed Langer's sentiments: "In a sense, such memories are not memories at all since their content has not been relegated to the past."[5] Reassured that I could count on the accuracy of what my parents remembered, I nonetheless adopted the motto "trust but verify." The real problem was that their recollections were incomplete. I decided I needed to fill in many of the missing details and turned, as everyone does today, to a Web-based search.

~

I went online, typing in "Jewish life Stettin 1930s." The first hit was a query posted on the website of the Association of Jewish Refugees, an organization of British Jews. Incredulous, I read "Ilse Woolf went to Jewish school in Stettin with my grandmother Ruth Isaac. Left on children's transport to Holland. Does anyone know what happened to Ilse?"

My mother's name was Ilse Wulff and she left Germany in 1939 on a children's transport to Belgium.

I showed the notice to my mother, who was at first convinced it must refer to someone else. "My name is spelled 'Wulff,'" she protested, "and I didn't go to Holland," she reminded me. But then she realized that the grandmother who as a child had been friends with "Ilse Woolf" was her old friend Ruth Isaac. "I remember her very well. She had a twin sister, Eva. They left on a Kindertransport to England. Their father was taken to a concentration camp after Kristallnacht." My mother admitted the notice had to refer to her. But when she sent email to the contact listed, it bounced back.

Undeterred, my mother contacted the Association of Jewish Refugees. The office had no other address for the granddaughter, but they did have an address for Ruth Isaac: the London house to which she had moved in 1947. My mother didn't think it very likely that Ruth still lived at that address, but just for fun, she mailed her a letter.

Two weeks later, Ruth Isaac Löwenthal replied. The two women in their eighties began to correspond, reigniting their childhood friendship. Sadly, Ruth's twin sister, who had lived in the United States—in Florida—and had died just months earlier.

Discovering Ruth was a boon for my mother but didn't provide me with much information about Stettin in the 1930s. The critical discovery, the treasure trove that made this book possible, was what my father told me was "a few letters" he had written to an American cousin during the war. I had heard about Cousin Bessie in Chicago and the letters he had sent her. I also knew that when Bessie died a few years ago, her daughter, Phylllis Tinsley, rescued all the letters she had received from Hans Garfunkel, beginning with his letter of introduction written shortly after Kristallnacht in November 1938 and ending with the announcement of his arrival in New York City almost exactly nine years later. Altogether, my father had written more than forty letters. Bessie had also saved the telegrams she got from my father's parents, a letter from my father's brother in Brazil, and other treasures. To my delight, the letters from my father, with one exception, were in English, an awkward, sometimes comical schoolboy English, but readily comprehensible nonetheless. Not only that, but they were all perfectly legible—many were even typed. And there, in black and white, were the answers to most of my unanswered questions, questions such as how and when he was notified of his mother's death and what he felt when the war finally came to an end. In September 1944 my father told Cousin Bessie that he had received a letter from the Jewish Council of Prague letting him know what had become of his mother. And on May 21, 1945, he wrote: "War is over in Europe! I can't still believe it!"

I now had accounts by a teenage boy of his experiences as well as his commentary about those experiences and his reactions to world events. These ranged from acerbic remarks about Swiss labor camps to a sentimental response to Franklin Roosevelt's reelection in 1944. Then my mother casually mentioned that she, too, had "a few documents" stemming from her years as a refugee in Switzerland. Several years earlier, she had requested copies of her file from the Department of Justice and Police in Switzerland. Shortly after September 11, 2001, in the midst of the American anthrax scare, she received in the mail a bulky package of uncertain provenance. With some degree of anxiety, she brought it to the post office for the authorities to open. Inside the envelope was no ominous white powder but instead an enormous number of documents, from her arrest record when she crossed the Swiss border on January 1, 1943, to the letter from December 1945 congratulating her on being "repatriated" to her "fatherland" and demanding that she appear at the Basel train station at a specified time to depart for Germany. Included were handwritten notes from my mother, age nineteen, respectfully requesting that she be permitted to withdraw funds from her own bank account to buy clothes and other essentials.

The materials were so remarkable that I asked my parents, somewhat petulantly, why they had not requested the analogous documents from my father's file. It turned out they had, and after rummaging through a few more drawers, they turned over another sheaf of papers. The entry tickets and the release tickets from each work camp to which my father had been sent were all there, providing the structure I needed to be sure of the exact timeline of his stay in Switzerland. And since requests for anything related to refugees were addressed to the Swiss Department of Justice and Police, I found letters from my father imploring the authorities to release him from the camps. I even found reports from one medical doctor and two psychiatrists who treated him summarizing their clinical findings—and asking the department to reimburse them for their consultations.

Other documents, long dormant, mysteriously resurfaced as I began work on this project. My mother found two poems she had written as a young teen while living with a group of a hundred Jewish children in southern France. She had saved a few letters sent to her by her mother from China, where she was a refugee for the duration of the war. And in the only history of the Château de la Hille, the castle where my parents lived from 1941 to 1942, I found several letters my father had sent to the former director of the children's home, one mailed from a Swiss labor camp and another from Brazil, where he had sought refuge after the war. In those letters, he commented angrily on the Swiss—"Switzerland may be 'God's own country' for tourists with a lot of money, but that's not how it's been for refugees"—and perspicaciously about the atomic bomb—"It is certain that these new and terrible weapons played a big part in Japan's surrender, but nevertheless, I'm not thrilled about this invention, because it's really too dangerous to entrust to human hands."[6]

As I delved deeper and deeper into my parents' story, I was struck that it was not just another story about remarkable escapes and the triumph of the human spirit, about courage and decency amid unimaginable barbarism. It was not so much a Holocaust story, or even a war story, as it was a refugee story.

When my parents left Germany in the winter of 1939, they were fleeing racial and religious persecution. They traveled to Belgium at a time when war had not yet broken out. And when war did erupt in September 1939, it was in faraway Poland; Belgium was still at peace. Once the German armies crossed into Belgium in May 1940, my parents fled to France, refugees once again. And even after France signed an armistice with the Nazis that same summer, southern France, where my parents lived in a children's colony, remained in the "unoccupied" sector. When their safety was threatened in 1942, particularly after German troops moved into Vichy France, they sought refuge again, this time in neutral Switzerland, where they stayed for the remainder of the war. And after the war, when the Swiss enforced their policy of "transmigration" (refugees could only stay in Switzerland temporarily), my father moved to Brazil and later to the United States; my mother went directly to New York.

In each of the countries where they sought refuge, they had to adapt to a new culture and often to a new language. They encountered scorn, prejudice, and hostility, as well as kindness and friendship. They endured poverty, insecurity, and fear. In short, they faced the same traumas that most refugees experience, including refugees in the twenty-first century.

While I was doing the research for this book, I read regularly in the newspapers about the world's newest refugees. Every month, 50,000 Iraqis fled their country, some simply in search of a better life, but most to escape persecution along ethnic or religious lines. By 2006 approximately 1.5 million refugees from Iraq had already made their homes in Syria and another 750,000 in Jordan, plus lesser numbers in Egypt (100,000), Iran (54,000), Lebanon (40,000), and Turkey (10,000).[7] At the same time, some of the several million Afghani refugees who had found refuge in Pakistan or Iran were at last able to return home, no longer afraid the regime would maim or kill them. And every day, thousands of people were fleeing the Sudan, where they were at risk of rape, enslavement, or murder at the hands of the Janjaweed because of their ethnicity.

For all the enormous differences between Afghan tribes today and middle-class German Jews in the 1930s, they share the experience of being strangers in strange lands. Their losses, their anxieties, their struggle to adapt are part of the all-too-universal nature of the refugee experience. Perhaps by reading my parents' refugee story, contemporary Americans will better grasp the plight of the 8.4 million people who currently meet the United Nations definition of a refugee: someone who "owing to well-founded fear of being persecuted for reasons of race, religion, nationality, membership of a particular social group or political opinion, is outside the country of his nationality and is unable, or owing to such fear . . . unwilling to return to it."[8]

Today's refugees, unlike my parents, have some protection, stemming from the Convention Relating to the Status of Refugees. Adopted by the UN General Assembly in 1951, extended to apply more broadly in a protocol added in 1967, and reaffirmed by the signatory states in a declaration issued in 2001, the convention lays out the international law governing the treatment of refugees.

By the time I got around to researching the history of international refugee law, I did not expect any more surprise discoveries. But when I actually read the text of the 1951 Convention Relating to the Status of Refugees, I was stunned. The centerpiece of the convention is article 33, the prohibition of expulsion of a refugee to a territory where his life or liberty is in danger. The convention calls this *refouler:* "No Contracting State shall expel or return ('refouler') a refugee in any manner whatsoever to the frontiers of territories where his life or freedom would be threatened on account of his race, religion, nationality, membership of a particular social group or political opinion."[9]

"Refouler" was what the Swiss police threatened seventeen-year-old Ilse Wulff with if they could prove she was over sixteen, and what they did to several of the teens from her children's colony who were caught trying to cross the border from France into Switzerland. To understand the origin of the provisions of the convention, all that's needed is to read my parents' story. The treatment they—and many others—received at the hands of the countries where they sought refuge is precisely what the United Nations agreed to outlaw.

The other provisions of the convention, one after another, are clearly responses to what the countries of the world *failed* to do for refugees such as my parents during the Second World War. Among other requirements, states that have signed the convention are obligated to provide elementary education for refugee children, to allow refugees to hold jobs for which they receive a fair wage, and to provide refugees with travel documents. The convention may not go far enough in helping today's refugees, and the office of the United Nations high commissioner for refugees, which is supposed to help implement the convention, may be limited in its resources and its power, but it is a magnificent start and it was woefully absent between 1939 and 1945.[10]

What follows is my parents' saga of harrowing escapes, overwhelming losses, surprising romance, and enriching community in a series of different countries—plus the story of their parents' experiences as internally displaced persons in Germany (Hans's parents) and as refugees in Shanghai (Ilse's parents). Its value, I hope, is in providing a window on life during wartime and life as a refugee. It is through stories such as this that the contemporary reader can begin to imagine what it is like to be uprooted from one's country because of a "well-founded fear of persecution" and learn to appreciate the origins of the contemporary system of aid to refugees.

1

Becoming Refugees

> The term "refugee" shall apply to any person who . . . owing to well-founded fear of being persecuted for reasons of race, religion, nationality, membership of a particular social group or political opinion, is outside the country of his nationality.
>
> —Convention Relating to the Status of Refugees, Article 1, 1951

The train station in Cologne was a noisy, chaotic place, filled with Germans fleeing the country and with Gestapo trying to prevent them from taking anything of value with them. On that momentous day in January 1939 when thirteen-year-old Ilse and fourteen-year-old Hans left their homeland forever, it was filled with soldiers, perhaps on their way to the Czech border. A mere six weeks later, German troops would cross that border and occupy all of Czechoslovakia, completing the takeover they had begun in October 1938 with their annexation of the Sudetenland, a part of Czechoslovakia with a large German-speaking population.

In Cologne, Ilse and the other Jewish children arriving from Berlin joined the rest of the group headed for Belgium. In Ilse's compartment, a young girl started crying bitterly. Determined to be brave, Ilse stifled her tears. Instead, she ate the white chocolate her family had given her as a special treat for the trip. After the first bite, her stomach began to churn. She opened the window to get some fresh air, oblivious to the freezing temperature outside. It would be a long time before Ilse, a fervent chocolate enthusiast, would again be able to eat white chocolate.

In a different compartment of the same train, Hans sat with other German Jewish boys. He didn't know any of them but he didn't feel sad or frightened. After all, his parents had assured him they would soon have visas permitting them to join him in Belgium and they would travel together to the United States. He had no way of knowing that the prospects were dim for obtaining visas for Belgium or anywhere else, even though just a week earlier, Reinhard Heydrich, head of the SS—who would be nicknamed "the Blond Beast" by the Nazis and called "Hangman Heydrich" by others—had been ordered to speed up the emigration process for German Jews.

Ilse also believed her parents would join her soon. In fact, most of the parents who handed over their children to an uncertain future, though one which they felt confident would be better than whatever awaited them in

Germany, told them they would soon be reunited. A girl Ilse would get to know in Belgium recorded in her diary that her parents reassured her, "Don't be sad; we will follow you soon."[1] Another child who had left Cologne for Brussels several weeks earlier reported that her mother's last words were that they would be together again in America.[2]

What Ilse did not know was that her parents had already made arrangements to leave for Shanghai, the only place in the world to which German Jews could immigrate without a visa. They would later tell her they hadn't taken her along because children were not allowed to travel to Shanghai. Much later, she would learn that was untrue: many families who escaped to China took their children. Michael Blumenthal, who would become U.S. secretary of the treasury under President Jimmy Carter, left Berlin with his parents in April 1939, when he was thirteen years old, bound for Shanghai. But the Wulffs believed that Shanghai, with its poverty and lawlessness, was no place for a cultured German girl; surely Ilse would be far better off in civilized Europe.

Several hours after the train departed from the Cologne station, it reached the Belgian border. German border guards stomped through the train, roughly opening suitcases, strewing the contents on the floor—clothing, perhaps a few dolls, or a photograph from home—searching for valuables that the children might be trying to smuggle out of the country. Michael Blumenthal had a similar experience when he crossed the border to Italy, the first leg of his voyage to China, reporting that the SS border guards "barked at the handful of Jewish emigrants to get off the train, and tore apart even the smallest piece of their luggage with sadistic delight. Men and women were strip-searched to ensure that absolutely nothing of value was being taken out."[3]

The children had received specific instructions listing what they could and could not take along. One Viennese child preserved a copy of the letter she received from the authorities prior to her departure on a Kindertransport to England. It specified that "jewelry and articles of value are absolutely forbidden." So too were cameras and musical instruments. Each child could bring exactly one suitcase and one backpack, and "persons accompanying the children must say goodbye before entering the train station as it is forbidden, without exception, to set foot on the departure platform."[4]

Ilse trembled as the Germans ransacked suitcases, but she was one of the lucky ones whose bag was untouched. After half an hour, the guards were satisfied and let the train continue on its way. As soon as they crossed into Belgium, Hans breathed more easily—he didn't need to open the window to feel the fresh air of freedom. Four hours after leaving Cologne, the train arrived in Brussels with its fifty children ranging from four-year-olds who had never been separated from their parents for even one night to eighteen-year-old adolescents. That morning, they had all been normal children living with their parents and, in most cases, attending school. Now they were refugees in a country where they did not speak the language and knew hardly a soul.

From the train station in Brussels, the refugee children traveled by bus to the local Jewish Community Center. It was evening by the time they arrived and the center was dark and disorganized, with dozens of friends and family members—it seemed like hundreds to Ilse—milling around, waiting. Ilse was met by her mother's close friend Friedel Brandenstein, who had for several years lived in Belgium with her husband, a prominent surgeon. Their daughter, also named Ilse, had immigrated to England. Ilse was tremendously relieved to see a friendly face, though Tante Friedel, as she was called, was one of those people she knew only secondhand, through her mother. But if Ilse thought she would be staying with Tante Friedel, she was mistaken. The Brandensteins lived in a small apartment, too small, evidently, for one young German girl. They had found a room for her in the house of a French-speaking Belgian widow. Friedel handed Ilse over to her new landlady and, mission accomplished, more or less dropped out of sight.

That night, Ilse climbed into an unfamiliar bed in a strange land. Her motion sickness had at last subsided, only to be replaced by intense homesickness. A sickly child who had always been coddled by overprotective parents, she had never gone on a sleepover to a friend's home or spent the summer in camp. She had never traveled outside of Germany. She wished desperately that she was home.

Home was Stettin, a bustling city with a population of just over a quarter of a million that was Germany's third largest port after Hamburg and Bremen. Stettin is a very old city, used as a stronghold by marauding Germanic tribes as early as the sixth century, and home to the dukes of Pomerania in the Middle Ages. By virtue of its strategic position near the mouth of the Oder River, Stettin has had many masters: at the conclusion of the Thirty Years' War in 1648, it was given to Sweden, only to be turned over to Prussia less than a century later. In the 1880s it was rebuilt with wide avenues and abundant parks like those found in Paris, which was designed by the same architect, Georges-Eugène Haussmann.[5]

Today, Stettin is no longer in Germany. A victim of the shifting borders that often follow wars, it is in Poland, sporting the name Szczecin. It was bequeathed to Germany by the major powers at the Potsdam Conference in the summer of 1945. But Joseph Stalin apparently had a change of heart and handed administration of the city to the Poles the following month.[6] Stettin won a place in the history books when Winston Churchill ominously intoned that "from Stettin in the Baltic to Trieste in the Adriatic, an iron curtain has descended across the Continent."[7] It was also the birthplace in 1729 of Sophie Friederike Auguste, a minor German princess who would one day become Catherine the Great, empress of Russia.

Ilse had lived all her life in Stettin, but with only 2,600 Jews,[8] it had become an increasingly frightening place over the previous six years. Ilse had been roughed up by bullies and humiliated in public school. But Stettin was where her parents were, and already on that first night away from home, she missed them terribly.

Ilse had brought a studio portrait of her family with her, a photograph she took out of her bag and gazed at longingly that night in Brussels as she would often during her years as a refugee. In the picture, Ilse is about five years old. She is wearing a pleated, light-colored dress with a Peter Pan collar—she is the only one in the portrait not dressed in black—and she is holding a bouquet of flowers. Her hair is cut short and she has bangs, which she evidently disliked so intensely that she was determined no daughter of hers would ever be coifed in that style. On one side of her is her grandfather, bald, with a goatee and a dashing upturned white mustache, looking very stern and very Germanic. On the other side is her father, also unsmiling, wearing a three-piece suit, a handkerchief poking out of his jacket pocket and a watch fob chain hanging down his chest. Her mother is seated in order to appear significantly shorter than her spouse. Her hands are folded in her lap, she is wearing a dress with a wide lace collar and cuffs, and she looks much like her daughter would look some thirty years later.

Ilse did not know how her parents came to live in Stettin—her mother, Charlotte, was from Saxony, a few hundred miles to the south—and she had no idea how her parents met. In fact, Ilse was not quite sure what her father did for a living. Her parents tended not to share personal information with their daughter, perhaps because they thought such details were somehow unseemly, hardly different, in their view, from sex, money, and other taboo topics. Hermann Wulff was probably a businessman of sorts—the majority of German Jews were engaged in trade or commerce in the 1920s.[9] He was definitely not a doctor, though in 1933, just over one-tenth of all German physicians were Jewish, nor was he a lawyer, though one-sixth of all German lawyers or notaries were Jewish. He might have been some kind of civil servant—the civil service in Germany was enormous—but as a Jew he would undoubtedly have lost his job much sooner than he did if he had been part of the Civil Service bureaucracy. Ilse remembers hearing the word "expediter," suggesting that Hermann, private first class in the German army during World War I, worked for an export-import business. Possibly his firm dealt in chinaware, as he sometimes brought home small sample cups that Ilse used for her dolls' tea parties.

As Ilse studied the picture of her father, she was reminded of how he could make her laugh, though he was also the disciplinarian in the family. Ilse liked playing pranks on her teachers, and when her parents learned of her latest infraction, it was her father who meted out punishment, usually by removing his belt and beating her. Corporal punishment was widespread in Germany in the 1930s, though it was on the decline compared to imperial times, when child-rearing practices were intended to foster obedience, orderliness, and thrift.[10] The Wulffs, who were not among the avant-garde of German society, whether in child-rearing techniques or anything else, simply did what everyone else in their circle did.

It was her mother whom Ilse admired and was close to. She wanted to be refined and educated like her mother, who could recite long poems by Goethe and Schiller by heart and had completed *Lyceum,* or academic high school, a fairly unusual accomplishment at that time. Only 1 to 2 percent of boys completed high school and obtained the graduate certificate, or *Abitur,* when her mother was growing up; far fewer girls reached that milestone.[11] After high school, her mother had gone to a finishing school in Switzerland where she met Friedel, the friend now in Belgium who had picked up Ilse at the train station. Lotte was also an accomplished pianist. A Bechstein grand piano graced the Wulff home, a symbol of the importance of *Bildung,* the love of literature, music, and theater so widespread among middle-class German Jews.[12]

Ilse looked at the picture of her grandfather, a far gentler figure than her father and far kinder than his picture suggested. Whenever her grandfather came to visit, he took Ilse on walks down to the pier. Holding her hand tightly—they were, after all, exploring an area that her parents regarded as off-limits, populated by sailors, prostitutes, and other "low life"—he let her watch the ships unload their wares. The docks of Stettin were a hotbed of crime, much as the piers in Hamburg, an even larger port, were, pilfered for food and other goods by the impoverished and unemployed underclass during the early twenties.[13] After their stroll, her grandfather let her indulge in another forbidden pastime: he took her to a *Konditorei* (café), where she could choose whatever pastry she wished, perhaps a chocolate covered, cream-filled *Mohrenkopf,* without any concern that she would spoil her appetite for dinner. Sometimes she chose a piece of *Pflaumenkuchen* (plum cake), a delicacy she would enjoy twenty-five years later when, on very special occasions, she celebrated with a cake from Bauer's, a bakery on the Upper East Side of Manhattan known for its traditional German desserts.

Missing from the picture was her Onkel Erich, her mother's brother. He was a stern, unforgiving figure, and Ilse could never understand what his wife, the good-natured, perpetually smiling Tante Trude, saw in him. Sometimes Ilse and her mother visited Trude's family on their farm, giving Ilse a chance to play with her cousin. The cousin's dialect was so thick that Ilse could scarcely understand her and she in turn made fun of Ilse's *Hochdeutsch,* the standard radio-announcer version of German that Ilse heard both in school and at home. She learned to feed the goats and milk the cows and played with her cousin, communicating without language. The two cousins were girls, relatives, and Germans. Nothing else really mattered.

Ilse had other relatives on her father's side who were not in the photograph, but they were shadowy figures, one of whom she saw but never actually met, and the other of whom she never even saw. The former was her father's brother Martin, who lived in Stettin but was estranged from Hermann. Ilse, who has an uncanny ability to remember faces and to recognize people twenty, thirty, and sometimes even fifty years after she last saw them, is not sure she would have known her Uncle Martin if she had encountered him later. Whenever her mother saw him from afar, she would announce "Da kommt der Martin"—here comes Martin—and promptly cross to the other side of the street, her dutiful daughter in tow.

The second uncle, Georg, lived in America, she thinks in Chicago, but perhaps he also became estranged, as there was never any discussion of trying to secure an affidavit from Onkel Georg to enable them to immigrate to the United States. All that Ilse knew about this other uncle was that at some indeterminate time in the past, he had sent Hermann "artifacts," which Ilse was only rarely allowed to look at. They were arrowheads, or at least she thought they looked like the arrows she had seen in the illustrations of the "Winnetou" books, Karl May's implausible story about a German who becomes the intimate of an Apache chief and nearly marries the chief's sister. Karl May himself was a con man and a petty thief who discovered his literary talents while in jail.[14] He went on to write some sixty adventure books, all featuring a thinly disguised version of himself as the hero, which were universally adored by German children in the 1930s.

The arrowheads, if that was what they were, would be at the center of a disagreement between Ilse's parents after the Nazis issued a ban on Jews owning weapons, on penalty of a twenty-year jail sentence.[15] Terrified that their apartment would be searched and the arrowheads discovered, Lotte implored her husband to dispose of the potentially incriminating items. Perhaps Hermann thought they were of some financial value or perhaps they were of sentimental value, representing his only memento of his brother Georg. In any event, family legend holds that Hermann eventually gave in to his wife's pleading, wrapped the arrowheads in newspaper, and threw the package into the Oder River.

Ilse put the photograph down. She could hear her mother's frequent exhortation, "Schlaf dich gesund und kugelrund" (sleep yourself healthy and round as a crumb), echoing in her head. The house in Brussels was very quiet. There were no loudspeakers blaring in the streets or heavy boots treading on the stairs. Ilse dozed off.

~

Hans was met in the Brussels Community Center by a distant cousin of his father's. Perhaps it was a second cousin—Hans didn't know the exact relationship. But they had never met before, and Cousin Adolph Rosengarde did not speak a word of German. Adolph took Hans to live with him, his wife, and their maid in an upscale section of town. The maid would be especially important to Hans because she was a Flemish speaker. Belgium, though a tiny country of only 11,700 square miles, is divided between the Walloon or French-speaking part and the Flemish part. Flemish is a dialect of Dutch, which in turn is related to German. The relationship was close enough that when Hans spoke German and the maid spoke Flemish, they could understand each other. The Rosengardes, by contrast, were French speakers. Two years of French at the Jewish high school in Berlin and frenzied private tutoring for a month before his departure from Germany helped a little, but not enough for Hans to speak fluently.

Hans was looking forward to exploring Brussels, though he regarded the city as provincial compared to Berlin, the lively metropolis where he had resided for the past three and a half years. His family had moved to Berlin when life became intolerable in the claustrophobic East Prussian town of Osterode where he spent the first eleven years of his life. He was more urbane and more experienced than Ilse in being away from home: he had spent several weeks at sports camp, first in Denmark in the summer of 1937 and then in the resort town of Schwartzort, Lithuania, as recently as the summer of 1938. But as he lay in bed in the Rosengardes' apartment, he missed his family. He, too, had brought studio portraits of his parents with him, which he looked at as he unpacked his suitcase.

In the photographs, his father, Julius Garfunkel, is a handsome man, pensive and intelligent, serious but not stern, with refined, regular features. Other photos show him dapperly dressed, with fashionable white shoes and spats. His mother, Paula Lonky Garfunkel, is a bit stocky, the quintessential *Hausfrau*—warm and motherly. Her clothes were always of fine quality, as befit the proprietor of a clothing store, but tended toward the dowdy rather than the chic.

Julius and his twin sister, Cecilia, were born in Lithuania in 1881. By the time the First World War broke out, Julius had married a German woman and enlisted in the German army. Possibly, he worked for the Lonky family and married the boss's daughter—Julius became an apprentice tailor when he left school at fourteen—but Hans didn't think so. Theirs may have been an arranged marriage. At the turn of the twentieth century, just about half of all Jewish marriages were arranged, though the proportion was probably lower by the time Paula and Julius married in 1914.[16] The woman's dowry often consisted of a share in the family business, so perhaps Paula's dowry was the 50 percent ownership Julius had in the business. He shared the responsibility for running what was by then a thriving concern with Paula's brothers Max and Siegfried. Siegfried had a small ownership share but did not actually work in the store: he studied for many years, earning him the nickname of "the eternal student," ultimately obtaining a law degree and becoming a judge, only to lose his job almost immediately after the Nazis came to power.

Paula Lonky was born in 1886 in Osterode, where her family had deep roots: several generations of Lonkys were buried in the Jewish cemetery of Osterode. Paula went through the local school system, including the *Lyceum*. Her father had established his own business, a clothing store, in 1878. Hans remembers the big sign that was draped over the storefront, "Jubileum: 1878–1928," on the occasion of the store's fiftieth anniversary.

The store was an imposing four-story building on prime real estate, right on the Marktplatz, the town's single main street, kitty-corner from the majestic town hall. On the ground floor were the ready-made clothes. On the second floor, the more affluent and selective customers could order custom-made clothing. On the top floors lived Max Lonky, the other partner in the business, with his Christian wife, Änne. Intermarriage, while regarded as faintly scandalous in Osterode, was in fact quite common in Germany. In neighboring Königsberg, the intermarriage rate soared from a scant 7 percent in 1885 to an astounding 35 percent in 1914.[17] But Tante Änne did not simply intermarry: each of her two successive husbands was Jewish; both were named Max; and they were brothers-in-law. Her first husband was Max Garfunkel (Julius's brother), a dentist, who died fighting on the western front in World War I. Thoroughly enmeshed with the Garfunkel-Lonky clan, she then married Max Lonky, who helped manage the clothing store in Osterode.

Paula married at twenty-eight, a bit later than average for the time. She was an accomplished musician—like Ilse's mother, she played the piano—

and as she came from a well-to-do family, she should have been eminently marriageable. Perhaps she was not satisfied with her suitors: she was, after all, better educated than many of them, having earned a high school diploma. Maybe Paula wanted to stay in Osterode, which was a far from appealing location for Jews, who were increasingly moving to Germany's largest cities, continuing a trend that had begun with the establishment of the German Empire in 1871. When Otto von Bismarck came to power, just under three-quarters of the Jews lived in the countryside; by 1910, the urban-rural ratio was reversed and three-fourths of German Jews lived in cities.[18]

If Paula Lonky was a bit older than most of her peers when she married, she was older still when she gave birth to her first child, Günther, at age thirty, and she was clearly past her reproductive prime when she had her second child, Hans Wolfgang Max, eight years later, on April 21, 1924. Had there been a series of miscarriages in the years between Günther's arrival and that of Hans? Was Hans a surprise? Whatever the circumstances of his birth, he was doted on by his parents, who loved him deeply and no doubt spoiled him. He had his own room in his family's spacious apartment, spacious at least in his childish eyes, or perhaps compared to the homes of his friends. His parents entertained frequently—customers and business associates of Julius often came for dinner, boring affairs that began with Paula serving an elegant meal and ended with a great deal of cigar smoke.

Hans did not give much thought to his brother, Günther, as he lay in the unfamiliar surroundings in Brussels. With the large age gap between the two boys, they had never been close. And two years earlier, Günther had effectively disappeared from Hans's life. He had shocked his family by taking off for Sao Paulo, Brazil, and then arranging for Friedel Kitkowski, his aunt by marriage, an "Aryan," and a woman fifteen years his senior, to join him as his wife.

Hans had no pictures of his grandmother Rahel with him—his father's mother, who lived with his maiden aunt Cecilia in the town of Tilsit. He did not see either of them very often. Perhaps there was some tension between the two branches of the family. On one occasion, Grandfather Isaac had become ill while visiting, which Aunt Cecilia implausibly attributed to Paula's cooking. Since Paula was reputedly an outstanding cook, perhaps the issue was that she did not keep a kosher kitchen. Grandfather Isaac was dispatched home in a specially rented ambulance train car to be nursed back to health by his Orthodox wife and daughter.

Thinking about his grandmother called to mind the first death in his family. The trouble began on a quiet spring day in May 1934, when a mirror spontaneously cracked in the Garfunkels' Osterode home, which Paula and Julius took as an indication of impending misfortune. In fact, within an hour or two of the crack's appearance, Julius's sister telephoned to report that Grandfather Isaac, whose eightieth birthday they were about to celebrate, had died of a heart attack. Instead of attending birthday festivities, Hans found himself at his first funeral. The mirrors in his grandparents' home were covered with sheets and the clock was stopped at the time of his grandfather's death. The family accompanied the plain wooden box to the gravesite, and Hans is convinced his father told him the coffin would be opened and he would have to kiss his grandfather goodbye. Orthodox Jews do not allow physical contact with the dead by men known as *Kohanim,* Jews such as the Garfunkels who are descendants of the ancient priestly class. Nor do they have open caskets at their funerals. So Hans's memory is more likely based on a childish fear rather than on a real event, but a fear so strong that he would remember the episode seventy years later.

Hans and Ilse, lying in their respective beds in different neighborhoods in Brussels, both vowed to be brave and to fight off homesickness. But in an era long before the invention of email and cell phones, when international telephone calls were a rarity and the postal service was slow, it would not be easy for the two young teenagers. That their parents, loving and devoted in their own ways, could have sent their children away to live as strangers in a strange land is almost unbelievable. Only a devastating and portentous event could have prompted their action: the November 1938 pogrom known as Kristallnacht.

2

The Alarm Sounds

Everyone has the right to life, liberty and security of person.
—Universal Declaration of Human Rights, Article 3, 1948

On her way to school on the morning of November 10, 1938, Ilse was shocked by the many shattered store windows and the piles of glass on the streets. The atmosphere was strangely quiet, ominous and oppressive. She sensed something was terribly wrong. She could never have imagined what lay in store for her, and for her family and friends.

Shortly after classes began, SS storm troopers in their signature high black boots and neatly pressed black uniforms burst into the school, pulled the teachers out of the classrooms, and lined them up in the hall. For what seemed like hours, the children heard the stomping of boots and the barking of orders. They were convinced their teachers were going to be shot right there, in the corridor. Eventually, the SS sent the children home with a curt "*Raus!*" (out). They never saw most of their teachers again.

Hans went outside that cold gray day but never made it to school. By eight o'clock that morning, thirty of Berlin's synagogues were in flames. With little effort by firefighters to extinguish the blazes, the fires were still raging that afternoon.[1] When Hans saw the Prinzregentenstrasse synagogue on fire, where his bar mitzvah had been held just a year and a half earlier, he turned around and went home. Fourteen-year-old German boys were supposed to be tough, but Hans threw himself into his mother's arms and cried. If God could not protect his own house, he thought, how could he protect the Jewish people?

Hans spent the next night in the relative security of Tante Änne's apartment in the fashionable Hessenallee in Berlin. Her husband had died of natural causes the year before, leaving her an unambiguously "Aryan" widow, her two previous marriages to Jews no longer jeopardizing her safety. The mobs had already ransacked the area when Hans reached his aunt's house—they had vandalized stores along the Kurfürstentdamm as well as the other majestic avenues and squares of the city, Unter den Linden and the Alexanderplatz. Armed with axes and hatchets, they had forced their way into private homes, beating up the residents and smashing furniture. As in the Russian pogroms earlier in the century, the crowds tore apart pillows and blankets, the most intimate symbols of security, sending feathers flying. The police stood idly by.[2] Across Germany, old age homes, orphanages, and Jewish hospitals were subjected to the same treatment. By the end of the day, 7,000 Jewish businesses had been destroyed; 100 people had been murdered; thousands more had been tormented, humiliated, and beaten. More than 1,000 synagogues had been torched with bombs or dynamite, including all the synagogues of Stettin and the six synagogues of Königsberg, East Prussia, Hans's birth place.[3] The synagogue in Osterode, which was no longer even functioning as a house of worship, was also destroyed.[4]

The following day, the SS forced a stunned and terrified Jewish population to sweep up the broken furniture and shattered glass that littered the streets. The Nazis then imposed a 1 billion mark "cleanup" fine on the Jewish community.

The prelude to Kristallnacht had come at the end of October 1938 when Ilse had heard a tremendous commotion during the night. Boots tramped up and down the stairs of her apartment building and the voices of the SS barked unintelligible commands. Her upstairs neighbors, a Polish Jewish family, screamed; their young daughter cried. The next morning, the family had disappeared. On the night of October 27–28, 1938, in a small-scale dress rehearsal of the deportations to come, the SS forcibly and brutally removed all Polish-born Jews living in Germany. Poland had just passed a law allowing the revocation of citizenship from Poles who had been out of the country for an extended period. The Nazis responded by hastily ridding themselves of Polish-born Jews.

Unsuspecting families, many of whom had lived in Germany for years, had only a few minutes to pack a handful of possessions before being herded onto waiting trucks and transported to the Polish border. The Poles did not want them, so the 17,000 men, women, and children languished in no-man's-land for weeks. Cold, without adequate food and shelter, many died. Ultimately, most found refuge in other European countries.

Among those gathered at the border were Sendel and Rivka Grynzspan and their daughter, Esther. In Paris, seventeen-year-old Herschel Grynzspan, learning of his family's fate, attacked an official at the German embassy in a fit of rage; he died of his wounds a few days later. That attack gave Hitler the excuse he was waiting for to launch a full-blown attack on German Jews.

Kristallnacht was the first battle in the war against the Jews—if war is the right metaphor for an assault by a heavily armed police state on the livelihood and dignity, indeed the very existence, of an unarmed civilian population. Ilse's Onkel Erich was picked up during the pogrom, one of the 30,000 men carted off to Dachau, Buchenwald, and Sachsenhausen, three concentration camps that had originally been set up to provide "protective custody" for political prisoners, principally Social Democrats, Communists, and trade unionists. Many became ill in the camps, a number went mad and committed suicide. About 5,000 died. Most were released if they could prove—usually through their wives' strenuous efforts—that they were about to emigrate and if they agreed to sell their businesses and other property for a pittance. When Erich was released exactly four weeks after his arrest, he stopped to visit the Wulffs on his way home. Twelve-year-old Ilse did not recognize him at first. He could barely walk and he looked like a living skeleton. Ilse began having recurring nightmares in which her emaciated Onkel Erich appeared at the door.

~

A few days after Kristallnacht, the Nazis issued the Decree on the Exclusion of Jews from German Economic Life, which eliminated Jews from any of the few remaining occupations in which they could still pursue their livelihood: they could not be retailers, exporters, business managers, or foremen. Jewish children were expelled from state schools, and Jews were banned from the few public places they could still frequent, such as theaters and movie houses. But Jewish schools reopened and Hans and Ilse returned to class, only to discover that many of their teachers had disappeared. Ilse's friends Eva and Ruth reported that their father had been taken away. From that moment, there was only one topic of discussion at home and in school—how to get out of Germany.

The Nazis in 1938 were still eager to promote Jewish emigration. Adolf Eichmann, who later became a linchpin in the plot to exterminate European Jewry, was put in charge of facilitating the Jewish exodus. Sending the German Jews to Madagascar was one of his more bizarre schemes; another one was sending them to Shanghai.

Eichmann dispatched a representative to the Chinese consulate in Vienna to explore whether the Chinese would accept German Jews. Concluding that they would, Eichmann gave his approval for the German government to charter ships to take the Jews of Germany to Shanghai. One ship actually made the journey: the *Usaramo,* a ship of the Hamburg-Amerika Line, set sail on June 29, 1939, chartered by the Nazis, carrying 459 refugees to Shanghai.[5]

The Wulffs and the Garfunkels, stirred from complacency, began trying to find a way to leave the country. But getting a visa was nearly impossible. Almost every country in the world either had a quota or barred immigration altogether. The day after Germany annexed Austria, adding nearly 200,000 more Jews to the Reich, President Roosevelt requested that Congress authorize an increase in the German quota to accommodate additional Jewish refugees, but the request died in the House Committee on Immigration and Naturalization. Harold Ickes, secretary of the interior, suggested settling European Jews in Alaska—a proposal vigorously rejected by Alaskans.[6]

Just months before, in July 1938, an international conference had been held in Evian, France, picturesquely situated on Lake Geneva, to address the plight of German and Austrian Jews. Instead of relaxing restrictions on immigration, the countries attending the conference, one after another, tightened them. A total of 115,000 Jews managed nonetheless to leave Germany between Kristallnacht and the outbreak of World War II on September 1, 1939. But getting out became increasingly difficult, not only because visas were unobtainable but also because of the cost. The now largely unemployed and unemployable Jews of the Third Reich could not afford to pay either their passage or the heavy exit tax levied by the Germans.

For the Garfunkel family in Berlin, Kristallnacht set into motion a plan for immigration to the United States, a plan that would take nine years to come to fruition. The key lay with Julius's cousin Bessie Silverman, née Garfunkel.

Bessie and Julius had a common grandfather, Abraham Garfunkel of Lithuania, who had been born in what was then part of imperial Russia. Abraham's seven children had scattered to various parts of the globe during the great migration of eastern European Jews in the 1880s. One son, Isaac, moved to Germany after his son, Julius, was born. Another son, Louis, moved to Chicago; he had four children, one of whom was Bessie. She lived in Chicago with her husband and two young children. Just two and a half weeks after Kristallnacht, Hans began a correspondence with Cousin Bessie that would serve as his lifeline during the war years to come. Writing in fractured English, he introduced himself, saying, "I was born April 21st 1924 in Königsberg." He continued, "Four years I have visited the public school and since Easter 1933 I go in the High School," clearly regarding as entirely unobjectionable his use of "Easter" rather than "Passover" or simply "April" to denote the beginning of the school year. "Now I am in the fifth class of the Zickel High School. A copy of my last school report you have received. I am very interested in mathematics and in history and I love the sport."

Then he addressed what would be the central theme of his correspondence, the efforts by the Silvermans to bring Hans to Chicago: "I am very glad that you are able to send the affidavit for me. To-morrow I shall go with my father to the American Consulate in Berlin. I hope the Consulate will have received the affidavit already. It will be very important to leave Germany in this year. You have no idea how grateful I am that you have made possible my emigration to America."

Addressed to "my dear cousins," the letter concluded: "I hope you are in the best health. I send you my best regards and all my love—your Hans."

A Western Union telegram from Hans's father to Bessie followed on December 29, 1938: WE MUST QUICKEN DEPARTURE WIRE IMMEDIATELY TO CONSULATE GENERAL BERLIN THAT YOU PAY SCHOOL-FEES AND LIVELIHOOD THANKS IN ADVANCE JULIUS. But before Bessie could respond, a new option presented itself and Hans left for Brussels.

Between 1933 and 1939, 400,000 Jews emigrated from Germany. By far the largest number (132,000) went to the United States, followed by Palestine (60,000). After the Arab Riots of 1936, the British drastically limited the number of "certificates" for immigration to Palestine, and many of the available certificates were awarded to nonrefugees. An additional 40,000 Jews went to England. In December 1936 Hans's brother, Günther, traveled to Brazil, leaving on a tourist visa with no intention of returning; 10,000 other German Jews also immigrated to Brazil that year. Other Latin American countries provided a haven for another 10,000 refugees, most of whom ended up in Argentina. No destination was too far: 7,000 Jews fled to Australia and 5,000 to South Africa. The remaining refugees escaped to other countries in western Europe, where the majority perished during the war. Approximately 200,000 Jews remained, penniless and persecuted, in Germany.[7]

After the November pogrom, one of the only remaining escape routes led to the international port city of Shanghai. Approximately 9,000 German Jews (along with an equal number of Austrian Jews) obtained permission to leave the Reich, paid a substantial fee for their passage, and embarked on the monthlong trip over land and sea to an uncertain future in China. Lotte and Hermann Wulff were among those who left Germany forever in April 1939, destined for the slums of Shanghai.

The other way out, available only to children and then only to a fraction of the under-eighteen-year-olds still living in Germany, was to take a Kindertransport, or children's transport. The British cabinet gave special permission to let 10,000 Jewish children, primarily from Germany and Austria, travel to England unaccompanied by their parents—provided that British refugee organizations guaranteed their support. They were housed with English families, and almost all survived the war. A few hundred children went on similar transports to Holland and Belgium. The Wulffs and the Garfunkels, desperate to save their children from the torment and penury that awaited them in Germany, though unaware that even worse was in store for those who stayed, succeeded in registering Ilse and Hans for the Kindertransport to Brussels, leaving January 30, 1939.

~

Kristallnacht was not the beginning of the end for the Jews of Germany. Even Hitler's assumption of power in 1933, an ostensibly democratic victory that belied the intimidation and violence behind his election, was not the beginning. Since 1916 Germany had become progressively more hostile toward Jews. During the First World War, Jews served in large numbers in the army. As soon as Germany began losing the war, Jews were blamed for the downturn. They were accused of profiteering and of laziness. Hans's father, Julius, who had been a soldier, told his family the story of how his regiment marched proudly behind their captain, who rode on horseback—and how he was given a bucket and shovel to scoop up the horse manure. The army high command had ordered a census in 1916, the primary purpose of which was to demonstrate that Jews were shirking their responsibilities. The expectation was the census would reveal that Jews were underrepresented in the army and that those who did serve were concentrated in desk jobs. In fact, the census revealed the opposite: Jews were overrepresented in the army and served disproportionately on the front lines. A chagrined high command suppressed the report and managed to convey the impression that their anticipated findings had been proven to be true.[8]

The years immediately after the end of the First World War had been tough for everyone, with hyperinflation eating up any savings a family might have had. At the height of the inflation, the average family devoted upward of 90 percent of their earnings to food alone. Inflation was so dramatic that, according to one typical though no doubt apocryphal story, a patron at a café could order a cup of coffee for 5,000 marks and by the time she got up to leave would be asked to pay 8,000 marks.[9] By 1925 the currency had been stabilized and both domestically made products and imports filled the stores. But economic prosperity was still tenuous, with 1 million Germans unemployed, a number that was to rise to 3 million within a year.[10]

During the "golden years" of the Weimar Republic, the period after the hyperinflation of the immediate postwar period and before the stock market collapse of 1929 triggered the Great Depression, anti-Semitism was a smoldering but not virulent presence in most of Germany. But after 1929, the generous Allied loans that had made Germany the most prosperous nation in western Europe disappeared. Investment capital dried up and trade fizzled, leading to massive unemployment. The worst year for Germany was 1932. The working class was affected the most severely, but the middle class, especially the Jews, also suffered. Following the pattern that was to be repeated again and again in the coming years, the very people who were among the hardest hit were blamed for the country's problems.

Anti-Semitism gained considerable momentum after Hitler's rise to power, but even after the January 1933 *Machtergreifung* (seizure of power), persecution was not yet systematic, universal, and unrelenting. German Jews experienced occasional lulls depending on where they lived as well as on political developments.

Hans spent his first eleven years in the picture-perfect town of Osterode. Situated on the sparkling waters of a lake, it was only a short distance from pristine forests known for their majestic spruce and fir trees. But Hans did not like the rides to the woods with his father to look for deer: to him, the tall, dark trees were forbidding, portending fear and danger, not tranquility. In the year of Hans's birth, Osterode had a population of only 18,000, including about 170 Jews.[11] Naturally, all the residents knew their neighbors. In particular, they knew who was Jewish and who was not. Well before Hitler came to power in 1933, it mattered very much if you were Jewish in a small town in Germany.

The town of Osterode was so small that it had neither its own maternity hospital nor its own rabbi. When it came time for Paula Garfunkel to give birth to Hans, she went to the hospital in the nearest city, Königsberg, fifty miles away, rather than depending on the local midwife. As a result, Hans was born in the hometown of the philosopher Immanuel Kant and the mathematician David Hilbert.

In lieu of a rabbi, Osterode had a preacher, or *Prediger,* a poorly educated, sadistic man, according to Hans, who ran the Jewish afternoon Hebrew school. Julius did not think much of the *Prediger* either. He threatened to throw him down the stairs when the preacher tried to meddle in the Garfunkels' affairs by objecting to the marriage of a family member to a non-Jewish woman.

Hans started elementary school, or *Volksschule,* in 1930, when he was six years old. His main recollection is that he was harassed by the other children, as was common throughout Germany in the last years of the Weimar Republic.[12] Hans is convinced his father paid protection money to the teacher in the hope that he would intervene on behalf of the sole Jewish child in the class. Fortunately, the school was only a block or two away from his father's store, so instead of going home after school, he could dash to the store and go home later in the company of an adult. He remembers on one occasion being accosted by a gang of stone-throwing older boys. His brother, Günther, eight years his senior, sent seven-year-old Hans scurrying to safety while he confronted the bullies.

As a successful Jewish establishment, the Garfunkel-Lonky store was the target of increasingly virulent anti-Semites. By 1931 *Sturmabteilung* (SA) gangs roamed the streets of German towns, meting out terror and humiliation. In 1932 Nazi hoodlums planted a bomb in the Lonky-Garfunkel clothing store. They proved to be incompetent arsonists and the bomb failed to detonate. Julius Garfunkel, who naively believed Jews could obtain justice in a German court of law, filed a complaint, only to find himself jailed in retribution on the trumped-up charge of being a Communist. But although law and order no longer prevailed in the early 1930s, bribery still worked. He was able to buy his way out of jail.

If the members of the Garfunkel family were identified by the surrounding community as Jewish, it wasn't because they were religiously observant. They did have a chicken coop in their backyard, but unlike Orthodox families that kept their own chickens so as to be able to slaughter them in traditional Kosher fashion even after the practice was outlawed, the Garfunkels did not observe traditional Jewish dietary laws. Hans painted and hunted for Easter eggs, hardly a pastime for the observant. Julius's parents had belonged to the only synagogue in Osterode, which was Orthodox, but their son did not receive a religious education. When Julius was called to the Torah for an aliyah—the blessing before the reading of a section from the scroll, an honor conferred on the most respected members of the congregation—he had to read a transliteration of the text. Julius Garfunkel, son of Rahel and Isaac, grandson of a distinguished Lithuanian rabbi, could not read Hebrew. Nor would his children be taught the language and customs of their heritage.

Hans's family did observe Rosh Hashanah (the Jewish New Year) and Yom Kippur (the Day of Atonement). They also celebrated Passover and Purim, holidays that are noteworthy for their historical references to times of oppression: Passover celebrates the liberation of the Jews from slavery with their exodus from Egypt; Purim commemorates the success of Esther, wife of the king of Persia, in preventing the slaughter of the Jews by the king's adviser, the evil Haman. Hans does not remember lighting Sabbath candles or observing other Jewish traditions.

Hans has no happy childhood memories from the time before the Nazis came to power, no images of playing on the soccer team—he was not allowed to participate in sports because he was Jewish—no fond recollections of playing with other children—there were no other Jewish boys his age in town, and the "Aryans" wanted nothing to do with him.

For Ilse, living in Stettin with its population of 250,000, the years before Hitler came to power were relatively serene. The Wulffs went on vacation in Swienemünde. A seaside town that would later become known for its munitions works, during Ilse's early childhood it was a popular resort. Ilse played on the beach with her dolls, a shy, sheltered, somewhat frail child. Back in Stettin her parents went out to the opera and to concerts but did not celebrate Jewish holidays except for the high holidays, when her father wore a top hat and accompanied his family to the local Reform synagogue. For the Wulffs, as for so many middle-class German Jews, it was *Bildung* rather than religion that shaped their identity. And nothing was more quintessentially representative of German culture than music, particularly the music of the great German composers.

As a very young child, Ilse wore leg braces, apparently to stretch the tendons of her legs, without which she would not have been able to walk properly. She must have had metatarsus adductus, the most common congenital foot deformity, occurring in about one in a thousand births, and more frequent in girls than in boys. The treatment, even today, consists of stretching exercises performed by the parents during the first eight months of life and, for more severe forms, casting. Ilse endured special exercises and manipulations as well as braces that extended to the middle of her chest. She also had "rheumatism" in elementary school, a somewhat mysterious condition that does not seem to have been either rheumatic fever (a not uncommon complication of strep throat in the pre-penicillin era) or juvenile rheumatoid arthritis (a form of arthritis that affects children). Whatever the condition, it led to an extra measure of protectiveness on the part of her parents. Her medical problems resulted in some degree of social isolation before she started elementary school, when she evidently shed the braces, though not the diagnosis of rheumatism. Her chronically anxious mother became alarmed when one of Ilse's playmates suddenly began limping, only to be diagnosed the very next day with polio. Ilse was spared, and although always pale and scrawny, she remained in remarkably good health for years to come.

Ilse's earliest political memory is the death of Field Marshal Paul Hindenburg. Hindenburg, who had been elected president of Germany in 1925, was reelected for another seven-year term in 1932. He had formed a coalition government with the Nazi party and, at the urging of assorted politicians, appointed Hitler as chancellor. A revered war hero from the First World War, Hindenburg reportedly became increasingly demented during his tenure in office, facilitating the assumption of total power by the Nazis. When he died, in August 1934, Ilse stood with her classmates, singing "Ich hat einen Kameraden, einen besseren findst du nicht" (I had a comrade, you couldn't find a better one), tears streaming down her face. Immediately afterward, Hitler made himself president as well as chancellor. As was his style, he then held a "referendum" in which the populace was asked to rubberstamp his decision—encouraged by club-wielding brownshirts who dragged voters to polling places, often giving them premarked ballots. Even in the elementary schools, children were told to support the führer. Ilse, too, came home and asked her parents, "You will vote for Hitler, won't you?"

Hitler's accession to power on January 30, 1933, would usher in an era of unprecedented repression, but to Hans and Ilse it was just the occasion for another parade. The Nazi consolidation of power was a gradual process, with the endless parades serving as repeated reminders of the party's inherent brutality. Since 1930, when the Nazis got only 17 percent of the vote in the Reichstag elections,[13] the marching, the chilling words of the SA "Fight Song," which spoke of Jewish blood spurting from the storm troopers' knives, and the propaganda had been incessant. Ilse and Hans lived through numerous elections, each preceded by violence and intimidation. The first big show of nationalist fervor came with the 1932 presidential elections, when the eighty-four-year-old Hindenburg ran for a second seven-year term—with Hitler on the opposing ticket. Hindenburg won the 1932 contest, though only after a runoff election, which afforded the Nazis yet another opportunity for raucous, flag-waving demonstrations.

In the second major contest, the Reichstag elections of July 1932, the Nazis outdid themselves with parades. Taking advantage of the fear engendered in the populace on Bloody Sunday, when the Red Front Fighters and the SA faced off in the working-class district of Altona, the Nazis proclaimed that a civil war was imminent. Using posters, leaflets, and speeches broadcast by loudspeaker in numerous public places, they promised a glorious future for Germany if they were elected.

The parades continued throughout the time Hans and Ilse lived in Germany. Whenever public support flagged or the regime wanted a distraction from the country's economic woes, the Nazis whipped up the passions of the people with a boisterous tribute to the glorious Reich. Three days a year were regularly designated for extravagant displays of nationalism: the Nazi Party annual September rally in Nuremberg; the Day of National Labor, a strange co-option of the traditional Communist May 1 celebration; and Hitler's birthday on April 20. The most magnificent of all was the Nuremberg Rally of 1934, when a quarter of a million people were brought by train to attend a one-week extravaganza. It was filmed, at Hitler's request, by Leni Riefenstahl. Her award-winning *Triumph of the Will* is widely considered a masterpiece of documentary propaganda.[14]

While the *Machtergreifung* failed to make much of an impression on seven-year-old Ilse and eight-year-old Hans, it ushered in a series of measures that would increasingly affect their daily lives. An early, tangible effect of Nazi rule was the economic boycott of Jewish-owned stores on April 1, 1933. Storm troopers stood menacingly outside shops, deterring patrons from entering. But Ilse's father did not own a store, and moreover, most Germans responded tepidly to the boycott. In the buildup to the March elections, the Nazi platform focused on the Communist threat, not so much on the Jews. Middle-class Germans did not want to forgo shopping at their favorite stores, many of which featured lower prices or a better selection than the competition. The level of intimidation was not yet so fierce that the shop owners themselves were cowed into silence. On the occasion of that first boycott, some Jews protested. In Stettin, for instance, a shopkeeper stood outside her store and explained to passersby just who she was—she was a loyal German subject, a widow whose husband had been awarded the Emperor's Service Cross in the Great War—and why they should not hesitate to come into her store.[15]

Immediately following that boycott, the Nazis promulgated a series of decrees limiting Jewish civil rights that affected the families of many of Ilse's friends but did not touch her directly. The prohibition against kosher butchery, instituted in April 1933, dramatically affected the 10 percent of German Jews who were Orthodox, but not the Wulffs, who did not keep a kosher home. The Law for the Restoration of the Professional Service, another April edict, forced the retirement of many Jewish physicians, lawyers, and civil servants. But Hermann Wulff was not a professional, and in any event would have been exempt by virtue of his service on the front lines during World War I.

The economic boycott of April 1 also did not amount to much in East Prussia. The Nazis themselves were reluctant to make too much of a stir, fearing condemnation by the international press. But by the Christmas season they felt bolder, and by the summer of 1935 the situation had become more virulent. The Nazis rounded up the entire Jewish population of Osterode and forced them to walk through the streets beating drums and wearing signs saying "Ich bin ein Judenschwein" (I am a Jewish pig). The Garfunkels had been warned in advance. Their chauffeur took them out of town while the "parade" took place. Similar episodes, many associated with violence, occurred in towns throughout Germany—shop windows were smashed in one town, a synagogue firebombed in another, a dozen Jews dragged to prison in a third.[16]

The Garfunkels were spared the humiliation of the "parade," but they did not remain unscathed for long. Suddenly, they faced a crisis: Hans was thrown out of school. At age ten, German children either continued in the *Volksschule* with the expectation that they would enter a trade at age fourteen, or, if they passed a qualifying examination, they transferred to the more academically oriented *Gymnasium* (high school). Hans passed the entrance examination in 1934 but that did not guarantee that he would actually be able to attend *Gymnasium*. The Law against Overcrowding of German Schools and Universities, promulgated in April 1933, had limited the number of places in public schools open to "non-Aryans" to 1.5 percent of the total number of seats. The *Gymnasium* initially accepted Hans since his brother had just graduated, which opened up a spot for another Jew. Then East Prussia excluded all Jewish students from the public *Gymnasium*.

Without a local Jewish *Gymnasium*, the Garfunkels were in a quandary. For Hans to pursue higher education, the family would have to move. After lengthy deliberation, Julius Garfunkel sold the family business, settling for a mere 10 percent of its value. In the next few years, 70 percent of the 100,000 Jewish-owned firms in Germany would either be closed or "Aryanized" (forced to sell to non-Jews).[17] Unemployed and unemployable, Julius Garfunkel abandoned small-town life and moved his family to Berlin, where one-third of all German Jews lived—about 144,000 people in 1935.[18] Max Lonky, Hans's uncle, refused to leave his hometown. The family doctor sedated him heavily and Julius transported him involuntarily to Berlin.

Moving to Berlin allowed Hans to breathe again—for a while. To a boy on the cusp of adolescence, Berlin was tremendously exciting. Everything was on a grand scale: the Kurfürstendamm cut a two-mile-long swath through the city, a wide boulevard lined by elegant stores and dignified residences, a sort of cross between Manhattan's Fifth and Park avenues. For those less interested in fashion, the Kaufhaus des Westes (KaDeWe), the city's most popular department store, sold everything from raincoats to radios. The economist Michael Blumenthal wrote of his Berlin childhood that though he "vaguely sensed the mood of helplessness, fear, and despair of the adults," it did not detract from his happiness.[19] Teeming with concert halls, theaters, museums, cinemas, and parks, Berlin was culturally vibrant. It provided the most positive experience German Jewish children could hope for in the 1930s.[20]

Nonetheless, an ominous undercurrent flowed below the vibrant pulse of Berlin city life. Nazi flags hung from every window and storm troopers patrolled every neighborhood. Each corner boasted a kiosk displaying the front page of *Der Stürmer* with its viciously anti-Semitic cartoons and outrageous headlines. And violent outbursts marred the fragile quiet of Berlin well before Kristallnacht. In fact, in July 1935, just before Hans and his parents moved to Berlin, groups of SA beat up Jews and smashed windows along the Kurfürstendamm, inaugurating a new wave of Nazi anti-Semitism. But since it was the German capital, and therefore more visible to the outside world than the rest of the country, anti-Semitism remained less conspicuous than elsewhere.[21]

The various regions of Germany issued their own anti-Jewish decrees: the residents of Pomerania (Stettin's province) and Prussia (Berlin's province) did not endure the same restrictions. But by the summer of 1935, both Stettin and Berlin had decreed public swimming pools off limits to Jews. The fantasy was ubiquitous that hook-nosed Jewish men were always on the prowl, seeking to seduce sexy blonde "Aryan" women.[22] Swimming pools, where scantily clad women were apt to be found, were obviously a high risk venue for innocent women. To uphold German morality, lascivious men needed to be excluded and that, of course, meant Jews.

It was life in the classroom more than the adult world that determined Hans's and Ilse's sense of well-being. For Hans, the Luise Zickels Höhere Privatschule, his new school in Berlin, was paradise. For the first time, he could participate in sports, joining the school track team and the soccer club. And unlike the *Gymnasium* in Osterode, his new school was coeducational. On the brink of puberty, Hans discovered girls and spent a considerable amount of time helping assorted female classmates with their math homework. He also studied French, which would prove very useful later on, and benefited from a series of outstanding, overqualified teachers who could not find positions in the German university system and were grateful for gainful employment teaching high school.

Ilse, too, was fundamentally content as long as she attended the local *Volksschule*. The principal showed respect to the school's three Jewish pupils. He greeted them with *Guten Tag* rather than the mandatory *Heil Hitler!* The children participated in school trips and received good grades if they performed well academically, unlike their counterparts in many rural schools who were left out of school activities and who could not succeed academically, no matter how diligently they worked.[23] But when Ilse took and passed the entrance exam to the *Lyceum* and moved on to high school, her world changed. For the first time, she experienced violent and outspoken anti-Semitism. Her books were roughed up—and so was she.

Ilse began at the *Lyceum* the year following the passage of the Nuremberg Laws, the laws of "German blood and honor." In mid-September 1935 all Jews in Germany lost their civil rights. Women under forty-five could no longer work as maids in Jewish households, ostensibly because they were at risk of falling victim to predatory Jewish men (a danger from which middle-aged and older women were evidently immune). Marriage and extramarital sex between Jews and non-Jews became a crime.[24] The Wulffs lost their tenants after the passage of the racial laws—and with them a significant source of income.

Home life had never been relaxed—Ilse's parents had always quarreled a great deal and the escalating Jew-baiting in the surrounding society did not help matters. They avoided discussing politics and actively discouraged their daughter from asking questions. Perhaps the decision to stay away from politics reflected their fear of the increasingly obtrusive "block wardens" who were hired by the Nazis to spy on neighborhoods. Block wardens were supposed to make sure that people displayed Nazi flags in their windows and attended party rallies. Whenever Hitler gave a speech, the wardens arranged to broadcast the speech over loudspeakers in public places. At the sound of a gong, everyone was supposed to stop whatever they were doing and gather around the loudspeaker. In addition, tenants could denounce their neighbors, leading to arrest under the Malicious Gossip Law and to torture, imprisonment, even death.[25] Lotte and Hermann Wulff worried that the superintendent of their apartment building might inform on them if Ilse ever commented that her parents did not support the Nazi regime.

Anti-Semitic incidents proliferated in 1936, except during a brief hiatus for the Berlin Olympics, when the Nazis temporarily abandoned overt racism. The Party Rally of Honor in September 1936, another massive parade, engendered a frenzy of Jew-baiting.[26] Ilse was attacked right outside her apartment building after she inadvertently stepped on and broke a boy's marble. The marble's owner punched her in the mouth, chipping her two front teeth. She would carry that reminder of German viciousness with her until a dentist fitted her with caps twenty-five years later.

Perhaps it was this attack that prompted Lotte and Hermann to put their daughter into a Jewish school. Growing numbers of parents chose the private school route: in 1932 only one-seventh of Jewish children attended Jewish schools; in 1934 the fraction was just under one in four; by 1936 it was over half.[27] After November 1938 Jewish children were banned from public schools entirely. Like many fathers of Jewish children, Hermann Wulff may have thought his daughter should tough it out in the public *Lyceum*. Maybe he thought it would give her a thick skin, despite studies even then that correlated signs of psychological disturbance among Jewish children with public school attendance.[28] But when Ilse's father could no longer deny the physical danger she was in, he agreed to send her to a private Jewish school.

Once Ilse started at her new school, shortly before the beginning of 1937, she felt secure. She started smiling again. But the sense of security was tempered by considerable instability as her classmates began moving away. Her closest friend, the girl who developed a mild case of polio, left for Argentina; other friends departed for England and South Africa.

The other girls at the Jewish school could read Hebrew, but Ilse had had no prior Jewish education. As was common among assiduously assimilated German Jews, the school provided Ilse's first meaningful exposure to Judaism, her first awareness that Jewishness could mean something other than what the Nazis said it meant. Early on, she realized how far behind she was academically: she understood nothing the teacher said and could not possibly take Hebrew dictation. Seventy years later she would still recall how mortified she was, reporting, "I was so embarrassed. I felt so terrible. I don't know how I did it, but I studied very hard. In fact I got an award in that class."

Ilse enjoyed religious rituals and was eager to light a Hanukkah menorah at home and to teach her mother the songs she learned. Once she had caught up with her classmates in Hebrew, she liked studying the language, but principally because of her facility with languages rather than out of an interest in reading the bible or the prayer book.

Hans had a bit more formal Jewish education than Ilse. He not only attended a Jewish school but also had a bar mitzvah, though the format of the ceremony was modified so as not to draw too much attention. The consensus of the members of the Reform Prinzregentenstrasse Synagogue was that group ceremonies were preferable to solo affairs, so Hans simply read a few lines of Torah along with nine other boys on a Saturday morning in May 1937. He wore a tallis (prayer shawl) and chanted in Hebrew. A year and a half later, he would see the synagogue in flames.

Neither Hans nor Ilse had much exposure to Jewish culture at home in the form of music or art or literature. *Bildung* for them meant Beethoven, Bach, and Brahms; Dürer, Schiller, and Goethe; not Klezmer music or Isaac Bashevis Singer. Their upbringing was much like that of their contemporary Peter Gay, who later wrote that "the idea of attachment to a social community or a common heritage was virtually meaningless to my parents. Jewish awareness? Jewish identity? These were empty slogans to them—and hence to me."[29]

Even more extreme were the views of Victor Klemperer, whose diaries reflect an enduring belief that he, unlike the Nazis, was a true German. Although his father served as a congregational rabbi in Berlin, his parents baptized him in infancy. Klemperer formally converted to Christianity as an adult, more out of opportunism than out of conviction. He married a Christian woman, further attenuating his ties to Judaism. In June 1934 he went so far as to write that "to me the Zionists are just as offensive as the Nazis, with their ancient cultural roots." As late as October 1938, Klemperer acknowledged that he had lost his nationalism and his patriotism but persisted in saying "no one can take my Germanness away from me." And when a friend suggested that the situation for Jews would not improve until they had a state of their own, Klemperer responded dismissively, saying "that is pure Nazism." In case his perspective was not clear enough, he went on to add that he would be "liberal and German forever."[30]

Ilse and Hans understood intuitively that they were both culturally similar to other Germans and biologically indistinguishable from them. It was obvious to them that the Nazis' racial ideology had no scientific basis. Every Jewish family seems to have its story of "passing," often in the form of a visiting "expert" in racial hygiene demonstrating "pure Aryan physiognomy" in school—and unwittingly choosing as a model a Jewish child.[31] And every family takes pleasure in recalling how they fooled their oppressors. Ilse remembers being called over by the SA to pose for a photograph intended to encourage donations to the *Winterhilfe,* welfare for the poor. "Making a donation" was a euphemism—for the majority of working-class wage earners, donations were compulsory: the SA simply knocked on the door and demanded money. In one movie house in Breslau, eight armed men showed up before a performance and announced that the exits were sealed to trap the "enemies of the state" inside. The police demanded a "gift" to the *Winterhilfe* from each moviegoer to "prove" he was not an enemy. Then fifty members of the SA came around with collection boxes.[32]

Donations to the *Winterhilfe* were mandatory, but the SA designed an imaginative advertising campaign in an attempt to make the population feel their contributions were voluntary. They told Ilse to stand next to a chimney sweep, widely held to be a symbol of good luck, and instructed her to pretend to drop a donation in his bucket. Terrified of disobeying, Ilse posed with the money and then scurried home. She told her parents nothing—but they found out when her picture appeared the following day on the front page of the *Stettiner Generalanzeigung,* the local daily newspaper, with the caption "young girl gives money to the *Winterhilfe.*" With her light brown hair, gray eyes, and straight nose, Ilse did not look Jewish to those Germans who believed in the stereotypes of the *Stürmer*. She generally enjoyed the freedom afforded by her appearance, though she never dared to sit on a park bench labeled *Juden unerwünscht* (Jews unwanted) or later *Juden verboten* (Jews prohibited) even in locations far from home, where no one was likely to recognize her.

As long as they lived in the Third Reich, Hans and Ilse thought of themselves as German and wanted to do what other children their age did. Ilse would have loved to belong to the Bund Deutscher Mädel (BDM), the Nazi equivalent of the Girl Scouts, with their smart uniforms, their tasseled knee socks, and their braids. She had little interest in the available Jewish youth groups—the Zionist Blau-Weiss (blue white) was out of the question for the Wulffs, who never considered immigrating to Palestine, and the Orthodox Essa was far too traditional for *drei-Tage Juden*—but she grudgingly joined the Bund der Jüdischen Jugend (Society of Jewish Youth), which appealed to middle-class and lower-middle-class German Jews. From Ilse's perspective, it was a weak imitation of the Bund Deutscher Mädel: no uniforms were allowed; hikes in the surrounding countryside were prohibited; and her mother refused to let her wear braids, associating them with the Nazi girls' groups.

Hans, too, was eager to belong to a club. In Osterode, he had joined the Jabotinsky League, a strongly Zionist organization that prepared its members for immigration to Palestine, because it was the only club open to Jewish boys. In Berlin, his youth group was one of two organizations devoted to sports, the Maccabis and the Hakoah. Hans played on his club's soccer team and further indulged his love of soccer by attending matches at a nearby stadium. He had to tone down his enthusiasm for Arsenal, the British team, at least in public: when he loudly applauded a British goal, his father gently chided him, saying that he really ought to root for the Berlin team, Hertha BSC.

The wave of anti-Semitism sweeping across the country, beginning with the infamous Nuremberg Laws, had a chilling effect on Hans's joie de vivre. His father was unemployed and Hans had no idea how he spent his days or what the family lived on apart from the proceeds from the sale of the business. He wanted desperately to go to the Olympic Games, which were held in Berlin in August 1936, but his parents were too concerned for his safety to let him go. Nonetheless, the excitement in the city was palpable and Hans was ecstatic when Jesse Owens—black, American, and a runner—took home four gold medals. Hans would have cringed had he known that the chairman of the American Olympic Committee and the coach of the U.S. track team quietly took the only two Jews out of the 4 x 100 meter relay.[33] And he could not help but notice that all the yellow benches with their *Juden unerwünscht* signs vanished, only to reappear two weeks after the games were over.

To escape the surrounding tension, Ilse read whatever she could get her hands on. She liked *Heidi,* a sentimental story about a Swiss girl, and she especially enjoyed a series about a little girl called Nesthäkchen who lived in Heidelberg and eventually married, had a family, and moved to Brazil. She also read Karl May, usually thought of as a favorite among the boys. Her other form of escape was to take long bicycle rides, typically through Stettin's many parks. Best of all was riding to majestic Auer Park and lying down in the grass with a book.

For many years, Ilse played with her Christian neighbor Edith, whose father owned a barbershop. The friendship came to an abrupt end the day Ilse came out to play and Edith simply turned around and walked away. Rejection by people she knew was more painful than insults from strangers. After the rebuff by Edith, all Ilse's friends were Jewish. Sadly, when it came to rejection and avoidance, the Jews of Stettin gave as well as received. They ostracized the Jews of eastern European descent, referring to them derogatorily as Ostjuden. Ilse's mother chastised her for playing with one of her classmates, telling her that she was never to bring "that child" to their home again. "That child" was a Jew of Polish extraction.

~

During Hans's years in Berlin, Germany grew progressively more militarized. Repeated international crises pushed the country ever closer to war. Until Kristallnacht, Hans, Ilse, and their parents remained largely oblivious to the brewing disaster. Hans read the *Frankfurter Allgemeine Zeitung,* the prestigious liberal newspaper that managed to retain some degree of editorial independence throughout the 1930s, but as long as he personally felt secure, he did not grasp what was happening. Ilse was similarly concerned with local dangers—the hoodlums lurking in doorways as she walked to school—but remained unaware of the looming external threat. Their parents, like so many other German Jews, believed that Hitler and his Nazis were just a passing phenomenon. The leaders of the Western world evinced little more concern. Only Churchill issued repeated warnings about the rearming of Germany, warnings that were consistently ignored. He would later write disparagingly in his memoir that "the English-speaking people through their unwisdom, carelessness, and good nature allowed the wicked to rearm."[34]

It should have been obvious that Germany was not a peace-loving nation when, in 1935, Hitler withdrew from the League of Nations. The German invasion of the demilitarized Rhineland the following year, in flagrant violation of the Treaty of Locarno, should have been a further warning sign. And the annexation of Austria by an emboldened Germany in March 1938 ought to have dispelled any remaining delusions about German intentions.

The thousands of Austrian Jews who fled after the Nazis arrived with their

Jew-hating, Jew-baiting propaganda sought refuge outside "greater Germany." Hans and Ilse would meet some of those refugees who escaped to Belgium, France, or Switzerland when they themselves became refugees. Perhaps this was when the Wulffs and the Garfunkels began to realize that Hitler and the Nazis were no mere ephemera. But maybe even the annexation of Austria did not strike them as an omen of what was to come. After all, the Austrians greeted the German army with flowers and kisses, in large measure acquiescing with enthusiasm to their incorporation into the Reich.

Even when Hitler seized the Sudetenland, part of Czechoslovakia, in September 1938, many Germans persuaded themselves that he was, as he said, simply following the wishes of the German-speaking majority in the area to be reunited with their brethren. The British prime minister Neville Chamberlain was also deluded; returning from a meeting with Hitler in Munich, Chamberlain proclaimed that he had achieved "peace in our time." If the politicians failed to understand Hitler's intentions toward his neighbors, surely two German teenagers and their parents, who just wanted to get on with their lives, could not be expected to understand. But his intention to marginalize and persecute the Jews could not be ignored after Kristallnacht.

3
From Bürger to Beggar

> States parties recognize the right of the child to education, and with a view to achieving this right . . . shall . . . make primary education compulsory and available free to all, . . . encourage the development of different forms of secondary education [and] make them available and accessible to any child.
>
> —Convention on the Rights of the Child, Article 28, 1989

In January 1939 Ilse's life had revolved around school, home, and a small circle of friends—that dwindled as, one by one, her classmates left the country. She was seldom allowed to go out on her own: it was too dangerous, with the Hitler Jugend on the prowl, looking for easy targets for their venom. Now it was February and Ilse was in Brussels, residing in a small room above her landlady's shoe store and living a largely solitary life. She spent her days reading, studying French, and, when the weather warmed up a bit, taking walks. Apparently, the women of the Comité d'Assistance aux Enfants Réfugiés Juifs, the group that had brought the refugee children from Germany and Austria to Belgium, had failed to make educational arrangements for their charges. The committee had arranged for the care of about 200 children, half in institutions and half in private families—perhaps there had simply not been time enough to make plans for schooling the children. Ilse was profoundly homesick.

Culturally, Brussels was not as exciting as Paris, London, New York, or Berlin for a teenager, though it was larger and freer than Stettin, a quintessentially middle- to lower-class small German city. To the chagrin of the Belgians, their most famous musicians and writers usually moved to France. Georges Simenon, the detective writer, had taken up residence in Paris. He was following in the footsteps of earlier prominent Belgians: the most eminent classical composer born in Belgium, César Franck, spent most of his career in France as did Belgian-born Adolphe Sax, inventor of the saxophone.

Belgium did have one prolific children's writer, Georges Remi, creator of the *Adventures of Tintin,* a sophisticated comic strip read by millions of children around the world. Writing under the pen name Hergé, Remi wrote "King Ottokar's Sceptre" in the late 1930s, a spoof that featured Syldovia, a small, peaceful agricultural country threatened by the neighboring country of Borduria, led by Mussler, a not-so-subtle combination of Hitler and Mussolini. If Ilse ever saw a copy of *The Adventures of Tintin,* she ignored it, since she regarded all comic books with unmitigated disdain. Her view of comics was no doubt influenced by the scurrilous cartoons that were regular features of German anti-Semitic propaganda. The "boulevard papers," sensational tabloids that were found on every street corner, caricatured Jews, routinely portraying them "with repellent curly hair, grotesquely hooked noses, evil eyes, sensual lips, busy cheating the world, orchestrating hostility to the Third Reich and, worse, lusting after blonde, often half-naked Aryan women."[1]

Ilse felt lonely, awkward, and unwanted in the apartment above the shoe store. She saw the bitter dislike in the salesgirl's eyes whenever their paths crossed. But it hadn't occurred to her that the older girl would scheme to get rid of a young refugee girl whom she perceived as her competition.

Although Ilse had never been happy with her landlady, she was mortified when Tante Friedel showed up to tell her she had to leave: she had been accused of taking a piece of fruit without permission and she was being thrown out. She felt deeply ashamed and wondered briefly what her parents would think. Her mother, after all, sent her regular reminders to "be a good girl" and "wear your rubbers when it rains."

Tante Friedel was no better equipped to take Ilse into her home than she had been on the child's arrival in Brussels—perhaps she was even less well disposed toward her, now that she had proved to be so ill mannered. Friedel brought Ilse to the Home Général Bernheim, a "children's home," effectively an orphanage.

The home, a three-story building on the outskirts of Brussels, was far from homey. The fifty girls lived in a huge dormitory room that afforded no privacy and made do with food that was so dreadful that Ilse ate very little and began losing weight. Responsibility for the girls fell to Elka and Alex Frank, a well-intentioned couple who had spent a few years on a kibbutz in Palestine and who were remarkably devoid of both compassion and common sense. Elka, a twenty-four-year-old nurse, was German, which meant that Ilse could in principle communicate with her. But Elka did not have the slightest idea how to relate to adolescent girls and did not make eye contact when she spoke to them. Her Belgian husband, a twenty-five-year-old with a background in agriculture, was just as ill equipped to work with children. One of the children in his care commented that she never saw him smile. But at least Ilse was together with other girls her age, and though they came from varied socioeconomic backgrounds—their parents were workers, businessmen, and intellectuals—and they had differing religious backgrounds—some were Reform, some Orthodox, some atheist—the girls were united by their language, their homesickness, and their experience as refugees.

Gradually, Ilse made friends with the eight or ten girls who were her age. Occasionally, Tante Friedel came on a weekend and took Ilse out for ice cream. Sometimes one of the wealthy ladies on the committee arrived in a chauffeur-driven black limousine and brought one of the girls to her house to play with her own children or perhaps with the dolls her children no longer found interesting.[2] Several of the older girls took bookkeeping and shorthand classes, but Ilse was too young. She was acutely aware of being pitied because she was thought to be poor, orphaned, and uncultured. In reality, she had, until very recently, been respectably middle-class, inculcated with *Bildung,* and attending school—and she still had loving parents who wrote to her weekly. Except for happenstance, which had deposited her in a foreign country with an unfamiliar language and an alien culture, she was not so different from the children of the ladies on the committee.

~

Hans, too, was homesick during his stay in Belgium, though he was too proud to admit it. Left to his own devices, Hans began exploring his Brussels neighborhood. He read the local newspapers, where he stumbled on an announcement of an upcoming track and field meet for teenagers at a nearby sports club. The Royal Racing Club de Bruxelles still exists today, although its focus is now on tennis and hockey.[3] In an astonishing display of initiative, Hans showed up at the club and signed up to compete in the 100 and 200 meter dash, and the broad jump.

The track and field coach at the club was intrigued by this intrepid adolescent who did not have proper track shoes and spoke broken French but who had managed to enter a competitive race. He was even more astonished when Hans won the 100 meter dash in 12.8 seconds —and was written up in the Brussels newspaper *Le Soir.* He took Hans under his wing, helping him particularly with the long jump—his best distance would be 5.6 meters. Hans's other event was the 200 meter dash. These were the three events in which Jesse Owens had won individual gold medals at the 1936 Berlin Olympics. (Owens got his fourth gold medal when his team won the 4 x 100 meter relay.)

He also continued his efforts to get out of the country. A scant two weeks after his arrival in Brussels, Hans had written to his cousins. "I have gone to Bruxelles," he announced, "where I live in the house of my relations. My parents want that I stay here—if it is possible—till my emigration to America." Cousin Bessie apparently did send an affidavit to Berlin as well as a letter to the Garfunkels expressing the hope that Hans, and perhaps the entire family, would soon make it to the United States. Hans replied, "I am very pleased to hear that you hope I shall go to America in a short time. In this country there is no possibility to stay a long time." It is not clear why he thought his stay in Belgium would have to be brief. Hans then asked Bessie to send a copy of the affidavit to the American Consulate General in Antwerp.

What he did not know when he wrote that letter on February 10 was that two days earlier, the American consul in Berlin had written to Bessie Silverman's congressman, responding to his request to expedite Hans Garfunkel's visa application. He wrote: "He [Hans Garfunkel] is, unfortunately, not in a position to qualify for a non-quota visa as a student for the reason that he is not in a position to present satisfactory evidence that he has a permanent domicile abroad to which he can return upon the completion of his studies." He added, helpfully, that Hans was on the waiting list for prospective immigrants under the German quota as of December 22, 1938, but "owing to the great number of persons registered before this date, it will be necessary for Mr. Garfunkel to wait for at least three years before his turn on the waiting list may be reached."

Undeterred, or perhaps simply uninformed, Hans continued to pursue the possibility of getting a student visa for the United States. On February 22, 1939, he again typed a letter to his "dear cousins":

> At the Consulate General at Antwerp we were informed that I can only get a visa for study, available for two years. In order to get this visa, we are in want of the following:
> a) A registration-slip of a school, which is accepted by the Departement [*sic*] of Labour;
> b) An affidavit, bearing only the following remark: Hans Garfunkel shall study (finish his education) in the United States.
> Your affidavit, which you have drawn up in December, cannot be used, because there is written: "he wishes to make his home here and to become a citizen of the United States."

A Western Union telegram from Julius to Bessie made much the same point, but Hans in his letter implied that his father might not fully understand the situation and begged Bessie "please, do so, as I have written." The telegram from Berlin, dated February 24, 1939, conveys a sense of desperation: HANS HAS GONE TO BRUSSELS. CAN GO TO AMERICA ONLY AS PUPIL. NEW AFFIDAVITS FOR TWO YEARS STUDY AND CERTIFICATE OF STATELY SCHOOL URGENTLY NECESSARY. NOT MENTION HIS BECOMING AMERICAN CITIZEN. EXCUSE TROUBLES. OTHERWISE IMPOSSIBLE. JULIUS.

Bessie supplied an affidavit and proof of admission to not one but two high schools in Chicago: the von Steuben High School and the Central YMCA High School of Chicago. She kept in her files a letter from the dean of the latter school dated March 14, 1939, stating: "This is to certify that Bessie G. Silverman . . . has this day enrolled her cousin, Hans Garfinkel [*sic*] of 197 de la Couronne, Brussels, Belgium, in the Central YMCA Day High School subject to his admission to the United States as a student. The usual financial arrangements have been made, and the Central YMCA Day High School is on the approved list."

There were no student visas, as the American consul in Berlin made clear, just the quota for immigrants for which the wait was at least three years. But Hans did not give up. He wrote to his cousins that he had been told that if the Silvermans congressman addressed a letter to the consul general in Antwerp, perhaps a visa could be arranged. He was not optimistic, however, saying, "I must confess that I am quite despaired. The worst thing is the uncertainty of the future."

Hans's training at the sports club ended abruptly when Hans learned he would no longer be living with the Rosengardes. After neglecting to send him to school for four months, the Rosengardes decided to enroll him in a Jesuit boarding school. A Catholic, French-speaking boarding school was an odd choice for a German Jewish refugee, but schools in Belgium were generally denominational and even the state-run schools provided either Catholic or Protestant instruction. Many of the private schools were also sectarian, and since Belgium was a predominantly Catholic country, most of these schools were Catholic. Hans speculates that the Rosengardes had been anticipating that he would stay with them for at most a couple of months. When the months dragged on, he outlived his welcome and they concluded that boarding school was a desirable alternative.

The Athenée Royale de Soignie was a top-ranked institution with a reputation for high academic standards, but Hans hated every minute he spent there. He found the other students provincial and he felt ill at ease in the exclusively French-speaking environment. He refused to cross himself and mumbled nonsense words instead of the requisite prayers before bed. And then, in an episode strikingly reminiscent of Ilse's experience, he was expelled after a few weeks for allegedly stealing a pair of running shoes.

Hans was picked up from the school by his previous benefactors, the Rosengardes, much as Ilse had been picked up by Tante Friedel after her supposed misdemeanor. He was brought to the Home Speyer, the analog for boys of the Home Général Bernheim where Ilse lived. Housing fifty German and Austrian boys, its barred windows faced a treeless, joyless street in the working-class section of Brussels. One of the boys likened Speyer to a prison, with its high walls and barren, desolate living quarters.[4]

Speyer was run by a Belgian named Gaspar DeWaay whose guiding philosophy was to "rule with punishment."[5] Reputedly a former streetcar conductor, he proved an incompetent administrator and an inadequate pedagogue. The home didn't provide enough food for its gaggle of growing boys, but at least Hans lived with other German-speaking refugees. He made friends: Addi Nussbaum, Edgar Chaim, and Leo Lewin would stay in touch with each other for the rest of their lives. Hans started a soccer team for the boys in the children's home. At the same time, he and his friends scavenged for cheap, slightly spoiled food in the markets of Brussels to supplement what they got at Speyer.

In less than a year, Hans had gone from being a well-fed, middle-class boy to a waif in an orphanage. Likewise, Ilse was no longer an obedient, dutiful, *bürgerliches Kind,* but rather an object of pity, a charity case.

Largely confined to their respective "homes," Hans and Ilse were insulated from the surrounding Belgian society. They were only dimly aware of the anti-German sentiment in the country. Despite Belgium's official neutrality, the country had been invaded by Germany in 1914 and occupied for the duration of World War I. The memories of the costly German occupation remained vivid in the 1930s. Belgium was a signatory of the Locarno Treaty of 1925, a follow-up to the Treaty of Versailles, in which Germany renounced any claim to the territory ceded to Belgium in 1919. France and England, the other Allied participants in the treaty, agreed to guarantee protection of Belgium's borders. Belgium also inherited the former German colonies of Rwanda and Burundi, a transfer that deepened Germany's already severely wounded pride.

In April, Ilse learned from her parents that they were leaving for China. Sailing from Italy, they would travel through Egypt, India, and Japan, finally docking in the international port of Shanghai in May. Ilse got one letter from her parents during their monthlong journey; enclosed was a handkerchief embroidered with a ship. Ilse carried that handkerchief with her for years to come.

Not long afterward the *St. Louis* steamed into the nearby harbor of Antwerp. Carrying 927 German and Austrian Jewish refugees, the ship had reached Cuba in May, but its passengers had not been allowed to disembark. One after another, seven other Latin American countries refused to let the refugees in. The captain appealed to President Roosevelt, who did not respond. On June 6 the *St. Louis* set sail for Europe. Thanks to the mediation of the Joint Distribution Committee, a leading New York–based Jewish refugee organization, England, France, Belgium, and Holland finally agreed to receive the passengers. Those accepted by Belgium were sent by train to Brussels and from there to a refugee camp in Liège.[6] This dramatic demonstration of world callousness to the plight of the refugees triggered alarm in Ilse, but she no doubt assumed the passengers would be safe in Europe. The father of two of the children who later joined her group—Manfred and Gustav Manasse—was on the *St. Louis* and would not survive the war.

In the summer of 1939, several of the children in the Home Général Bernheim were sent to a more healthful environment. Ilse, who had been thin even before she began losing weight because of the scarcely edible food, was sufficiently pale and scrawny to be among the chosen. She traveled to a village in the countryside with two other girls, Edith Moser and Lixie Grabkowicz, where they lived with a strict, authoritarian woman. Their stay was tolerable only because the landlady had a kind and considerate eighteen-year-old daughter who knew how to have fun with the three young girls.

The European school year resumed in August after a summer break, and Ilse was sent to the village school. It was run by nuns who were even stricter and more authoritarian than Ilse's landlady. They demanded that the children sit motionless and silent at their desks, their hands folded. After a few weeks, Ilse had had enough of the toxic atmosphere dominated by uneducated and narrow-minded teachers. To the astonishment of the other girls, a very authentic sounding meow suddenly emanated from Ilse's seat. Everyone began to giggle. The nun at the front of the class scowled, her triple chin quivering as she waddled across the room, searching for the perpetrator of this terrible sin. "Who did that?" she demanded, her angry red face framed by her white wimple. Fearful that the nun would impose collective punishment on the class, Ilse confessed. Then it was Ilse's turn to be surprised—because she had admitted her "terrible deed," she was spared and the nun meted out no punishment that day. The other children thought Ilse was remarkably brave.

The sojourn in the village came to an abrupt end with the outbreak of war on September 1, 1939. Germany invaded Poland and, honoring their mutual assistance treaty in word if not in deed, England and France declared war on Germany. Belgium remained neutral, dependent on the French and British to come to her aid if attacked. Ilse and her friends Edith and Lixie returned to the children's home in Brussels.

Hans spent much of his time in the Home Speyer scheming to leave the country. His correspondence with Cousin Bessie, which he had initiated while he was in Berlin and continued after his arrival in Brussels, heated up at the time of his move to the orphanage. One letter, handwritten on August 21,

1939, in understandable if not always grammatical English, was sent without the assistance or knowledge of the Rosengardes:

> You must forgive me for my impatience. As I have already written to you, we must find as soon as ever possible a new solution. You know Mr. Rosengarde is not willing to pay further my stay in Belgium and therefore intends to place me in the home for the German Refugees at Brussels. He says that his decision is as a result of the political situation in Europe. To his mind I should be more safe in case of war being in that home. But his exact reason . . . I already told you. I have as good as no hope to go straight on for America in a very near future. Therefore I ask you to try everything and have me go to England. I am so sorry that I must trouble you continually. I really don't know how to thank you for your kindness and I am afraid you are considering me ungrateful. With all my love and my best regards to you. Your affectionate cousin, Hans.

Paula Garfunkel sent a telegram conveying a similar message, minus the dig at the Rosengardes: CONSUL BEACH HAS REFUSED VISA. PLEASE TO TRY AFTER PERMIT TO ENGLAND. CORDIALLY. PAULA. His American cousins were in no position to arrange for Hans to go to England. For the time being he had no choice but to remain in Belgium.

~

The children in the refugee homes had an inkling of trouble on the horizon when the Nazi-Soviet Non-Aggression Pact was signed on August 23, 1939. Since Germany and Russia had spent much of the previous six years vilifying each other and had been the prime supporters of opposing sides in the Spanish Civil War, the world was shocked when they joined forces. It was clear to many observers that Hitler would march next into Poland, reassured that his aggression would go unchallenged by the Soviets. After staging a fake attack on a German radio station near the Polish border, an "attack" blamed on the Poles but in fact carried out by German prisoners acting on Gestapo orders, the German army crossed into Poland on September 1. Two days later, in keeping with her treaty obligations, England declared war on Germany. France followed suit in a few hours. Hans and Ilse must have fervently hoped that the British would join the Poles in repulsing the Germans: Hitler would be defeated and they would all be able to go home. But neither England nor France mobilized their armies. The Poles tried to defend themselves, but they were no match for the German Wehrmacht with its 750,000 troops and another million men in the reserves (notwithstanding the limit of 100,000 men imposed by the Treaty of Versailles).[7]

By September 17, the western half of Poland was in German hands and the eastern half was under Soviet control, as spelled out in the secret protocol contained in the German-Soviet pact. On September 27, Warsaw capitulated, and the Polish campaign ended. Horrors raged in Poland: the Nazis and their Polish accomplices rounded up Jews and shot them or herded them into buildings that they then set on fire; Torah scrolls were desecrated and burned as well. By the end of December, 250,000 Jews had died in Nazi-occupied Poland, whether by shooting, starvation, or from disease in what was, from the beginning, "a war of racial conquest, subjugation and extermination."[8] Parts of Poland were annexed to Germany proper—these areas were to be "cleansed" of Jews and Poles. Other parts of Poland, chiefly the *Generalgouvernement* under the control of Hans Frank, were to be the dumping ground for the population expelled from the now-German sections. All told, over a million people were displaced during the early months of the Nazi occupation.

The children in the Home Général Bernheim and at the Home Speyer believed they were safe in western Europe. Terrible things might be happening in faraway Poland, but the war had not reached Belgium. There were fascists in Belgium when Hans and Ilse arrived in 1939, but they were neither strong nor popular. The Belgian fascist party was the Parti Rexi (Rexist Party), founded by Leon Degrelle, whose only prior claim to fame was that he had failed his final law school examinations three times. The party was overwhelmingly defeated in the Belgian national elections of 1938 and its newspaper *Le Pays Réel* was banned along with *Der Stürmer* in October 1939.[9] Belgium's 90,000 Jews—just over 1 percent of the population—lived primarily in the two largest cities, Antwerp and Brussels, where they experienced little discrimination. Fully 15,000 of the Jewish population were refugees from Germany.

The children's sense of security suffered a major setback with the fall of Norway and Denmark on April 9, 1940. Then, on May 10, German troops invaded Belgium.

Air raid sirens awakened the fifty girls sleeping on their cots in the dormitory of the Home Général Bernheim. All except Ilse, who slept through both the shrill alarm and the anxious chatter of the other girls as they grabbed a few belongings—pictures of their parents, a letter from a best friend still living in Germany or Austria—and clattered down the stairs to seek shelter in the basement. Not until the entire group sat at the long dining room tables for the dry toast and dilute coffee that passed for breakfast did fourteen-year-old Ilse learn that the German army had invaded Belgium.

Ilse couldn't eat any breakfast. Her stomach was slightly queasy and her chest felt tight. But a day later she felt better—she and her friends witnessed a dogfight between a British and a German fighter plane. The aircraft were close enough for them to make out the Union Jack on one and the black swastika on the other. The Messerschmitt burst into flames and fell out of the sky—to the cheers of the girls and the Belgian civilians who were watching with them. Finally, England had been jolted out of its complacency. The "phony war" that had lasted more than eight months was over. No longer would England and France sit back while Germany overran her neighbors, as she had Poland and Czechoslovakia, beating, humiliating, enslaving, or murdering the Jews in every town her troops entered. Now that the war had arrived in western Europe, England had at last been prodded into action. England would win the war, Ilse was confident, and then she would be reunited with her parents.

No air raid sirens awoke the refugee children in the Home Speyer the night of May 10, 1940—they were too far away from the airport, the principal target of the German bombers, and the center of town, the second target. But the following morning, the newspaper headlines screamed the news. Hans, who had turned fifteen three weeks earlier and was one of the more urbane of the boys in the home, was a news junkie. The local paper ran the story that had also been transmitted by wireless to the *New York Times:* "Brussels Is Raided: 400 Reported Killed—Troops Cross Border at Four Points." It continued, "The invasion Belgium had feared since the outbreak of the European war came before dawn this morning. About a hundred German planes flew over this city and bombed the airport." Starting at 5:30 a.m., Belgian antiaircraft guns responded from the center of the city.[10]

Hans, like Ilse, was confident the British would prevail, but his most immediate concern was to get out of the path of the German Panzers. He knew from some of his friends in the Home Speyer what had happened in Austria after the Anschluss. Emboldened by the enthusiastic crowds that German troops encountered when they crossed into Austria on the morning of March 12, 1938, the new Nazi government immediately introduced laws depriving Jews of civil rights. Within weeks, they ousted them from the professions and the civil service. Even more ominously, they instituted a "general cleansing of jewified Austria."[11]

Terrified by the German invasion, tens of thousands of Belgians began fleeing the country. And on May 11, just one day after the first German tanks rolled into Belgium, Hans Garfunkel made two telephone calls. The first call was to Adolph Rosengarde, his father's cousin. The Flemish maid answered the phone. She was happy to hear from Hans but said no, the Rosengardes were not in. They had left earlier that day by plane for the Belgian Congo. Hans never heard from them again. The second call was to Mrs. Goldschmidt, the head of the Committee to Aid Jewish Refugee Children. Hans learned that she, too, along with the other women on the committee, had fled the country.

What Hans did not know was that behind the scenes, the women of the Comité d'Assistance aux Enfants Réfugiés Juifs were busily trying to make arrangements for the children. The chair of the committee, Marguerite Goldschmidt, whose husband was a businessman and treasurer of the Belgian Red Cross, together with the committee's treasurer, Lily Felddegen, provided the funds and the means to enable Elka and Alex Frank to take the children to France.[12]

The Franks, who were Jewish, realized they needed to get out and agreed to escort the children. Gaspar DeWaay failed to see what all the fuss was about, but when two train cars headed for France were reserved, one for the girls and one for the boys, he agreed to come along. Alex Frank's brother worked for the Belgian railroad and reportedly helped reserve the cars.

On May 14, 1940, four days after the German troops crossed into Belgium, the fifty boys from the Home Speyer and the fifty girls from the Home Général Bernheim arrived at the railroad station in Brussels. Elka instructed the girls to take extra clothes, which they did by wearing two or three dresses, one on top of the other. Gaspar advised the boys to pack food. The net effect was that the girls sweltered and starved on the way and the boys were cold for months afterward. The abandonment of Hans's few possessions made a strong impression on his parents, whose subsequent letters repeatedly referred to the clothes that were languishing in Belgium and who continually asked whether the children had been reunited with their missing clothing.

All fifty girls were crammed into a single car of the hot, dark, and windowless train. They had no idea where they were going and whether their parents would be able to find them at their new destination. The cars moved steadily for a while, then lurched to a halt, stood still for no apparent reason, and then began moving again. All the stopping and starting was too much for Ilse. Waves of nausea overcame her and she was terrified that she would throw up, creating an unbearable stench in the already airless car. Frightened, sick to her stomach, and embarrassed, Ilse began to cry.

Elka Frank worried that Ilse's sobs would set off a chain reaction: the prospect of fifty wailing, inconsolable children was too much for her. It did not occur to her to say something reassuring or to put her arm around the thin, fourteen-year-old who lay moaning on the floor, clutching her stomach under her three layers of clothing. Instead, Elka pushed her way over to Ilse and kicked her, yelling at her to shut up. She did not stop until one of the older girls told her to leave Ilse alone.[13]

Ilse never forgot those blows.

For hours, the train continued on its stop-and-go journey. At one point it completely changed direction—Hans was at first hopeful that they were heading toward a port since they seemed to be traveling along the coast. Perhaps, he speculated, the plan was to board a ship for England. But then the train headed southeast again. Sometimes when they stopped, the doors opened and the local people gave the children bread and water. Apart from those sporadic donations, the girls had nothing to eat or drink.

Later during the seemingly endless journey, the children heard the alarming roar of low-flying airplanes. They heard a tremendous ruckus and learned that one of the other cars in the long freight train had been bombed.

At another stop, the children saw a second train across from theirs, filled with British soldiers. They joined in the chorus as the soldiers sang, "It's a long way to Tipperary, but my heart's right there." The youngsters could not imagine that the soldiers they saw on the adjacent train—young and energetic and patriotic—would fail to crush the Germans. But within days the German army had cut off the British Expeditionary Force from the main French army and from its own bases in western France. Trapped, with their backs to the Atlantic Ocean, the British troops were at risk of being driven into the sea. Thanks to a gallant effort by soldiers and civilians alike, the Dunkirk evacuation, code-named Operation Dynamo, rescued 338,226 men in one week. Commencing on May 26, a grand total of 222 naval ships and 665 civilian boats would ferry British, French, and a few Belgian soldiers from Dunkirk to the British coast.[14]

After four days and five nights, the train stopped its zigzagging course through Belgium and France. The doors opened and the hundred children tumbled out into a magnificent spring day. They had reached Toulouse, a city in the southern part of France, a mere fifty miles from the Pyrenees. From there, they boarded a bus to the village of Seyre.

Outside their windows, they saw fields, small farms, and acres of vineyards. The countryside was quiet, with no armored trucks spewing exhaust fumes, loudspeakers blaring directions, or uniformed policemen and soldiers. Hans sat next to Hanni, a girl he had had a crush on in high school in Berlin. Looming ahead, the refugees saw a magnificent white castle on top of a hill. Just as they began imagining the marvels that lay in store for them in this storybook destination, the bus veered off in a different direction and brought them instead to an abandoned barn that was to be their home for the next year. They slept in the vermin-infested stables on uncovered palettes of straw. The Home Général Bernheim, even the prisonlike Home Speyer, were luxurious by comparison. But for the moment, the children were safe.

~

Belgium was soon under German control. The Belgian army resisted bravely, holding off the Germans for eighteen days before King Leopold III unconditionally surrendered, an act regarded as treasonous by many of his countrymen. Leopold was an overt anti-Semite who would later say about the 30,000 Jews who had entered Belgium since September 1939, "action against them cannot be harsh enough."[15] The Belgian cabinet fled to London to establish a government in exile. The royal family stayed behind, under house arrest, until they were deported to Germany in 1944. When Leopold returned in 1945, after being liberated by American troops, he hoped to resume his role as monarch. But the demonstrations in Belgium were so massive that he chose instead to abdicate in favor of his eldest son, Baudouin.

Within months of their arrival, the Germans set about depriving the Belgian Jews of their civil rights, their economic livelihood, and their dignity. They proceeded more gradually than they had in Poland, where they found many of the indigenous population eager to carry out their most heinous schemes with unexpected cruelty and thoroughness. The Belgians, by contrast, did not have a long tradition of anti-Semitism and had suppressed the relatively small fascist Rexist Party in recent years.

The existing civil service continued most of its routine functions even after the German occupation. The German general Alexander von Falkenhausen, who became the military commander, supported the anti-Jewish measures, and as early as 1940, Jewish lawyers and civil servants lost their jobs. German racial laws were imposed and kosher slaughtering was banned. Starting in May 1941, Jewish businesses were "Aryanized," that is, sold to non-Jews for a token amount, leading to the impoverishment of the community. In October 1941, a strict curfew was put in place for all Jews; in December, they were excluded from public schools. In May 1942 Jews were required to wear a yellow star; males age sixteen to sixty and females sixteen to forty were conscripted into forced labor. While no friend of the Jews, von Falkenhausen was opposed to the most extreme deprivations of life and liberty advocated by his Nazi superiors. He was arrested after being implicated in the abortive 1944 conspiracy to kill Hitler.[16]

The Belgian people, as a whole, did not cooperate with Nazi efforts to round up and deport the 65,000 Jews who had remained behind at the time of the invasion. Railway workers left the doors of deportation trains open so that those inside could escape. Postal workers read letters addressed to the German authorities and made sure that those containing personal denunciations were not delivered. The Belgian police proved singularly incompetent at finding the Jews they were supposed to deliver to assembly points for deportation. And the Belgian clergy were among the most active in Europe in rescuing Jews.[17]

Despite the resistance of the Belgians, the Nazis succeeded in bringing their iniquitous final solution to Belgium. From the first transport to Auschwitz in August 1942 to the liberation of Belgium by the Allies in September 1944, 26,000 Jews had been sent to their deaths. The first to be taken were those, like Hans and Ilse, who were foreign born.

4
Refugees in the Free Zone

> The Contracting States shall accord to refugees lawfully staying in their territory the same treatment with respect to public relief and assistance as is accorded to their nationals.
>
> —Convention Relating to the Status of Refugees, Article 23, 1951

The dazed, dirty, and hungry children who emerged from the bus into the French sunlight were so glad to have arrived somewhere, anywhere, that the youngest ones forgot to cry and the oldest ones forgot to worry. Many of them were excited about the new adventure they were about to begin in southern France.

But even the most upbeat of the children were stunned when they saw their new home was an abandoned stable. The accommodations, Ilse would say more than sixty-five years later, were "truly deluxe: we had rats and mice and fleas and lice and whatever else you can imagine." Behind the stables was an outhouse; the children used leaves for toilet paper.

After the initial shock, the older children began as thorough a cleaning of their quarters as they could manage without either scouring powder or vacuum cleaners. Within days of their arrival, the villagers had supplied some rudimentary furniture. The older boys in the group fashioned simple tables and primitive beds of wooden planks. The small stipend provided to refugee children by the French government sufficed to purchase basic supplies from local farmers, though the children primarily subsisted on turnips—turnip stew, turnip soup, turnip mush. All the survivors of those years remember the turnips, and most of them would never be able to eat turnips again. They also ate cornmeal in the form of cornbread and cornmeal stew. Their cook, Flora Schlesinger, who had come along from Belgium, was a veritable magician in the kitchen, turning what little she had into dishes that, if only barely palatable, were at least nutritious. Sometimes the stews had bits of meat—usually animal lungs or stomachs that the local farmers did not deign to eat.[1]

A single main street comprised the entire commercial area of the nearby village of Seyre, which boasted a church with a clock tower and a small general store. Most of the village men were in the French army, leaving behind perhaps 300 of the very old and the very young. The village idiot remained behind—a man of indeterminate age who always wore the same dirty clothes and sported a beret that had seen better days. Fields of thistles and weeds grew beyond the town.[2]

The adults in charge of the refugees were a motley crew: Alex Frank had rejoined his regiment in the Belgian army, his wife, Elka, Ilse's tormenter on the freight train, stayed with the children. Both Flora the cook and her husband had traveled with the group from Belgium. Gaspar DeWaay, the reviled director of the boys' refugee home in Brussels, was in charge of the colony.

In his thirties, with wavy blond hair and glasses, DeWaay insisted that the children call him "Uncle Gaspar." Accompanied by his wife, Lucienne, who wanted be called "Tante Marie," he was "our most terrible scourge," according to one of the older girls.[3] He treated the children with contempt and required that they speak French exclusively. Legend has it that he heard one of the younger children ask "*was?*" (German for "what?") and immediately ordered her into seclusion, with only bread and water for a week. But already in those early days at the farmstead in Seyre, the children had banded together and they sneaked food to the hapless victim of DeWaay's harsh discipline. The boys were even worse off—Gaspar beat them with a cane if they disobeyed him. One of the boys, Edgar Chaim, ran away when he found his nemesis from Brussels in charge once again. Edgar stayed on a local farm until DeWaay left, which happened mercifully soon.

According to one account, rebellion to protect then three-year-old Manfred Manasse precipitated DeWaay's departure.[4] Manfred—now Fred—was a strong-willed child. Today he lives in the Boston area, is friends with Hans and Ilse, and is still strikingly strong-willed. The fight, or near-fight, started when Manfred refused to eat his gruel, pronouncing it disgusting, a sentiment that the other children clearly shared. In a bizarre reversal of the orphan Oliver Twist asking for more, Manfred Manasse brazenly asserted he was not going to take another bite. Gaspar DeWaay was unmoved by the outspoken preschooler: if Manfred did not eat every morsel on his plate, it would be bread and water for him. At that point, one of the older boys, incensed by this abusive behavior, approached "Uncle Gaspar" menacingly. Only the intervention of one of the other adults prevented a fight from breaking out. Shortly afterward, DeWaay and his wife left Seyre without a word. Some claim they absconded with supplies that had been intended for the children; some are sure they took what little money the group had; everyone agrees they did not say goodbye and they were not missed.

Alex Frank, who had been serving in the Belgian army, soon rejoined his wife and the refugees. After Belgium capitulated to the Germans on May 28, the military no longer needed his services. Frank was a humorless man, with no experience as a schoolteacher or the headmaster of a boarding school or a summer camp counselor—any one of which would have better prepared him for leadership of an assortment of three- to eighteen-year-olds than his time on a kibbutz and in the army. But he meant well and he did what his limited skills and equally limited imagination allowed. He set up a routine, dividing up the chores and organizing the children into groups, with the oldest ones caring for the youngest ones.

Ilse, in a long poem called "A Day in Seyre" written in her neat, schoolgirl penmanship, commented that the "chores are not always well done, which makes Mr. Frank enraged." Alex Frank, like his predecessor Gaspar DeWaay, believed in bread-and-water treatment for youthful offenders: Ilse wrote that "dry bread and water are his [Frank's] favorite punishment." But she did not seem overly upset by his discipline, adding that "a neighbor smuggled something in a cup."

The poem summarized a typical day. "A day passes approximately as follows," she wrote. When the bell rang at 7:00 a.m., the group leader would try, usually unsuccessfully, to roust her girls from bed. They would finally bounce out of bed when they heard the whistle blow for breakfast; they would then dash into the dining room, which was furnished with tables and benches. The meal was followed by chores, including sweeping, sewing, and laundry. Each girl had a single needle that she guarded like a precious jewel. Nobody was particularly good at sewing—the seams were crooked, the stitches uneven. Then came lunch, followed by rest period and outdoor activities, at least until the weather was too cold. They walked in the blissfully serene countryside, often in search of blackberries or figs: "the figs taste so good!" the poem proclaimed. In the evening, after yet another dispiriting meal—Ilse diplomatically omitted reference to the endless turnip stews and cornmeal mush—they see "what's on the program" for the evening. All in all, she said, writing before the bitter cold winter days made their lives very hard to bear:

Über ein halbes Jahr in Seyre wir sind
Und ganz gut eingelebt ich find.
(We have been in Seyre for over half a year
And are well settled in, I think.)

The poem ended on a bittersweet note, expressing contentment but a looming anxiety about the future:

Neigt der Tag seinem Ende zu
Legen wir uns mit Freuden zur Ruh'
So vergeht nun Tug um Tag

Weiss wer, was die Zukunkft noch bringen mag.
(As the night draws nigh
We lie down joyously to our rest
So go the days
Who knows what the future will bring.)

Ilse did not mention the French soldiers stationed near the barn who were all too interested in the teenaged girls now living in their neighborhood. She later recalled that when the girls went to use the outhouse, they had to go in pairs or carry a stick or take one of the boys along for protection. Another girl remembered that they boarded up the windows and doors of the barn at night to keep the undisciplined, often intoxicated French soldiers away.

Ilse also did not mention in her poem the skin problems that so many of the children developed. They got scabies, which causes profound itching as the tiny mites burrow under the skin of the abdomen, chest, arms, and legs. Scabies are notoriously difficult to eradicate; even with the effective medications now available, the challenge is to destroy the mites in clothes and bedding so the infestation does not recur. The standard procedure today is to wash every article of contaminated clothing in industrial strength washing machines and to discard items like pillows or at least stash them away in plastic bags for months until every mite has starved to death. The only hot water the children had at Seyre was the water they pumped from a well and heated over a fire. And they had no medications to apply to their raw, itchy skin.

Malnourished, the children also developed boils and hepatitis.[5] One of the girls described recurrent skin problems for the rest of her life—rashes that flared up and wounds that did not heal. Hans had a particularly severe case of boils or furuncles. One of the older girls ran the makeshift "infirmary" and drained and dressed the pus-filled sores. Hans came to the infirmary often, between his various chores, for treatment of his recalcitrant furuncles. He and Inge Berlin, the seventeen-year-old "nurse," used the time to discuss politics. Always eager for an intellectual discussion, Hans provocatively suggested that many assimilated German Jews would have been supporters of Hitler if only the Nazis had not been such vicious anti-Semites. Inge was outraged, but when she became a professional historian decades later, she would express agreement with Hans's position.

Hans argued about all kinds of issues, not just politics. He protested against the treatment the Franks instituted for the various skin problems. Their approach was to heat up a tub of water, add some powdered sulfur, and have one child after another bathe in the same water. Hans took one look at the crusts floating in the tub and concluded that the "treatment" was completely unhygienic. Its one incontrovertible effect was to make all the children reek of sulfur, a smell indistinguishable from that of rotten eggs. Despite his entirely justified criticisms, the group bathing continued.

By the fall of 1940, the situation at the barn had worsened. It was unseasonably cold and the few articles of clothing the children had brought with them from Brussels were not warm enough. In a letter to his Cousin Bessie, Hans wrote: "That is a splendid idea that you will send me some clothing because I didn't take with me anything besides a shirt, two pairs of stockings, 1 pair of shoes, and some handkies. Underwear and a sweater I don't have at all, I shall be very thankful for a package with some warm clothing."

Despite the adverse conditions, the children still grew—perhaps not as much as they would have in other circumstances (Ilse would reach a maximum height of 5 feet 1 inch and Hans, 5 feet 3 inches), but just enough so that the clothes they had barely fit. Each child had a single, thin blanket. The French refugee organizations that had been supplying provisions were stretched to the limit, and their priority was French children orphaned during the brief fight against Germany, not a group of non-French Jews.

In May 1940 when the 100 refugee children arrived in Seyre, France was still a free country, though already under siege by the Germans. The very day the group reached their destination in France, Churchill gave his first address as British prime minister. The children would have been inspired and reassured by his words: "The long night of barbarism will descend [on the Czechs, Poles, Norwegians, Danes, Dutch, and Belgians] unbroken by a star of hope, unless we conquer, as conquer we must, as conquer we shall."[6] They learned before the end of the month that Belgium had fallen to the Germans and were greatly relieved that they, along with 25,000 other Belgian Jews who had fled to France, had gotten out just in time. But with Norway, Denmark, Belgium, Luxemburg, and Holland all coming under Nazi control in a few short months, the German army believed it was invincible. Its next target was France, its longtime enemy.

Germany's most recent humiliation at the hands of the French had been at Versailles, the magnificent palace with its elaborate gardens, its chandeliers and ballrooms. Versailles was symbolic of the 1919 peace process, which virtually all Germans regarded as reprehensible and dishonorable. That France had later taken a hard line on reparations had not helped heal the wounds between the two countries: when Germany asked for a moratorium on its payments in 1923, Prime Minister Poincaré responded by sending 40,000 troops into the Ruhr, thus rubbing more salt in Germany's wounds.

France between the wars had been weak, hurting from the worldwide depression, from inflation, and above all from its tremendous losses during the

Great War. A total of 1.5 million Frenchmen died during the war, and another 3.5 million were injured.[7] During the twenty years following the armistice, France went through a succession of governments, some lasting only a few months, one only a few days. Some were socialist in flavor, many were solidly bourgeois, defending private property and lower taxes. All were strongly anti-Bolshevik, as Russian Communism and to a lesser degree, the Catholic Church, rather than fascism, were held to be the greatest threats to the French way of life. By 1939, what united the nation was the memory of the horrific losses of the Great War and a strong sentiment against renewed fighting.[8]

In light of the apathy of the French public, it was not surprising that the government did nothing concrete after declaring war on Germany on September 3, 1939. The provocation for the declaration was the Nazi invasion of Poland; France was treaty-bound to come to Poland's defense. Had France immediately challenged Germany in the west, the Nazis would have faced a two-front war at a time when they might not have had the strength to respond. Instead, France entered the *drôle de guerre,* or phony war. During the nine and a half months between the declaration of war and the fall of France, another series of ineffectual governments came and went: the indecisive regime of Edouard Daladier, the short rule of Paul Reynaud, and ultimately the leadership of Pierre Laval, who happily cooperated with Hitler and Mussolini. When the Germans invaded France in early June 1940, they encountered very little resistance. Millions of Frenchmen fled to the countryside by bicycle, car, train, or on foot, as the German army marched inexorably toward Paris. On June 14 the Nazis paraded down the Champs d'Elysées, having taken a million French prisoners of war in the previous eight days. They hung a swastika from the Arc de Triomphe. On June 25, France formally surrendered to the German army in the very same railroad car in which the Germans had surrendered in 1918.

A few short weeks after Hans, Ilse, and their fellow refugees reached Seyre, the French prime minister resigned and a new government was formed in France. The eighty-three-year-old Marshal Phillipe Pétain, hero of the Battle of Verdun in the Great War, became head of state and Pierre Laval, the real seat of power, became vice president of the council of ministers. While only the northern two-thirds of France was directly under German military occupation, with the southern part constituting the so-called free zone, in fact the Vichy government had jurisdiction over the entire country. The puppet masters manipulating the strings were the Germans. All decrees of the Vichy government required approval by the Nazi military authority. Conversely, the Nazis could force the Vichy government to institute whatever decrees they wished.

Not much pressure was required for the authorities in Vichy to suspend the political and civil liberties of Jews throughout France. All the Jews in the country—the 270,000 who had lived in France before the outbreak of the war (230,000 in Paris, including 30,000 who had emigrated earlier from Germany), as well as the 40,000 refugees from Holland and Belgium—were at risk.[9] As early as July 1940, SS Commander Reinhard Heydrich instituted wholesale expulsions of Jews, driving out 22,000 Jews from Alsace Lorraine, which Germany had reannexed in 1936, and unceremoniously dumping them on country roads in the south of France. By autumn the Vichy government had passed a Statut des Juifs, or Jewish statute, without much prompting from their Nazi minders. This law ousted Jews from all administrative positions and prevented them from teaching in colleges or high schools. The same law made foreign and stateless Jews—Hans and Ilse were both—subject to internment in the barbaric prisons at Gurs, Rivesaltes, and elsewhere, camps initially created for political prisoners, much as the Germans had originally established Dachau and Buchenwald for political undesirables.[10]

With the local situation in Seyre increasingly precarious—the French refugee organizations announced they were cutting off aid to the children's colony—and the noose tightening for Jews in France as a whole, the women of the Belgian refugee committee appealed to the Swiss Red Cross for help. Several of them, including Mrs. Alfred Goldschmidt, the former head of the Belgian Refugee Committee, had fled to Vichy France in the same exodus as the children. At a meeting in September 1940 set up by Alex Frank and Mrs. Goldschmidt, the Swiss Red Cross agreed "to assume full responsibility for the upkeep and education" of the children's colony at Seyre.[11] The hope at the time was to create a camp on a farm for the older children and to find a separate facility for the younger ones. An additional plan was to integrate other refugee children, such as those displaced by the Spanish Civil War, into the same sites. Mrs. Goldschmidt made a donation of $918 in U.S. currency, a substantial sum in 1940, earmarked to help the children immigrate or to provide for urgent necessities.

On October 1 the Swiss Red Cross formally assumed responsibility for the 100 refugee children in Seyre and dispatched the director of its Toulouse bureau, Maurice Dubois, to visit the group. He was appalled at the conditions and immediately started looking for better quarters in which to house the young refugees.

As soon as the Swiss took over, even before a new facility was found, the living conditions improved for Hans and Ilse. Hans wrote to his Cousin Bessie: "The Swiss Red Cross sends lots of milk and cheese and sometimes corn." He did not add that often the milk was sour and tasted so terrible the children could hardly swallow it. Though he felt more secure once the Swiss were in charge, Hans was still lonely and frightened, commenting: "I get as good as no news from my dear parents, nor from my brother. You can also imagine that it is very hard to be alone and without news."

At the beginning of autumn, Hans and some other boys worked on neighboring farms, helping with the potato crop. The work provided a distraction from their wretched living conditions—and a chance to obtain additional food. Hans was also in charge of a group of younger children: "I take care of a group of 12 boys from 12–15 years. In the morning we go to work and in the afternoons, I am giving different lessons."

As winter approached, the temperature dropped precipitously. All the children would remember the extreme cold that winter and how early the bad weather began. Hans wrote to his Cousin Bessie in October, "I shall be very thankful for a package with some warm clothing" and then, in mid-December, "though we live in the south of France, the climate is rather cold and sometimes we have much to suffer from it." Ilse was relatively fortunate: she slept with eight other girls in an unheated room, but her bed—a wooden plank with a sack of straw for a mattress that she shared with two others—was on the inside wall of the room. Inge Berlin, by contrast, slept under a window frame that had long ago lost its glass panes. When it snowed, which happened not infrequently that winter, the snow fell on Inge, who developed frostbite. By the end of December, Hans wrote to his cousins, "The last two weeks have been very cold here. Everybody likes to stay in the big eating room. It is the warmest place in the house and there is also our most beautiful diversion: a very nice wireless set. Sometimes we even heard the news from the broadcasting station [in] Boston." He of course had no inkling that he would one day live in the Boston area. The uncertainty about the future was terrifying and access to the news, along with the letters from his relatives, were his lifeline to the outside world.

~

Since their arrival in Seyre, living in a country effectively conquered by the Germans, the refugees found that mail was erratic, even more unpredictable than it had been since the outbreak of war in September 1939. Sometimes the children went for weeks without any news. The letters brought little information—except when a friend or family member had been imprisoned or was ill. Nonetheless the children yearned for contact with their parents and were always excited and hopeful when the postman arrived. In October 1940 Ilse received a postcard from her mother; the mail had taken a month to reach her from Shanghai. When she read the card, she screamed. Then she fainted.

Ilse's mother reported that her husband, Ilse's father, had died from liver cancer on September 4.[12]

Ilse had not seen her father in nearly two years. She had not been close to him and he had not written to her in Belgium or France except to add "Dear Illa, my regards to you and your friend Edith, from your father, Hermann Wulff" at the bottom of her mother's letters. However stern and rigid, he was her father. The realization that she would never see him again shattered her tenuous self-control. Ilse sobbed almost without interruption for days. And when she stopped crying for her father, she cried for her mother, so faraway, so alone, and without any means of support. One by one, the other children would receive similar news in the coming years.

~

Not everything was bleak at Seyre: Alex Frank's mother, Irène, nicknamed BliBla by the children, had joined the colony and begun teaching French. She taught the older children literature. Another teacher stayed for a brief period, taking groups of children on long walks and teaching them songs. One of his favorites was "La haut sur la montagne était un vieux chalet" (high up on the mountain was an old lodge), a song Ilse would sing twenty years later while washing the dishes in her New York City apartment.

Shortly after the group had become settled in Seyre, Hans renewed his correspondence with his Cousin Bessie, once again pressuring his American cousins to try to get him out of Europe. Frustrated by the slow and unreliable transatlantic mail, he wrote: "Sunday, the 29th of September has been the happiest day for me since long time: after having waited during weeks and months for your knews [*sic*], I finally received your kind letter from September 9. You can imagine that I was awfully glad to hear from you and I thank you a thousand times. The next day I got by American Express 860 fr (equivalent to $20). I really don't know how to tell you my gratitude for this wonderful present."

He was, as always, acutely aware of the political situation. The Vichy government had just issued a decree authorizing the internment in a French concentration camp of all foreign-born and stateless Jews over age sixteen. Alluding to this edict, he wrote: "My situation is not very agreeable. As I am aged of more than 16 years, I must always fear that—according to recent law—I shall have to go in a camp." The letter ended, as did all his letters, with a plea for his cousin to work on his immigration. The key, he increasingly believed, was interceding with someone in Washington who had clout. "If you could take steps at the right authorities, perhaps they would give me the permission to enter the USA."

The news from Hans's parents was more and more pro forma—declarations that "we are in good health and that is the most important thing" were about all they could hope to get past the German censor. Hans wanted desperately to feel that he belonged to this American family he had never met. He revealed in a postcard just how lonely he was. "I should be so awfully happy if you would be so kind as to write me every week by airmail. I am really ashamed of my request and you will certainly believe that I am very pretentious." He closed with the usual request to "continue your efforts to try everything" to support his case for immigration.

The prerequisite for obtaining a visa was still an affidavit from a U.S. citizen, as it had been since Hans had begun his quest for emigration in November 1938. When no visa arrived from the Silvermans, Hans became irritable, frustrated by what he suspected was negligence on the part of his cousins. His tone bordering on accusatory, he lashed out at Bessie: "You told me that you would send the new affidavits next week. Unfortunately they didn't arrive . . . and you will understand that I am a little unquiet." He was, however, optimistic that their new benefactors, the Swiss "will also care about our emigration" and hoped that "they will succeed to hasten our departure."

Hans continued to believe that if only he had that elusive affidavit, he would surely be able to get a visa. On November 5, 1940, he again harangued Cousin Bessie: "I hope that the papers have not gone lost. They are [of] first importance. The ladies who are occupied with our emigration to USA take only an interest in those children who are in possession of valuable [valid] affidavits. I am always afraid that I shall not be among those children because I shall not get the papers at time."

He did not put his faith entirely in the "ladies" who were busy working on the children's emigration—the same members of the Belgian refugee committee who had arranged the escape from the Reich to Belgium, the support in Brussels, and then the departure to southern France. He was confident that if only Bessie could find the right person or organization to appeal to in Washington, all would be well. "I have been told," he explained, "that if you could interest an American Committee or the right people in my case, they must have the possibility to get the permit for me to enter the USA."

Hans was frustrated that there was nothing he could do in France—he would have preferred to take matters in his own hands and not to depend on anyone else. "I must repeat that I can't make any steps here. The American Consulate in Marseille is entirely overburden and doesn't reply to any demand." The tension between seeking to be self-sufficient and recognizing the importance of influence, of pulling strings, would remain with Hans through out his adult life.

Hans was extremely vigilant, his antennae always ready to receive news of changes in the political situation or new possibilities for emigration. On December 18, 1940, he wrote to his cousins: "There is a rumour abroad that it is now much easier for refugees living in France or Spain to go to the USA. I have been told that there is a possibility to get a visa of visit." This would prove to be false. Just a few days later, he wrote again, expressing anxiety about the fact that quota numbers were routinely ignored by the American Consulate: "There are many children who are in possession of quota numbers which have been called up since long time. Nonetheless, the American Consulate at Marseille doesn't give the visa, even he doesn't reply to any request." Hans again concluded—or was told—that the only way to get results was via pressure from Washington. He ended his December 22 letter again requesting a weekly letter form the Silvermans, asking "could you give me this beautiful present?"

What Hans did not know was that Assistant Secretary of State Breckinridge Long had sent a memo to his staff in June 1940 outlining ways to obstruct the granting of American visas to undesirables such as European Jews. "We can delay and effectively stop . . . the number of immigrants into the United States," he wrote, "by simply advising U.S. consuls to put every obstacle in the way and to require additional evidence and to resort to various administrative devices which would postpone and postpone and postpone the granting of the visas."[13]

On Christmas Day 1940 Hans received a letter from Cousin Bessie with a copy of the affidavits she had sent to the U.S. consul in Marseilles. He seemed to have forgotten that he had recently argued that the consul in Marseilles did nothing, no matter how many affidavits he received, unless he was told to act by his superiors in Washington. For the moment, Hans was ecstatic: "Really I couldn't imagine a more beautiful present. I thank you a thousand times for it. To vent my joy I jumped through the house and played foolish tricks to everybody." In a burst of optimism about his future, he wrote that he wanted to continue to study English but complained that "we can't obtain any books for this purpose. Couldn't you send me an English compendium?"

~

The children decided to do something special for Christmas and to invite Maurice Dubois and his American-born wife, Eleanor, to their festivities. Inge Joseph later maintained that some of the children protested the very idea of celebrating Christmas. She also wrote in her memoir that Dubois gave a talk extolling the virtues of Christianity and suggesting that if only all the Jews had converted, they would not be in such terrible straits.[14] Ilse remembers getting some treats at Christmas time, but no speech. Hans, who later worked in the Red Cross Office under Dubois, dismisses such claims as preposterous. He wrote to his cousins in Chicago about the visit in a letter dated December 30, 1940: "On Christmas we had a little festival. The delegates of the Secours Suisse were invited and a performance took place. Every child had got a present which was put on the table. So we spent a very nice afternoon." Maurice Dubois had a deep-seated commitment to humanitarian work. During the Spanish Civil War he had worked tirelessly to help orphaned Spanish children. When the Second World War was finally over, he would run a children's home for former concentration camp victims in the town of Adelboden, Switzerland. In 1985 Dubois would be named one of the "Righteous among the Nations" by Yad Vashem, the Holocaust Martyrs' and Heroes' Remembrance Authority in Jerusalem.[15]

Soon after Christmas, the Swiss Red Cross found a new home for the 100 refugee children—an abandoned castle some twenty miles away from Seyre. Once the worst of that bitter cold winter was over, when the first hint of spring was in the air, the older boys moved to the castle to ready it for occupancy. Hans was among those who left Seyre in February 1941 to work on preparing the Château de la Hille. Under the guidance of Ernst Schlesinger, the cook's husband, and several other adults, they dug a cistern and hooked up pipes for running water. They tried to install showers, but that proved beyond their plumbing abilities. They repaired the electrical system so there would be electricity in the kitchen and main dining room, though how they managed to perform this feat without electrocuting themselves is unclear.

The advance brigade also built simple furniture: beds, tables, and chairs for the children and their adult supervisors. It was hard work, and the few surviving letters from his parents to Hans during that time express the hope that he would soon do something less dangerous, such as office work; their anxiety over his safety is palpable. On March 2, 1941, his father wrote: "You are probably busy with the renovations of your castle. Hopefully the food and accommodations have not gotten worse." His mother added, in the same letter: "Hopefully we will hear something encouraging from you—that you are settled in your home and that you are satisfied with the work you have been doing—which was hopefully not excessively demanding for you young children."

Shortly before the castle was ready, in April 1941, the children got some very good news. Thanks to the tireless efforts of the women of the Belgian refugee committee and the good offices of the Quakers, twenty children received permission to go to the United States.[16] One of the committee women, Lily Felddegen, who in the interim had immigrated to New York, was instrumental in securing visas for the children and finding them homes in their new country. The children chosen were the youngest of the group, those who were orphans, and in some cases siblings. All the children had been asked to provide copies of their birth certificates, which most got after scrambling madly, writing to their parents who struggled to extract an official document from the invariably uncooperative Reich authorities. The hope had been to bring the entire group to the United States, but there were many children in France in need of rescue and a total of 300 visas granted, so only 20 visas were allocated to the colony in Seyre. Far from expressing jealousy of those who escaped, Ilse reported being overjoyed that so many would have what she was certain was a safe and promising future.

Hans was convinced that this partial success boded well for him. Confirming his belief that further visas would materialize, Hanni Schlimmer also left for the United States in May 1941. Her father had been a diplomat in Berlin and had international connections. He had been trying for more than two years to emigrate and finally in the spring of 1941, he and his wife received visas and arranged for their daughter to join them. This miraculous rescue did not include permission to travel to Vichy France to pick up Hanni; she had to make her way to Bilbao, Spain, where she was reunited with her parents in time to board a ship bound for New York.

In one of many heart-wrenching twists of fate during the war, Hanni's father contracted typhus while on the ship and died within days of their arrival in New York. As if that were not tragedy enough, Hanni's mother had a psychological breakdown. Years later Hanni told Hans and Ilse that her mother began saying that she hated Hanni and she wished she had never been born. Abandoned emotionally by her own mother, Hanni yearned for the camaraderie of Seyre. Hans continued to write to her for the duration of the war. Almost every letter he sent to his cousins in Chicago ended with a postscript such as the one he appended on July 2, 1941: "I am enclosing a letter for Hanni Schlimmer. Please be so kind as to mail it to the indicated address." Hopefully Hanni derived some comfort from remaining in touch with her friends in France—and realized that however painful her relationship with her mother, at least her survival was assured and her future prospects, for education, a career, and a family, were more than a mere dream.

During the year the children spent in Seyre, Hans repeatedly implored his Cousin Bessie in Chicago to send books and clothing, emotional support, and above all, help in escaping from Europe. The rescue of the twenty children, together with Hanni's departure, made clear that it was, occasionally, possible for refugees to leave Europe. It took constant pressure, vigorous exploration of new avenues, endless entreaties to the American authorities, and a large measure of luck. Seventeen-year-old Hans Garfunkel demonstrated in his letters to America that he had all of the necessary attributes, except the luck.

Writing to Bessie in early May 1941, Hans made a seemingly audacious request: "Please, be so kind as to book the passage [from Lisbon to New York] immediately and advise me as soon as the passage is paid. There are far more chances to obtain the visa if I can show the booking and date of sailing is fixed. The delegate of the 'Swiss Help' promised to accompany me to the consulate in Marseille when I shall get the passage." This was not just chutzpah. Another boy in his group, Werner Rindsberg, had gotten a visa thanks to the intervention of an aunt and uncle in the United States who bought him a ticket from Lisbon to New York. Werner, at age eighteen only a year older than Hans, made his way alone over the Pyrenees, traveled from Spain to Portugal, and in August boarded the ship *Mouzinho* to New York. He had beaten the odds, gotten a visa to the United States, and put the nightmare years behind him.

If Werner Rindsberg could get out, so, in principle, could Hans Garfunkel. Even Maurice Dubois, head of the Secours Suisse in Toulouse, believed the children would eventually get visas. In a letter to Mrs. Felddegen in New York, updating her on the planned move to the Château de la Hille, he wrote: "You must recognize the difficulties in France. . . . But thanks to foodstuffs we have been able to get from Switzerland, and from others of our contacts, we can continue to take care of the children in an absolutely satisfactory fashion, until they emigrate."[17]

Hans continued his relentless exhortations to Bessie Silverman in Chicago, to the American consul in Marseilles, and to the offices of the Secours Suisse aux Enfants. Increasingly he believed that success depended not on merit or fairness but exclusively on exerting pressure in high places. His May 4 letter to Bessie ended: "There are thousands of people who want to go to the United States, and visas are given by ordinary way very scarcely. There is only the hope for me that you will succeed to obtain in Washington the permission which enables me to enter the USA." In the meantime, the work on the Château de la Hille was complete. The rest of the group moved in at the end of May 1941.

5

Lord of the Flies in Reverse

> The Contracting States shall apply the provisions of this Convention to refugees without discrimination as to race, religion or country of origin.
> —Convention Relating to the Status of Refugees, Article 1, 1951

The refugee children's new home, situated at the foot of the Pyrenees, was an imposing structure surrounded by ivy-covered stone walls. A massive door led to a courtyard, framed by towers on both sides. Green hills surrounded the castle, with groves of cypresses and chestnut trees nearby. Inside was a giant dining room with a parquet floor and several dormitory rooms, each containing ten to fifteen beds.[1]

Along with smaller rooms housing four or five people, set aside for the oldest children, and running water and electricity, the château came with a new leader. The Swiss were not happy with Alex Frank's management and sent a nurse, recently returned to Europe after working for Albert Schweitzer in Africa, to run the home.

Rösli Näf was tall and thin, all sharp angles, her blonde hair pulled back in a bun to give her a no-nonsense look. She was a strict disciplinarian, almost military in her bearing, and had little understanding of the emotional needs of teenagers. Sometimes what they needed more than books or nutritious food, although those were in short supply, was underwear. The adolescent girls were mortified that they had to make do with reusable rags for sanitary napkins, hanging up their blood-stained garments to dry along with their handful of other clothes. They did not have enough underpants and had to wear the same clothes for a week. And many of them did not have brassieres, which led the boys to tease them mercilessly. Ilse felt that Rösli Näf simply did not grasp the amount of emotional space occupied by underwear in the mental world of adolescents.

Rösli brought order to life at the château. Every child had an assigned task: in the sexist division of labor common at the time, the girls were responsible for kitchen work, for cleaning, and for setting the table. The boys did the heavier labor: cutting wood, digging ditches, and carrying barrels of water. Ilse did not like Rösli, but she later understood that the discipline she instituted helped the children cope with daily life. She took what she learned from

Rösli and fashioned it into an educational philosophy—as a nursery school teacher fifteen years later, she would believe strongly in the utility of a structured day for the children in her class.

Ilse also discovered that Rösli Näf was not as severe and unfeeling as she appeared—but it was only later, when she risked her life for the children, that they came to understand how deeply she cared about them. Her experiences dealing with the recalcitrant Swiss authorities, like Moses asking Pharaoh to let his people go and finding, each time, that Pharaoh hardened his heart, profoundly affected her understanding of herself and the world.

A few of the children found Rösli intolerable. As part of her passion for order, a relic of her nurse's training, she insisted that the beds be made with hospital corners, whatever that meant when your bed was a pallet of cloth-covered straw. If the beds were not made just so, the offender was punished—perhaps not with solitary confinement and a diet of bread and water, in the style of DeWaay, but punished nevertheless. Ruth Schütz, one of the oldest and most outspoken girls, could not stand Rösli Näf. Infuriated by her obsession with bed-making etiquette, Ruth lashed out at Näf. She wrote in her memoir that the world was going up in flames, the children were sick with worry about their parents—and Rösli treated them as though they were simple-minded. Ruth left the château and found work on a nearby farm.[2]

Alex Frank and Rösli Näf also proved to be incompatible. The Swiss had insisted when they took over responsibility for the group that they would have the final say about the employees. While they promised to try to retain the existing staff, the regional director of the Secours Suisse, Maurice Dubois, made it clear from the outset that he would bring in new, more suitable staff if necessary and that he had the prerogative to dismiss any employees with whom he was dissatisfied. Näf thought Frank was not the right man for the job and believed there was no room for two directors of the château. Not long after her arrival, Frank left to work elsewhere in southern France. His wife, Elka, and his mother, Irène, remained at La Hille.

Rösli did much to bring a semblance of learning and culture into the lives of the children. Several of the children were musical, and Rösli managed to procure a piano for the castle. It was old and not in very good shape, but it had eighty-eight keys. A few of the children played casually, providing musical accompaniment for skits they put on. Several were extremely talented, so gifted that when Maurice Dubois heard them play, he arranged for them to have music lessons in Toulouse. Rösli also found an old violin for another very gifted child who would later become a professional musician.

Concerned about the children's health, one of Rösli's first projects was planting a vegetable garden. The colony could not become self-sufficient, but the home-grown produce would supplement what the Secours Suisse provided and what the boys got by working on neighboring farms. Näf liked talking to the children about her experiences in Africa. And as she was after all a nurse, she taught them a little about nutrition and health, and led them in exercises. But any discussion of sexuality—menstruation, intercourse, pregnancy, childbirth—was taboo.

Naive as the children may have been, and stunted as their natural development was—Ilse did not begin menstruating until she was sixteen—they had normal adolescent urges. Several romances flourished in the spring and summer days. Hans, bereft after the departure of his sweetheart, Hanni, competed unsuccessfully with Edgar Chaim for the affection of Lixie Grabkowicz. Ruth Schütz was paired with Werner Rindsberg until he left for the United States. Inge Joseph found a soul mate in Walter Strauss. Ilse was so quiet and discreet that many of the group did not know she, too, had a special relationship. Her first love was Kurt Moser, the brother of her best friend, Edith.

Kurt was one of the oldest *Kinder,* and together with one of the oldest girls, Lotte Nussbaum, was in charge of the little ones. He was gentle and affectionate—like a parent to them. Kurt was among the seven Jewish teenagers who had been freed from the French internment camp of Gurs and brought to Seyre on the pretext that they were needed as "assistants."

Tall, serious, with dark wavy hair and glasses, Kurt dreamt of becoming a physician. He was extremely protective of his sister—every group picture of the children at La Hille seems to show Kurt with his hand resting gently on Edith's shoulder. And he saw in Ilse Wulff more than a thin young girl with a tendency to develop motion sickness. He recognized that beneath her quiet demeanor, she was observant, insightful, intelligent, kind, and, in what was no doubt an important coping strategy, able to find humor in almost any situation.

~

For the first three months after the group moved into the castle, Hans worked for Maurice Dubois in the office of the Secours Suisse in Toulouse. He liked the work—at least, he preferred it to construction work. He felt useful and wanted Mr. and Mrs. Dubois to be pleased with him. He wrote to his cousins: "I am always [still] at the Office of the Swiss Help and I do like work very much. I believe that Madame Dubois is content with me." Perhaps Mr. and Mrs. Dubois served as surrogate parents for him. It is striking that Hans has no recollection of where he lived during this period—it was too far to commute from La Hille to Toulouse. He has repressed just how isolated he felt.

Hans was in touch with some of his friends at the château by mail. Charley

Blumenfeld, his closest friend, clearly missed him, too, and turned to Hans for consolation when he learned that his parents had finally received the affidavits needed to apply to go to the United States—simultaneously with their deportation notification: "Yes, we have more worries. I wish you could come back here. I would so like to speak with you again." He also longed for a companion with whom he could discuss politics. Charley wrote on June 24, days after Germany flagrantly violated the Ribbentrop–Molotov Pact by invading the Soviet Union, "What do you think about Russia? Actually, we can't say anything. We'll have to wait and see."

In June 1941 Ilse wrote "Unser Schlossleben," a poem about her life in the castle:

Nun auf dem "Château" angekommen
Ein neues Leben hat begonnen.
Ganz angenehm; mal so allein
Denn Ruhe ist ja doch ganz fein.
(Now arrived at the castle,
A new life has begun.
Very nice, but so alone,
Quiet is very good.)

Most poignant is the final couplet:

Doch bis dahin nicht verzagen,
Und mutig unser Schicksal tragen.
(Until then, don't lose heart,
And bravely bear our destiny.)

~

The Château de la Hille was not the only children's home in France in the early 1940s. It was one of dozens of havens for foreign-born refugees, orphans, and French Jewish children fleeing from the occupied zone that had sprouted up after the Nazi invasion. A handful, like La Hille, were run by the Secours Suisse, and a far larger number by Oeuvre de Secours aux Enfants (OSE), the Children's Welfare Organization.

OSE (pronounced o-zay) was founded in Russia in 1916 by physicians as an aid organization focused, not surprisingly, on health. After the Russian Revolution, its headquarters moved to Berlin and then, after the Nazis came to power, to Paris, where its mission shifted to the sustenance and ultimately the rescue of Jewish children. Already at the outbreak of the Second World

War, OSE was caring for 300 children, primarily refugees from Germany and Austria, in special children's homes near Paris. After the fall of France, OSE quickly emptied its Parisian homes, transferring their occupants to convents, private families, and new homes in the southern, unoccupied zone.[3]

By 1942 there were fourteen OSE homes in operation, housing about a thousand children. In addition, OSE established a presence in the more than thirty "internment camps" in existence in France. The organization not only sent medical teams into the camps and provided clothing, drugs, and supplementary food for the children held there, but also managed to persuade the Vichy government to release a total of about 2,800 children, including Ilse's friend Kurt.[4]

In addition to the children protected by OSE, several thousand Jewish refugees were taken in by individual families. Most striking was the resistance offered by the residents of Le Chambon-sur-Lignon. A small town in rural France with a strong Protestant heritage and a memory of its own oppression by French Catholics, Le Chambon became known as a safe harbor for Jews. Most of those taken in by the townspeople were hidden in plain sight by families. Some lived in one of seven group homes supported by a variety of welfare organizations, including three by the Secours Suisse. Like the children of La Hille, the residents lived in poverty but relative security until the fateful summer of 1942.[5]

~

Hans and Ilse were relatively content and secure at the Château de la Hille in the fall of 1941 and on into the first part of 1942. They were happy to be taking a few classes: in October, Rösli brought Eugen Lyrer to La Hille, a bona fide teacher who would be regarded by all the children as a friend and confidant. In his forties, with black hair and a very serious demeanor, he taught history, math, and, in the hope of preparing the children to earn learn a living some day, shorthand. He arrived with a suitcase full of books including *Treasure Island* and *War and Peace.* Lyrer sometimes read aloud to the children in his sonorous voice, particularly from *Das Totenschiff.* A singularly apt choice, this classic by B. Traven was about the plight of merchant seamen who had no documentation of citizenship and could not find legal residence in any nation. The narrator was an American sailor stranded in Antwerp. Repeatedly arrested and deported, first by one country and then by another, he finally found work on a dangerous and decrepit "coffin ship," a ship whose owners wanted it to sink so they could collect insurance money. An apocryphal story holds that Albert Einstein said that *Das Totenschiff* was the one book he wanted to have with him if he were stranded on a desert island.

Lyrer, according to Ilse, was a warm human being who was concerned about the children's future. When La Hille was no longer a safe haven and the children were forced to flee, leaving behind the few photos and letters that were their only mementos of their parents, it was Eugen Lyrer who would send the children their precious possessions once they reached safety.

Evening was a time for reading aloud and for other homegrown entertainment. The group held concerts featuring Walter on piano and Heinz on violin. And while daytime was devoted primarily to chores and only peripherally to learning, there were occasional footraces; there were also math competitions in which Addi Nussbaum and Peter Salz, along with Hans, participated.

Ilse thrived during the fall of 1941 at La Hille. She had recovered from the shock of her father's death and had adapted to the castle routine. Eugen Lyrer bought more books in Toulouse, spending what was probably his own money to restock the castle's library for the children. He purchased French classics, the plays of Corneille and Racine, along with the works of Tolstoy and other masters. Ilse had matured in the last year: no longer a skinny, overprotected child, she had become a pretty young woman.

In addition to her romantic relationship with Kurt, Ilse had several close friendships with other girls. She was one of a triad that included Edith Moser (Kurt's sister) and Helga Klein. The three sat together at meal time, chatting the way teenage girls do. Photographs of the older children show Helga as a sturdy girl, almost stocky, and well developed. Ilse, by contrast, was thin and delicate; Edith wore glasses and was perpetually smiling.

Despite its overall harmony, the château community had its trouble spots. Two of the children had significant mental illness: one girl, who had fantasies that she was going to have a baby, was ultimately admitted to a mental asylum, where she later died. Minor disagreements and petty quarrels occasionally disrupted the colony's tranquility. Ilse did not care for some of the other girls and she thought that some of the boys, particularly Hans Garfunkel, were aloof and arrogant. But they all felt responsible for each other. "We were family," Ilse would say. "It's hard to imagine 100 people being family, but we were all close to each other"—closer in many ways than they felt to their blood relatives whom they had not seen for more than three years. In an increasingly barbaric world, the children and the handful of adults who supervised them established an oasis of civility. It was *Lord of the Flies* in reverse.

~

While the residents and staff of Château de la Hille went about their daily routines, Germany continued to achieve one military victory after another. The news on the precious wireless set was alarming. Yugoslavia and Greece had fallen to the Nazis in April 1941. The optimism Hans had felt in June when Germany had audaciously invaded the Soviet Union seemed to have been misplaced: while Russia had huge manpower reserves, less than a third of her soldiers had automatic weapons and they were facing more than 3 million well-armed and well-disciplined German soldiers.[6] In the fall of 1941, when the German army was unbeaten, in control of much of continental Europe, and facing a strong defense only from England, Hitler's designs on Moscow did not seem far-fetched.

The turning point came in December when Hitler's Japanese ally attacked Pearl Harbor, destroying 188 U.S. aircraft on the ground and killing more than 2,000 American soldiers. In a moment of supreme miscalculation, Hitler declared war on the United States. With Japan engaged in the fray, he thought Germany would be victorious over the United States. Instead, he roused the sleeping giant out of its neutrality. America would supply Britain with aircraft, warships, and, ultimately, manpower. Churchill grasped the full import of Germany's December eleventh declaration of war, writing in a telegram to Anthony Eden, his foreign secretary: "With time and patience [the American entry into the war] will give certain victory."[7]

The older children at La Hille, too, sensed that the tide was turning. Seven months of war with Russia had resulted in 200,000 German soldiers killed in action or dead from their wounds. And now winter had begun, delivering a devastating blow to the German troops marching toward Moscow. On a single day at the end of December, fully 14,000 German soldiers underwent surgical amputations because of frostbite.[8]

But on the day Pearl Harbor was bombed, Hitler took another step toward fulfilling his dream of exterminating European Jewry. In the town of Kolo, Poland, special commandos began experimenting with gas to kill Jews. Seven hundred Jews were loaded into trucks and driven to the town of Chelmno. There they were forced into special vans in which the exhaust fumes were pumped into the vehicles, killing the hapless passengers, who were then dumped into burial pits. Each day, the trucks returned to Chelmno from Kolo and the surrounding villages until 360,000 Jews had been murdered.[9]

Inspired by the success of the Chelmno killing operation, SS Commander Reinhard Heydrich convened a meeting in the Berlin suburb of Wannsee on January 20, 1942, to discuss further strategies for exterminating the Jews of Europe. He announced that Europe would be "combed from West to East" to locate the 11 million surviving Jews. The gassing vans of Chelmno would serve as the model for a series of new camps to be built along existing railroad lines. The sites had already been chosen: Belzec, which would become operational in March; Sobibor, which would follow in April; and Treblinka, which would also open for business in the spring. No longer was emigration or forced labor to be the "solution" to the "Jewish question." Elimination was the goal and mass murder the means. Adolf Eichmann was charged with implementing the plan.

Word got out quickly—but listeners were skeptical. On the day of the Wannsee meeting, a Jew from Chelmno escaped and found his way to a nearby Polish village. "Don't think I'm crazy," he implored the local rabbi. "They're killing the whole nation of Israel. I myself have buried a whole town of Jews: parents, brothers, and the entire family." He had been forced to bury the bodies thrown from the gas vans in Chelmno.[10]

Ten days after the Wannsee Conference, Hitler gave a speech revealing the broad outlines of his plans. Addressing a crowd at the *Sport Palast* (sports palace) in Berlin on the occasion of the ninth anniversary of his accession to power, Hitler prophesied that "the result of this war will be the complete annihilation of the Jews."[11]

The first deportation to Auschwitz took place in March 1942. In that same month, more than 1,000 Jews were deported from France. Typically, victims were rounded up and brought to a "holding camp," before being sent to their deaths. Hans and Ilse knew about these holding camps—southern France boasted several of them. All the children of La Hille would soon understand that something was terribly amiss, as they learned, one after another, of their families "going on a trip" to the east.

Hans knew his parents' deportation was inevitable and imminent. In a letter to the Silvermans written on March 16, 1942, he reported: "Sometimes I have some letters from my parents (only by the Red Cross, most 25 words). It is quite possible that they will have to leave for Poland in a short time." When he had not heard anything further from his parents a few days later, he wrote again to the Silvermans, palpably anxious: "The last news from my dear Parents are from beginning of last month; at that time they were still in Berlin, but it is quite possible that they have already had to leave for P[oland]." To add to his fears and sense of isolation, he had not heard from his brother, Günther, in Brazil: "From my brother I have not any news since October 1941, and I wonder what may have happened that he does not write anything."

The letter ended with a desperate plea for an end to the war. The words sound stilted and contrived in his fractured English as he translated literally from German: "I only wish that this terrible war will be over and that a freedom—such as we want him!—will reign in the world again," he wrote. He seemed to believe, however, that he personally was safe: "Since a month or two we depend directly on the Swiss Red Cross [he dated the "dependence" to the move to the Château de la Hille]. This guarantees us to live a rather good security with regard to the constant fear of being sent to a camp."

His everyday life continued in its established routine. "We have hard work in the fields and the garden. Moreover, we cut some big woods. . . . Just on Sunday there is some time for my personal affairs." He was not disturbed by the irony that his day of rest was the Christian Sunday rather than the Jewish Sabbath: "Then I read a book or I write my letters. Sometimes we play a match of football [soccer] with the boys of the farmers." A week later, on March 28, Hans dashed off another letter: "Perhaps I have become an optimist for I do not give up all my hope that you will manage the visa still during the war and I shall come to you very soon. I can't imagine all your troubles have been in vain. That would be too cruel."

Hans did not mention his parents. He did not know that as he wrote those words, his father lay in a hospital bed in Berlin. One month later, Hans received the news that his father had died—not at the hands of the Nazis, at least not directly, but following an operation. He did not learn the news from his mother. In fact, his mother wanted to protect him from this trauma and wished to keep Julius's death a secret. But she was in contact with another family in Berlin, the Lewins, whose son, Leo, was also at La Hille. Mr. Lewin wrote to his son, who told his friend Hans. Hans has the letter from Leo's father, dated April 30, 1942:

> First I have to tell you something sad about Hans Garfunkel's father and have to ask you not to say anything about it. His father unfortunately died after a bladder operation. We were with his mother. She sends Hans kisses (that you can tell him, and also say his father isn't entirely well, but in no case should you tell him that his father is no longer alive). Eventually he will hear the sad news. So please keep quiet—it is the special wish of his mother.

Of course Leo Lewin did no such thing. How could an eighteen-year-old keep such a terrible secret from a close friend? What could Paula Lonky possibly have been thinking? Several months later, she gathered the courage to tell her son the news. It was the last letter Hans received from his mother.

The literature on the effect on adolescents of the death of a parent indicates that extensive stress-related symptoms develop in the year after the loss of a parent, including strained peer relations and trouble sleeping.[12] Psychiatrists emphasize that what helps teenagers cope is their social network. The assumption is that this social network includes a caring surviving parent, dedicated and concerned teachers, and perhaps an experienced social worker and an astute physician. Hans had virtually none of these.

Adopting a pattern that would be repeated over the coming years, Hans sublimated his grief by taking action. On May 5, 1942, immediately after seeing the letter from Leo's father, he arranged for "some friends in Switzerland" to send a cable to the Silvermans: "I had wanted you to send a wire to my brother in Sao Paulo telling that our Father died in April and that I am very anxious about him, as I am without any news from him since Oct 1941." He picked up on this theme in another letter to his cousins on May 25: "In case you did not yet inform my brother, please would you be kind enough as to wire to him with paid-answer, and then let me know his reply at once, if ever possible by telegraphic way." And then he added, implying that he expected to lose his mother as well, "Now, as I have lost my poor Father, you are my only hope for a better future."

The exchange of telegrams did not take place, and at the end of July Hans again wrote his cousins, "I am really very sorry that I don't hear anything from you for such a long time." He assumed that they had in fact received the various letters he had sent in the interim, "so you will know that poor Father is dead in April after a short and painful illness."

Hans was very worried about his mother. He wrote on August 7, 1942, to his cousins: "From my dear mother I didn't hear for some weaks [*sic*], as we have been learned by many letters, all the Jews will have left Germany for Poland in a month or two. So I know that dear mother will have to go off too, that must be quite terrible if someone is quite alone and has already about 55 years."

Concerned as he was about his mother, Hans had become painfully aware of the precariousness of his own position: "Perhaps you will already know that Jews will be deported from the unoccupied zone in France; they are speaking from 10,000 persons who will be sent off for . . . nobody does know in which destination. In any case about 1,000 are gone off till today." He added, "Of course I am very unquiet [*unruhig*]." Then he continued with his customary plea to "do anything possible to get the permission in Washington."

Sounding as though he was working hard to persuade himself, Hans went on: "If in our sad situation I keep as much faith as I can, it is because I know you are taking care of me, even if I do not hear from you. I know that you want me coming to you and this is the principal thing for me."

~

It was Hans who sounded the alarm about the impending deportations from the unoccupied zone. He listened to the radio whenever he could, and he knew that Prime Minister Laval had authorized the roundup of foreign-born and stateless Jews in August 1942. Children over age sixteen were at greatest risk. The Vichy government had not yet approved the deportation of those under sixteen except to achieve "family reunification"—a policy that would "enable" children to join their parents who were interned in French camps so they could all be deported "together" to Poland. Pétain seems to have come up with this plan on his own; his Nazi minders were pleasantly surprised by his creativity.[13]

Hans suggested that the older children hide in the woods rather than sleeping in the castle, and by early August, he had already stashed away some supplies. The oldest boys discussed the proposal but most felt Hans was unduly concerned, perhaps even hysterical. Bowing to the will of the majority, he abandoned his plans for camping out. And then, on August 25, Hans heard an alarming broadcast on the BBC program *The French Talk to the French:* "We know based on an absolutely reliable source that a roundup . . . of 640 foreign-born Jewish refugees will be carried out starting in Lyons as of tomorrow, the 26th of August."[14]

Hans became restless. Some of the other children remember him pacing the halls of the castle. He awoke around 4:30 the following morning and went to the outhouse to relieve himself. On the way back, he suddenly found a flashlight shining into his eyes: "Stop! You're under arrest," he heard. A policeman was pointing a gun at him. The French police—there must have been a dozen, dressed in full regalia—followed Hans into the castle. "Mademoiselle Näf!" he called, in as calm a voice as he could muster. "The police are here!"

Rösli appeared, shaken and angry. She insisted the gendarmes could not take her children but they ignored her protests and insisted in turn that the children get dressed and pack a few belongings. Leering and smirking, they stood in the girls' dorm to watch the teenagers dress. Rösli snarled at them like a furious mother protecting her young and this time they heeded her demand to wait downstairs.

All the inhabitants of the Château de la Hille stood in a line outside the sheltering walls of the building that had been their home for nearly fifteen months. The police, who had been given the names and birth dates of all the children, read aloud a list of some forty names. Those called were loaded on to waiting vehicles. Every child over age sixteen was taken away, along with the Jewish staff members.

Watching the proceedings, the younger children were terrified. Rösli Näf was stunned. The police refused to tell her where they were taking the children, but a few hours later, Rösli went to the nearest town and began making inquiries. After considerable arm-twisting, she learned that the children had been taken to nearby Le Vernet, one of the most notorious transit camps in southern France.

When they pulled up to Vernet, Hans and Ilse saw a desolate collection of barracks surrounded by barbed wire. The girls were separated from the boys.

Each barrack was divided into two tiers, with twenty bunks on the upper level and another twenty beneath them.

The newcomers quickly learned the camp routine. In the morning, each person had to stand next to his or her bunk—really just a slab of wood—for inspection. Then they were given the universal camp fare of tasteless brown liquid that was euphemistically called coffee and a chunk of bread. Once a day, a meal of watery soup was provided; it sometimes included an unidentifiable morsel of something solid. The rations were meager and the children were all constantly hungry. Some of the girls saved a few pieces of bread and gave them to the boys.

There wasn't much to do all day—they whiled away time participating in interminable inspections, Vernet's analog to the humiliating, endless, and pointless roll calls that were standard operating practice in German-run concentration camps. Some of the other inmates—the political prisoners—had been there for months. New arrivals came each day: French Jews who had been born in another country and refugees like the group from La Hille. They all understood that as soon as an unspoken quota was reached, they would be transported by train to an unknown destination to the east. The train tracks ran straight into the camp. Many of the children knew their parents had been sent from Germany for "resettlement" in Poland. They also knew that most of those who had been deported had never been heard from again.

Hans managed to notify Otto Grädel in Switzerland of his arrest, the *Pate* (godfather) assigned him by the Red Cross to serve as an intermediary for letters to and from Germany. He asked Mr. Grädel to contact the Silvermans in Chicago, naively suggesting they might be able to intervene. Otto Grädel immediately wrote to the Silvermans, in a letter dated August 31, 1942: "Hans Garfunkel shared with me today via a card that he and all the other boys over 16 from the Red Cross Colony, Château de la Hille, were interned in the Concentration Camp Vernet. The reason—unknown. Nothing good can be expected from this. Can you do anything for him?" The letter continued with additional news: "From Tilsit [where Hans's aunt lived] came the news a few days ago that Mrs. Garfunkel in Berlin, Hans's mother, has gone away and that Miss Cecilia Garfunkel [his aunt] and Hans's grandmother are also going away. That means, in plain Swiss-German, being sent to Poland. Terrible times! Hans doesn't know anything about this yet."

~

Camp Vernet already had an illustrious chronicler: the Hungarian-born writer Arthur Koestler had been interned at Vernet for several months during the winter of 1939–40. He described his experiences in his memoir *The Scum of the Earth,* written in English and published in New York in 1941.

Koestler, who had been a Communist for seven years, had become disillusioned with Marxism, recognizing that "Stalinism had soiled and compromised the Socialist Utopia."[15] When the phony war began in September 1939, Koestler had been living and working in France for ten years. He was arrested in October in a roundup that the newspapers alleged targeted "the most dangerous elements of the Paris underworld—the real scum of the earth," principally foreigners who had fought against Franco in the International Brigades.

In December, Koestler was transferred to Vernet. The camp would remain virtually unchanged over the next few years except that a growing proportion of its inhabitants would be Jews rather than antifascists, and it would become a transit camp rather than a final destination. The camp stretched over an area of about fifty acres. The barracks were wooden huts, each of which contained the same double layer of sleeping platforms that Hans and Ilse would find on their arrival in the summer of 1942. There were no real windows, simply a few rectangular slats cut out of the planks that constituted the walls.

During Koestler's incarceration at Vernet, he was one of 2,000 prisoners. His overall assessment was that "in Liberal-Centigrade, Vernet was the zero-point of infamy; measured in Dachau-Fahrenheit it was still 32 degrees above zero."[16] But he went on to say that "in Vernet beating-up was a daily occurrence; in Dachau it was prolonged until death ensued. In Vernet people were killed for lack of medical attention; in Dachau they were killed on purpose." Commenting on the material conditions of Camp Vernet, Koestler concluded that it "was notoriously the worst in France. But . . . as regards food, accommodations and hygiene, Vernet was even below the level of Nazi concentration camps."[17]

After Hans and Ilse's group had been at Vernet for several days, they heard a disturbance at the entry to the camp. There was shouting and a flurry of activity. And then there was a familiar voice, a woman's voice, demanding the release of her children.[18]

It was Rösli Näf. She stormed into Vernet, leaving the camp commander wondering what to do with her. Visitors were prohibited and discharging the children was out of the question. Nobody entered the camp voluntarily—but here was a thirty-something-year-old woman wearing a Swiss nurse's uniform, insisting that she be allowed to join forty young Jewish refugees imprisoned at Vernet. The commander opted to let Rösli stay for the time being.

The children, after all, would be leaving for Poland in a few days. He would see then whether this tall blond woman still wanted to remain with "her children."

As soon as the French police had driven off with their catch, Rösli had gone into action. She notified Maurice Dubois, director of the Secours Suisse in Toulouse, that the older teenagers' had been arrested. After she found out where they had been sent, she set out to join them, traveling by bicycle and by taxi to reach her destination.[19]

Mr. Dubois, in the interim, had also taken steps, appealing to his superiors in Bern. They arranged for him to meet with a high official in the Vichy government's Department of the Interior. Dubois traveled to Vichy to meet face to face with the official. Realizing that neither polite requests nor righteous indignation would be effective, Dubois decided to deliver an ultimatum. The Swiss Red Cross, Dubois pointed out, provided relief for thousands of French refugee children in a number of locations throughout the country, many of them orphaned or separated from their parents during the chaotic exodus of hundreds of thousands of French families from Paris in the summer of 1940.[20] If the children of La Hille were not released, he threatened, the Swiss would withdraw their support for the French children. Dubois was bluffing—he had neither the power nor the authorization to make good on his threat—but his ruse worked. The official informed the commander at Vernet, who in turn informed Rösli Näf, that the children were to be sent back to their castle.

Before they left, they had an experience that Ilse would describe as the second of the three worst moments of her life. On the morning of September 1, the third anniversary of the outbreak of war, all the camp inmates were told to pack their belongings and stand by the platform that served as their bunk bed. A camp official then read a list of names. Anyone whose name was called was sent off to a waiting freight train.

However awful the conditions at Vernet, everyone knew that what awaited them at the end of the train ride was worse. The train ride itself, in cattle cars without windows or seats, was sure to be horrific. When the children of La Hille did not hear their names called out, they realized they had been spared. They watched in horror as hundreds of others were herded into the train, prodded, kicked, and shoved. Hans saw a man carried on a stretcher, too sick to walk on his own. Ilse saw women imploring those who were staying behind to take their children and keep them safe. They thrust their babies toward the children from La Hille, who had no choice but to turn away. Ilse can still hear the cries of those mothers and of their children.

Hans saw a rabbi outside the train and was convinced he was reciting Kaddish, the prayer for the dead. Rabbis do not chant Kaddish for people still living, but Hans is convinced he could hear the Aramaic words with their strange and mystical sound, a prayer that is recited at every Jewish religious service.

The following day, the entire group of forty, together with their brave and determined leader, Rösli, boarded buses bound for the Château de la Hille. Their reception was extraordinary. The younger ones at the castle, who in their precocity had concluded they would never see the older ones again, cheered when the buses rolled onto the grounds. They sang, they cried, they hugged.

Waiting for Hans were two letters. The first was from his mother, who had finally written to her son, to "Hansimann," as she called him, of his father's death the previous April. Most of her letters had been typed; this letter was handwritten and the ink ran in spots where her tears had fallen. The second was from his Tante Cecilia—the letter to which Otto Gräbel, his *Pate,* had referred in his correspondence with the Silvermans. She wrote that Paula Garfunkel had been deported on August 15, 1942, and that she herself and her mother, Hans's grandmother, were scheduled to leave in August as well.

Almost immediately after his safe return, Hans fired off a letter to Bessie Silverman: "I can't still believe it myself that we are here at our Château again. You will certainly know that all our children of 16 and more have been interned in a camp on Aug 26. Owing to the superhuman efforts of the Swiss Red Cross the miracle has been fulfilled and all our children have been put in liberty yesterday. The Swiss Red Cross had to do many demarches [take many steps] at the authorities in Vichy in order to get us out and to allow us to remain in France." He acknowledged that he had received the letter from his aunt referring to his mother's deportation, but euphoria over his personal liberation temporarily overshadowed his grief, as he wrote matter-of-factly, "Mother has gone off too and besides you I am now quite alone."

The mood at the Château de la Hille was tense. The teenagers' brush with death had been too close to ignore. And a brush with death it had been—the train carrying the inmates from Vernet to Auschwitz had been bombed, killing everyone on board. Ilse, who had written in her poem about La Hille that the she and the others had to "bravely bear our destiny," understood that passivity was no longer compatible with survival. She hoped that Rösli Näf and Maurice Dubois, who had come through for them so magnificently, would be able to persuade the central office of the Swiss Red Cross in Bern to evacuate the entire group to Switzerland. Hans, as usual, was hoping that the Silvermans would be able to obtain a visa for him from the U.S. State Department.

Less than two weeks after the dramatic rescue from Vernet, Hans again wrote to Bessie. His letter was a mixture of cynical pragmatism and wishful thinking. Recognizing that almost all the Jews of Germany and Austria had already been deported by September 1942, he concluded that the United States, if it was going to honor its quota system, should move quickly through the list: "Of course we do not know if we shall be quite in security and rather it seems to be the contrary. . . . In any case, I beg you very heartily to try everything in order to get me out as fast as you can. As most of [the] people had to go off unfortunately, there can't be more many requests for visas at the States [*sic*] Department in Washington and I think it will be now much easier to get the permission for me to enter the United States."

For the next two weeks, Hans and many of the other boys picked grapes in nearby vineyards. The official justification for their release from Vernet had been that the teenagers would be inducted into the Corps de Travailleurs Étrangers (Foreign Worker Service) to do agricultural work. The stint in the vineyards was an attempt to legitimize the virtually unprecedented liberation from the camp. Hans found the work a welcome distraction, except that he ate far too many grapes, with the expected digestive consequences.

As soon as Hans returned from grape gathering, he again wrote to Bessie. He indicated that life at the castle was getting back to normal. "Tomorrow the lessons will begin again. I shall take part in shorthand and in English." For the moment, he shared the no doubt widespread view that those who were "sent away" were still alive, just out of touch. He was therefore not grieving for his mother. Instead, he was experiencing an overwhelming sense of isolation: "In all the terrible moments we had to face, it was a wonderful comfort to know that there is somebody who takes care of me and will not forget me."

Then, abruptly, the letters from Hans stopped. He had promised to write every two weeks, so most likely the mail did not get through. The major change in local circumstances, perhaps accounting for the absence of mail, was that the fiction of a free zone in France had come to an end. The Allies invaded North Africa on November 7, seeking to repel the advance of the German army under Rommel, and in retaliation, the German army moved into the southern part of France. Stationed not far from La Hille was a German regiment.

Hans became viscerally aware of the new development when, in mid-November, he made up his mind to try to leave France illegally. He felt he could no longer wait for the illusory visa to the United States. Bessie Silverman and her husband, it would later become clear, had done everything in their power—and all that their pushy and desperate young nephew suggested—to try to get a visa for him, but to no avail. Mr. and Mrs. Dubois had appealed to the director of the Red Cross in Switzerland and had discovered to their dismay that he had not the slightest interest in antagonizing the Germans by bringing a group of eighty Jewish children from France to Switzerland.

Two potential escape routes remained: four hundred miles away lay the Swiss border, and a tantalizing thirty miles away lay Spain. Between Ariège in France, where the Château de la Hille was located, and the orange groves of Spain stood the Pyrenees, mountains that were difficult to cross at the best of times. In November 1942 it was already cold and snowy in the mountains. The only hope for crossing into Spain was by enlisting the help of a guide, though some of the "guides" supplemented their income by delivering their clients to the Gestapo.

Hans decided he would try the route over the Pyrenees. Through Rösli, he was put in touch with a possible guide and a rendezvous was arranged in a town a few miles from the château. Hans set out to meet the man to whom he was hoping to entrust his life.

He never met the guide. As he walked along the road to the town—there was only one road and walking was the sole means of travel—he saw German troops in the distance. He would have to walk directly past their camp. During the three and a half years he had been away from Germany, he had not seen or heard the SS storm troopers. He had seen the French police in action and that had been awful enough. But the sight of Germans in uniform, the guttural sound of German commands issuing from their lips, was overwhelming. Hans decided he would not keep his appointment; he headed back to the castle.

The over-sixteen-year-olds spent most of the daylight hours doing chores and most of their leisure time talking about how to flee. Two children did venture across the Pyrenees—successfully. A few went to work and live on nearby farms, trusting the farmers to claim they were distant relatives, orphaned by the war.

Rösli Näf and Maurice Dubois realized just how dangerous the situation was. They were well aware that Jews had been rounded up and interned in French camps since 1941. And since March 1942 foreign-born Jews had been transported by train from those internment camps—primarily from Drancy, outside Paris—to a concentration camp in Poland called Auschwitz. Since March, more than 40,000 Jews had been sent from France to Auschwitz, including 6,000 children.[21] Three-fourths of all the victims had been picked up since mid-July.

What Näf and Dubois had no way of knowing was the arrangement Adolf Eichmann had reached with Pierre Laval, who was once again prime minister in the Vichy government. On June 11, 1942, Eichmann had set a quota of 100,000 Jews to be deported from France over the next three months. All those between the ages of sixteen and forty-five were to be sent to their deaths in Auschwitz. Insufficient numbers of trains put a damper on the plans, and Eichmann revised the schedule, calling for the deportation of 22,000 Jews from occupied France and another 10,000 from the so-called free zone. Laval exceeded the quotas. He made a deal with Eichmann that if the French provided the police for the arrests, the Germans would spare French citizens.

The first 25,000 to be deported came from the occupied zone. But starting in the middle of August, the net was cast more widely to include foreign-born and stateless Jews in the free zone. By September 1, 9,000 Jews had been rounded up in the free zone and turned over to the Germans for transport to the killing centers in Poland.[22]

A few Frenchmen protested. The Swiss minister to Vichy, Walter Stücki, who was also the acting delegate of the International Red Cross Committee for France, complained. He complained to Marshal Pétain specifically about the arrests at La Hille, where the children were under the protection of the Swiss. Pétain reportedly said he "deplored" the situation but that it was "a matter of internal concern" and nothing could be done.[23]

Mrs. Dubois did more than complain. She traveled to Bern to meet with the director of the Secours Suisse aux Enfants, Colonel Hugo Remund, to ask that he arrange for the entire group of children to immigrate to Switzerland. He said he would take up the matter with Swiss government officials. But as early as 1940, the Swiss authorities had begun rejecting applications for asylum, informing the Swiss delegate to Vichy: "It unfortunately will not be possible for us to admit into Switzerland German emigrants living in France who fear deportation to Germany. Admitting persons threatened with extradition would create a potential burden that would be completely untenable today."[24]

Representatives of Swiss relief organizations, concerned about the roundups taking place throughout occupied Europe in August 1942 and distressed by the Swiss government's decision to tighten its borders, met with the head of the Federal Department of Justice and Police, Heinrich Rothmund, on August 24. The meeting was not amicable. It did have one positive outcome: refugees who had entered the country before August 13 were deemed to have the right to a "detailed review of their personal case."[25]

The Swiss compromise was of no use in the fall of 1942, when the children of La Hille again faced the risk of being arrested. Rösli Näf and Maurice

Dubois had exhausted all legal avenues available to them; they had appealed to non-governmental organizations such as the American Friends Service Committee, which was eager to help but had no leverage over the Swiss. The only remaining option was to arrange for the older teenagers to cross illegally into Switzerland. Solo or in small groups, in the dead of winter, they would set out in search of freedom.

6

"The Lifeboat Is Full"

> No Contracting State shall expel or return ("refouler") a refugee in any manner whatsoever to the frontiers of territories where his life or freedom would be threatened on account of his race, religion, nationality, membership of a particular social group or political opinion.
>
> —Convention Relating to the Status of Refugees, Article 33, 1951

By December 1942 the children and the director of La Hille realized they no longer had any legal means of leaving France. In desperation, and without the authorization of the Swiss Red Cross, Rösli Näf mapped out an escape route to Switzerland for the older teenagers, those at greatest risk of arrest and deportation. She acted in violation of the dictates of the Swiss Red Cross, which faithfully upheld the Swiss policy of excluding refugees, because she was appalled by the prospect of "her children" being sent to a concentration camp. She had identified a French town from which it would be possible to walk across the relatively unguarded border. She figured out how the children could travel from La Hille to the border town and she worked with a colleague in another children's home to find a guide to take them to the border.

The first group left on December 22. Four children set out with no identification papers, no maps, and just enough money to buy train tickets and a little food along the way. The youngest was fourteen; the oldest, seventeen. Two days later, on the day before Christmas, Hans set off by himself. Traveling alone was safer—one boy could blend into a crowd more easily and would not be dependent on the sangfroid of others—but also more frightening. On December 31, once Rösli Näf was confident that the first groups had been successful, it was Ilse's turn.

Rösli awakened three girls before dawn. They had had no advance warning. The departures were kept secret so that, if questioned, the children who remained behind could truthfully say they had no idea what had happened to their friends: they simply woke up one morning to discover that several of the older children were missing. First Rösli chose Ruth Klonover, a seventeen-year-old from Dortmund—the site of the Aplerbeck Hospital, where disabled people were "euthanized" by the Nazis. Next she selected Else Rosenblatt, also seventeen, from Aachen, burial place of Charlemagne. The third girl was Lixie Grabkowicz, but she had menstrual cramps and did not think she could make the trip. Rösli awakened the girl in the next bed and asked her whether she wanted to try to cross the border to Switzerland. Without a moment's hesitation, Ilse agreed. She and the other two girls would be the third group to leave France for Switzerland along the route Rösli had plotted.

As the girls were dressing, Rösli gave each of them a pair of shoes instead of the wooden clogs they normally wore. They also received standard schoolgirl briefcases to bolster the cover story that they were pupils on vacation, going to visit their aunt. They had just a short time to get ready, but packing was easy since they could not take anything along that might reveal their true identity—no photographs of their parents, no letters from home, nothing in German. Rösli gave each girl a hunk of cheese and a bit of bread and sent them on their way.

They left the château before five in the morning and walked to the nearest train station, in the town of Varilhes, about a two-hour hike. The ground was snow-covered and in the predawn darkness they did not even have the benefit of the sun's rays to keep them warm. They planned to throw themselves into the ditch that lay alongside the road if they saw anyone suspicious, but the road was deserted. They walked in silence, clutching their satchels.

At the station, Ilse bought the tickets to Toulouse because her French was the most fluent. She got them without difficulty, exactly as Rösli had instructed her, and the girls caught the train. The first leg of their journey was uneventful, but they had a long layover in Toulouse before the next train departed, the one that would take them to Annemasse, near the Swiss border. They could not stay in the train station as it was crawling with soldiers and police—people in uniforms of various kinds, any of whom might demand to see identity cards, which they did not have. The consequence of failing to have the requisite papers was almost invariably arrest.

Loitering in the station was out of the question, but outside it was bitter cold and the girls had no boots or warm winter jackets, no hats or gloves. The three explored the area around the station and found a movie theater nearby where they spent the next few hours. The cinema was crowded and full of soldiers, but they decided nobody would notice three schoolgirls, not even if they stayed through two performances. They watched *Taras Bulba,* a movie based on the novel by Nikolai Gogol. The plot revolves around an old Cossack and his two sons who set out to join other Cossacks fighting against the Polish nobility. First made into a movie in 1909 (a second version starring Yul Brynner would be made in 1962), it features lots of blood and gore and more than a smattering of anti-Semitism.[1]

When they finally boarded the train headed for Annemasse, Else, Ruth, and Ilse found themselves in a compartment with several young German soldiers who tried to flirt with them. The soldiers attempted to communicate, using a dictionary to utter a few French words. The three girls acted as though they could not understand anything the soldiers said. After a while, they closed their eyes and feigned sleep. But then the soldiers began telling each other jokes. The girls, of course, understood every word. Else and Ruth remained impassive but Ilse began to smile. One soldier said to his buddy, "Look at the little one! She's pretending she understands us!" Else and Ruth maintained their poise. Terrified that she would give them all away, Ilse made a break for the bathroom, where she pulled herself together and then rejoined her friends.

After a couple of hours the train stopped at Annecy, where the girls thought they needed to change trains for the last segment of the trip. They got off, asked what train to take next, and were told the train they had just come from was continuing to Annemasse. As they were about to reboard, they saw the police enter the car they had been on to check papers. The three waited until the police moved on to the next car. Then they got back on the train, confident the inspectors would not return to their car. Their calculation was correct and they arrived at Annemasse without further incident.

To exit the train station, all passengers were required to pass through another set of guards and show their papers. Else, Ruth, and Ilse got in line like everyone else. They had no idea what they would say when they were asked for identification. They were not eager to say anything: one spoke French moderately well, the other two spoke French poorly and with a German accent. They reminded themselves that they were supposed to be students on their way to visit family. Ilse struggled to recall the name of her alleged school and her supposed relatives. She was convinced the plan was going to fail: they were not going to be able to bluff their way through *Kontrolle.*

Else and Ruth started whispering to each other. As they began to giggle, Ilse joined in. Only a few more people stood in front of them. Each passenger dutifully showed his identification to the guard and was waved ahead. The girls were next. They continued whispering and giggling. They did not make eye contact with the guard, but kept on walking through the checkpoint. Bored, the guard ignored them and went on to the next traveler.

The three girls continued walking at the same leisurely pace until they emerged from the station into the bright, cold sunlight of Annemasse. Ilse was sweating and her heart was still pounding. Her hands were trembling. She thought she might faint. The other two girls linked arms with her and together they kept walking. By prearrangement, they made their way to a café across from the station, where they met a young woman named Renée Farny who worked for the Secours Suisse at another children's home in the nearby town of Saint-Cergues. She accompanied them by bus to the home, where they hid in a dark, unheated basement room. There was just enough light to make out a knapsack, which they identified as belonging to Hans, who had evidently left it behind. But they were encouraged—the backpack proved that he had gotten at least that far.

The girls were told to be absolutely quiet. The director of the home, it was rumored, worked for the Germans and would not hesitate to turn them in. The need for secrecy was not farfetched—when Renée's role in the illegal escapes was subsequently discovered, she would lose her job and be sent back to Switzerland in disgrace.

Shortly before 11:00 p.m., a young scout appeared, about the same age as the girls, and beckoned them to follow him. He whispered that they would have to cross a broad snowy field, a wide-open space with no trees. He emphasized that they would have to cross the field as quickly as possible since there was no place to hide. On the far side of the field, the scout said, they would find a fence. Past the fence lay Switzerland. He walked with them a short way, pointed them in the general direction of Geneva, and left.

The threesome had expected to be accompanied across the border. It was dark, it was cold, and they were scared. They followed the guide's directions and made their way across the seemingly endless field. After what felt like hours, they came to the fence. It was made of barbed wire and the only way to get to the other side was to crawl underneath. The wire was rusty and the girls were not wearing gloves, but they managed to lift the wire high enough to wriggle underneath on their stomachs.

The other side did not look any different. There was no sign saying "welcome to Switzerland," just snow, lots of snow, and a few bushes. They did not have a compass. They walked on, not knowing whether they were going in the right direction. And then they encountered another barbed wire fence.

The girls thought they might have walked in a circle and that the second fence was actually the first fence. They worried that if they crossed it, they would be back in France. But they didn't *think* they had turned around. With nothing but their instincts to guide them, they decided to crawl under the second fence.

This fence was as rusty as the first one—suggesting that maybe it *was* the first one. But they persevered, again forcing the bottom of the fence up with their bare hands just far enough to squeeze underneath, and then continued walking. They had no idea whether they were in France or in Switzerland.

In the distance, they saw a house and decided to go inside to find out where they were. But as they approached, they suddenly heard gunshots. The girls threw themselves on the ground, convinced they were being shot at. As they lay in the snow expecting the end to come, church bells began to ring. It was midnight and the gunshots and the bells were ushering in the New Year.

The three girls got up and walked steadily toward the house. The door was unlocked so they entered, deliberately making a great deal of noise to indicate to the inhabitants that they were not thieves. As they stood in the kitchen, a stout, broad-shouldered woman barreled down the stairs, yelling at them. They were clearly not the first refugees to walk into her house in the middle of the night. Furious at the disturbance, she chased them away, gesticulating and screaming invectives. But before they left, Ilse noticed a brand new 1943 calendar on the wall advertising a bank in Geneva. Suddenly the unfriendly woman bearing down on them was merely a minor nuisance. What was important was that they were certain they had reached Switzerland.

Not long afterward, a Swiss border guard showed up, shining a flashlight in their faces and demanding to know who they were. Scarcely older than the girls, the guard saw they were shivering, soaked, and frightened. Before radioing his superiors, he brought them to his house, took them into the kitchen, and asked his wife to give them each a bowl of hot soup and a piece of genuine Swiss cheese. They relaxed, convinced their ordeal was over and that they had encountered civilization at last. The guard brought them by truck to the Charmilles assembly camp where refugees were processed.

More than fifty years later, Ilse requested and received copies of the documents the Swiss had kept about her. Included in her file is the *Rapport d'Arrestation* (report of arrest) submitted by the Department of Justice and Police. Even the name of the agent whose wife gave the girls something to eat is recorded. The time of arrest was 3:00 a.m. on January 1, 1943; the location, the district of Geneva. The reason given for the arrest was that Ilse Wulff, daughter of Hermann and Lotte, born in Stettin, a German Jew, had clandestinely crossed the border in order to "avoid deportation to Germany."

On the truck with the girls were two other children from the Château de la Hille who had come via a different route. They all arrived at the camp where officials promptly informed them that anyone caught lying about his or her age would be sent back. The youngsters knew that a new rule, just promulgated, required that anyone over age sixteen be sent back. The Swiss ruthlessly enforced the rule: they sent eighteen-year-old Inge back to France, even though her mother was already in a refugee camp in Switzerland. Ilse Wulff had turned seventeen on Christmas Day. Her path was clear: If she told the truth about her age, she would be handed over to the French police. If she lied about her age and was found out, she would be handed over. Her only hope was to lie and not be detected.

After two days at the first camp, Ilse was transferred to another camp, Champel. The director of that camp would become known for his abuse of the inmates and his overt anti-Semitism. For some reason, the authorities at the camp believed Else and Ruth when they said they were fifteen, but they did not believe Ilse though she looked even younger than the others.

Her first night at Champel, Ilse was hauled out of bed at 2:00 a.m. and interrogated with bright lights shining in her face. The second night she received the same treatment, and again on the third night. She decided she could not take any more—if she was questioned again, she would admit the truth about her age.

Shortly after making that fateful decision, Ilse was summoned to the office. "That's it," she said to herself. But this time she was asked a different question. She was asked whether she would be willing to work as a maid for a Swiss family. Apparently a local Protestant chaplain was looking for a young girl to help his wife care for their three daughters. For a moment Ilse was speechless. A secretary working in the office quietly signaled Ilse to say yes. It had to be better than *refoulement,* being sent back. She agreed.

The interrogations stopped and Ilse was left alone. She remained in the camp barracks until she was introduced to Pastor Charles Brütsch a few days later. Ilse liked him immediately. He smiled and asked her if she needed anything. She blurted out the first thing that popped into her head—soap. He smiled again and told her not to worry. He brought her a bar of soap and some chocolate. The paperwork took a few more weeks to complete, after which Ilse went to live with Charles and Marguerite Brütsch and their three daughters in their Geneva apartment.

Upon her release from Champel, Ilse had to sign a document: effective February 8, 1943, she promised to abstain from all political activity and to remain in Geneva unless authorized to leave by the police. She also promised "on her honor" to live at the home of Mr. Brütsch and not to move without official permission, as well as to remain indoors between midnight and 6:00 a.m. Ilse agreed not to attend any bars or dances, not to go out in groups of more than five people, and to behave "on all occasions, with the greatest discretion." She also agreed, consistent with Swiss policy that refugees could only remain in the country temporarily, to "commit to taking active steps to obtain, as rapidly as possible, the documents necessary for [her] to leave Switzerland."

~

Hans had followed the same route from La Hille to Geneva. He had walked in the early morning hours to the train station in Varilhes and traveled the forty miles to Toulouse. He had whiled away the hours before taking a second train to Annemasse. He also pretended to be a student on vacation and wore the standard schoolboy uniform of shorts and kneesocks. And he had gotten past the *Kontrolle* on exiting the station in Annemasse through another stroke of luck: as the train approached the station, he heard someone calling "Hans!" At first he ignored the voice; he was after all supposed to be French and his name was "Jean." The calls became more insistent and suddenly he recognized their source. It was Renée Farny, whom he had met when he was working for Maurice Dubois at the office of the Secours Suisse in Toulouse. Renée worked at the orphanage in Saint-Cergues. She told the guard when they got off the train that "Jean" was an orphan whom she was taking to the "home" and he did not ask to see any identification papers.

Hans also was taken by a scout—he thought the young man was in the French resistance movement—and told to run across the snowy field, past the barbed wire fence. He also heard church bells at midnight, in his case marking the beginning of Christmas Day. And he also encountered two barbed wire fences and went under both. But he was convinced that he had doubled back and was again in France. When he was picked up by the police, it was still dark so he did not recognize that they were wearing Swiss uniforms. He had told them that he was a French boy who had gone to midnight mass and then gotten lost. On learning that he had strayed across the border in error, the guards politely and generously offered to escort him back to France.

When Hans realized that he had in fact made it to Switzerland, he quickly changed his story, admitting that he was originally from Germany and was seeking refuge in Switzerland. The guards contacted the military police, who brought him by army truck to the same reception camp outside Geneva where Ilse and her friends would be sent a week later. The Swiss regulation of December 29 ordering that refugees over age sixteen be sent back over the border had not yet been issued, so the guards did not press him about his age. Finally, on January 1, just before the three girls from La Hille arrived at Charmilles, he and fifty other refugees were awakened at 2:00 a.m. and taken by cover of darkness to the train station in Geneva, and from there to another camp.

The group sat for three hours in the dark, kept discreetly out of the public gaze. If they had to go to the bathroom while they waited, they were escorted by a rifle-toting Swiss guard. Eventually they were transported to Büren, a different reception camp, this one in the canton of Bern. It was, Hans would say many years later, the worst of the various refugee camps he would experience.

The winter of 1943 was another mercilessly cold season and Büren had no bathrooms, just outhouses. The commander was unsympathetic to the pleas of some of the older inmates that it was too cold to go to the bathroom.

Ashamed but desperate, they occasionally could not make it to the outhouse in the dark and cold nights and urinated in the barracks. The commander responded by barking at them, "If you think it's cold here, we can arrange for you to go to Stalingrad to find out what cold really is."

Hans knew nobody at Büren. Inmates were not allowed to send letters abroad, so on January 28, 1943, Hans wrote to Mrs. Goldschmidt, the former head of the Belgian Refugee Committee, who had found refuge in Basel, Switzerland, asking her to notify his American cousins of his whereabouts. He said: "You will surely be amazed to get a letter from me from a Swiss camp. I arrived in Switzerland on Christmas day." He then proceeded to describe how eight others had successfully reached Switzerland and one girl had been sent back. "The news from 'gentle France' [the letter is in German but he wrote 'la douce France' in quotes] is disturbing and I often ask myself what has become of my friends there."

He went on to explain: "I reached the border, traveling as a 14½ year old French child in short pants and a boy scout shirt," a ruse apparently undertaken in case the anticipated new regulations had already gone into effect. He had not brought anything with him and was pleased that his godfather had provided him with the essentials on his arrival.

Hans was hopeful that he would be able to leave the camp and live on a farm: "My *Pate* [godfather], Mr. Otto Grädel, has already applied for me to stay on a farm belonging to one of his relatives in a neighboring village." But that was not to be. The Swiss did not want to let refugees work, potentially taking a job away from a Swiss citizen and, more importantly, becoming integrated into Swiss society. Hans was sent to a work camp instead.

The camp was called Girenbad and Hans found it a notch better than Büren. It had been notorious for its poor conditions but had improved somewhat since the death of one of its best-known residents the previous November. Joseph Schmidt, a Romanian-born opera singer, had been interned at Girenbad since 1940. In the fall of 1942, he developed chest pain and went to the camp infirmary, which refused to send him to the hospital. Ultimately he was hospitalized but was thought to be malingering and was released. He was sent back to work digging ditches, only to die shortly afterward of a heart attack.[2] Concerned that reports of such episodes would damage Switzerland's reputation, the military, which was in charge of the camps, agreed to increase the food rations and make other modest changes in the living conditions.

~

Since the summer of 1940 the Swiss had dealt with refugees by placing them under the jurisdiction of the army. The "assembly camp" was effectively a prison in which the military police interrogated their prisoners to decide whether or not they would be expelled: they photographed and fingerprinted the inmates much as they would common criminals. The next step, for Hans and Ilse as for almost all refugees, was the "reception camp," which was also run by the army. Daily life included inspections and roll calls, much like in French or German concentration camps. The decision to put the military in charge was deliberate, intended to show the refugees that they would be "subject to strict discipline during their stay." The need for such discipline, one officer reported, resulted from the "racial" characteristics of the Jewish people: "Only with strict military discipline is it possible to maintain a certain degree of order among Jewish refugees. . . . The Jew has great respect for uniforms and keeps his distance from those wearing them. With civilians he would immediately want to do 'business'. . . . Nor should one forget the sexual problems that play a large role especially with Jews."[3]

In January 1943, when both Hans and Ilse were in reception camps, twenty-six such facilities were in operation. Typically the camps were set up in old factories, poorly heated plants with minimal sanitary facilities. Büren, where Hans was taken, was probably the worst. Initially established to accommodate a large influx of Polish soldiers who were members of the 45th French Army Corps, which fled in the face of the German invasion in June 1940, the camp was eventually viewed by the Swiss as misguided. The Poles were then dispersed throughout Switzerland. The facility was reopened as a reception camp for Jewish refugees in the late fall of 1942 and housed on average 600 to 700 people at a time. The Swiss Report of Experts, written about the Swiss treatment of refugees more than fifty years after the fact, would say about Büren: "The accommodations were completely inadequate and the mass operation was strained to its organizational limits. Moreover, the camp commander and some of the staff were considered notorious anti-Semites. Food was one of the major problems. . . . Fresh fruit was never seen and most people in the camp suffered from hunger."[4]

Refugees in the camp were cut off from civilian society and the outside world. Unlike prisoners in Swiss jails, they were not allowed to receive visitors. The camp of Charmilles (where both Ilse and Hans were sent initially) and of Champel (where Ilse was for some time) were surrounded by barbed wire fences. Mail was censored; writing in Hebrew was forbidden; and, as Hans indicated in his letter to Mrs. Goldschmidt, sending mail abroad was not allowed.

The Swiss Report of Experts notes that "the officers and soldiers working in the camp often lacked the necessary training and personal qualities to work with refugees." The experts go on to give examples of "incompetence" and "lack of understanding" at Charmilles where "Captain Rehfus inspected the . . . camp with a whip, threatening refugees at every opportunity with expulsion and molesting women." The head of another Geneva facility, Captain Quillet, openly acknowledged that he "could not stand Jews."[5]

The conditions at the two Geneva camps were widely known, but the military evinced no interest in improving them. Captain Rehfus and Captain Quillet had the support of the chief of police. The prevailing view among the officers was that "people who entered the country illegally were, without exception, common criminals and swindlers" who deserved punishment for any infractions.[6] Conditions at the camps were so poor and the focus on order and discipline so pervasive that the facilities won themselves comparisons with French internment camps. In one camp, according to an internal Swiss memorandum, the "treatment of refugees was worse than in the internment camp Gurs in southern France." A few officials worried that "the way in which the Swiss show hospitality is not likely to increase its moral stature."[7]

~

Once Ilse was released from the reception camp, her life changed dramatically. Very gradually, she warmed to her new "family." Charles Brütsch, the minister who took her into his home, was an erudite scholar who wrote biblical commentaries. Ilse, a native German speaker who was quickly becoming fluent in French and who had learned to take shorthand while in France, took dictation and proofread the minister's papers. She assisted Mr. Brütsch with his correspondence and in editing his work. She had found both a home and a protector.

Ilse also helped Mrs. Brütsch around the house, vacuuming, preparing vegetables, and sometimes putting the children to bed. Ilse—or Illie, as they called her—told stories to Charlotte (age six), Anne-Claire (age eight), and Marguerite (age ten). They liked her stories, and even Marguerite, who had to give up her room and move in with her two younger sisters so that Ilse could have a place of her own, became fond of the seventeen-year-old who had been foisted upon her. The family lived in a three-bedroom apartment in Geneva that included a study for Mr. Brütsch and a dining room to accommodate their frequent guests.

Immediately after her release from the reception camp, Ilse wrote a letter to Mrs. Goldschmidt, the wealthy head of the Belgian refugee committee that had arranged for the initial Kindertransport to Brussels, for the departure for France, and for the transfer of responsibility for the colony to the Swiss Red Cross. Evidently the refugee children were aware that she, along with Lily Felddegen in New York, continued to advocate for them. Dated February 3, 1943, the letter is in impeccable French: "You can imagine the joy I feel in writing to you that as of yesterday, I am free. A lovely minister's family has welcomed me into their home, and I already feel at home. For the moment I will help Mrs. Brütsch but maybe later I will be able to go to school. Your niece told me at the Camp Champel that you took steps for my two friends and me and that you had even found a family to take us in. In any case, I sincerely thank you for the efforts you made on my behalf. My two friends, Ruth Klonover and Else Rosenblatt, are still in the camp, but will also be freed soon." She again thanked Mrs. Goldschmidt and her husband for all they had done.

But for all her bravado in saying she felt right at home, and despite the objective reality that the Brütsch family took good care of her, a pall lay over Ilse. She learned after her release from the reception camp that although the first three forays into Switzerland by the teenagers of La Hille had been successful, the fourth was not.

Several days after Ilse, Ruth, and Else left La Hille, another group followed the same path. Three girls (Adele and two girls both named Inge) and two boys (Walter and Manfred) made it to the no-man's-land between France and Switzerland outside Annemasse, near Geneva. They passed under the two barbed wire fences, just as Hans and then Ilse had done. One member of the group, Walter Strauss, noticing a house in the distance, decided to find out whether they were in Switzerland. When he did not return, the other four followed. Like Ilse and her friends, they came upon a house and entered. But the house they entered did not belong to an overweight, unfriendly Swiss civilian. They had stumbled onto a guard house and were immediately arrested by patrolling soldiers, just as Walter had been earlier. Walter was ultimately freed and returned to La Hille; Inge Joseph jumped out of a bathroom window in the guard house and also made it back to La Hille. The other three were deported, first to Gurs in France and then to Auschwitz, where they perished. Inge Joseph tried again to reach Switzerland, this time successfully. Walter Strauss was once more rounded up by the French police. His luck ran out and he ended up in Majdanek, where he was murdered.[8]

The route that the group of five had taken was identical to that followed by Ilse and her friends. Ilse became convinced that it was her footprints in the snow that had led to the capture of the others. In her nightmares, German soldiers followed the footprints directly to the unsuspecting teenagers. She could hear the patrol's harsh voices in her head, calling out "*halt*!" to terrified Adele and Manfred as they cowered in the snow, wet, cold, and with no place to hide. Over and over, she saw in her mind's eye the Gestapo beating the children until they broke down, abandoned their story about being French pupils who had lost their way, and revealed that they were Jews, born in Germany, who had been living at the Château de la Hille in southern France. No matter that the group had walked up to the guard house and knocked on the door, perhaps disturbing the soldiers' card game. Ilse felt responsible and she was devastated.

She slept poorly and cried out in her sleep. She became withdrawn and often stayed in her room and cried. She had difficulty concentrating. Mr. Brütsch recognized that Ilse was depressed and took her to a psychiatrist. After only a few therapy sessions she quickly improved. Ilse was inherently a cheerful person: sixty years later, one of the other graduates of La Hille would still remember her laughter. She laughed often, sometimes so hard that she cried. Ilse quickly regained her focus and devoted herself to fitting in to the Brütsch household.

Mail from her mother in Shanghai arrived only sporadically, but Ilse's spirits were buoyed up by letters from her boyfriend, Kurt, who was still in France. He told her he was working on a farm near La Hille. He imagined the time when they would be together again. And then, in June, Ilse got word that Kurt had been arrested.

By 1943 life had become increasingly dangerous for those teens who remained at La Hille. After a brief lull in the deportations to Auschwitz, transports resumed in February. There was another roundup at the château on February 23, leading to the arrest of four children as well as the cook's husband. The border near Geneva had been sealed more tightly after Inge Joseph and her companions had been caught. The Swiss Red Cross summoned Rösli Näf to headquarters in Bern after learning of her complicity in the escape attempts and fired her, along with Renée Farny, who had provided shelter at the children's home in Saint-Cergues outside Annemasse. Without the Geneva escape route and without guidance, money, and local contacts, the prospects for reaching Switzerland were bleak. Once winter was over, the daunting route over the Pyrenees to Spain began to seem more attractive.

A group of boys from La Hille decided to risk the dangers of the mountains. They included Hans's good friends Edgar Chaim and Addi Nussbaum; Ilse's first love, Kurt Moser; Hans's closest friend, Charley Blumenfeld, along with Werner Epstein and Fritz Wertheimer. It was May; the snow was melting; the fields were green; and hope was in the air. The Germans were in retreat after their defeat at Stalingrad—surely they would have better things to do than expend their diminishing resources on capturing a few teenaged Jews. The six found a guide to escort them over the Pyrenees to Andorra and prepared to leave the castle. In the last minute, Edgar and Addi chose to stay behind. They did not trust the guide.

The four who continued reached the Spanish border where, in exchange for a modest reward, their guide turned them over to the Gestapo. The Gestapo took them to a jail in Toulouse and interrogated them for three weeks. From there they were sent to the French concentration camp of Drancy. One of the boys managed to throw a card out of the window of the transport, addressed to his friends at La Hille, letting them know what had happened. From Drancy, the next stop was Auschwitz.

The news spread quickly through the La Hille grapevine and word soon reached Switzerland, where Hans and Ilse learned that those closest to them had been taken away. They never head from them again. The information that the Nazis had caught Kurt in their net was the third of the three most traumatic moments in Ilse's life.

Of the boys from La Hille who were arrested along with Kurt and Charley, only Werner Epstein survived the extermination camps. Werner would be liberated by the Russians at the end of the war, one of the few to live through the SS death march from Auschwitz to Breslau. He would report to his friends how he and Kurt Moser had worked together in the coal fields for several months until Kurt developed severe diarrhea and was admitted to the infirmary. Finagling a rare visit, Werner found his friend weak and emaciated. Kurt knew he would soon be sent to the gas chambers and said he was glad his suffering would be at an end. Fifteen months later, Werner would relay to the other La Hille children Kurt's last words to him: "Little Eppelstein, you must survive and put up with everything. You have to visit my dear sister—I think about her all day long. But my parents must not know what happened to me. . . . Listen, my little Eppelstein, it's very important—don't forget—greet Ilse Wulff and all our comrades."[9]

Two days later, Kurt was sent to the crematorium at Auschwitz.

~

On March 2, 1943, Hans was transferred from Girenbad to the labor camp at Bonstetten. Otto Grädel's offer to take Hans into his own home—he was a teacher in a small village—was rejected by the Swiss authorities. The offer by Grädel's father-in-law to let Hans live with him and work on his farm had also been quashed by the authorities. The explicit goal of the Swiss refugee policy was to make life unpleasant for the undesirables so that they would leave the country as soon as possible. At Bonstetten, Hans's job was to clear the forest for new farm lands by chopping down trees. He was supplied with an ax and when that proved insufficient to fell the huge trees, he and his work detail were given dynamite. No one in the group had any experience felling trees. As in the previous camps, inmates were not allowed visitors nor were they given information about the outside world. They lived in primitive conditions with inadequate amounts of food. As had happened at Girenbad, only when one of the laborers was injured would conditions improve slightly.

The pay was a miserly 1.5 francs a day, of which the Swiss kept half to cover "room and board."

While Hans was in the work camp, the German army suffered its first major defeat. The battle of Stalingrad was the bloodiest, most horrific battle of the war to that time. Russian casualties were estimated at over a million, and the Axis lost about 850,000 men. The battle raged for 199 days, ending when the Russian army surrounded the German 6th Army. Stalingrad was retaken by the Russians on February 2, 1943, after General Friedrich von Paulus, newly appointed field marshal, surrendered, handing over his 60,000 surviving men to serve in Russian POW camps.[10]

Hans sensed a change in the attitudes of the Swiss after the defeat at Stalingrad. The atmosphere of the camp became less oppressive once the Swiss recognized that the Germans might not win the war. He felt there was a glimmer of understanding that they would be accountable for their behavior and that it would be the Allies, not the Nazis, who would set the standards by which they would be judged. Small things changed in the camp: he could, for instance, receive mail from abroad.

In the spring of 1943, Hans received news from his Aunt Cecilia and Grandmother Rahel. They were still alive but had been sent to the concentration camp in Theresienstadt. They could only send postcards with twenty-five-word messages, but Hans knew enough about conditions in German camps to realize they were considerably worse off than he was. He decided to collect donations from his fellow inmates in Bonstetten and send care packages to Theresienstadt. He was an *Unterleutnant,* a group leader, and was able to capitalize on his position to organize support for his family members in the Nazi camp. Hans had heard nothing from or about his mother since her deportation in August 1942.

As part of the camp improvement plan, the commander at Bonstetten introduced athletic activities and put Hans in charge of organizing a sports program. Hans assembled a cross-country running team and received permission to take the group out for practice runs. To make sure that none of the athletes got any ideas about running away, the commander ordered a guard armed with a rifle to follow the team.

Hans was tired of being viewed as a worthless refugee and he was fed up with Swiss superciliousness. He decided to have a little fun with the guard, a middle-aged man who looked as though he had not been through basic training and wouldn't be able to make it if he tried. Hans whispered to his cross-country squad that instead of jogging at a leisurely pace, they should sprint. He blew his whistle—and the runners were off. The Swiss guard tried in vain to keep up, sweating and panting. Finally he fired his rifle in the air, shouting "Stop or I'll shoot." Hans reined in the other boys and returned to the camp, where he reported to the commander with a straight face that the guard had shot at them. Neither Hans nor the guard was punished—but the sports activities came to an end.

Sunday was the inmates' day off. Hans often walked the twelve miles to Zurich to see Peter Salz, one of his friends from La Hille. For some reason Peter had been allowed to live with the Dyms, who were his godparents; their home would become a central meeting place for those *Kinder* of La Hille who reached Switzerland. From Peter, Hans learned of the Juventus Institute, a private high school that Peter attended. Hearing that the Swiss Jew who owned the school accepted refugee children without charge, Hans enrolled as an evening student.

Six days a week, Hans lived in the labor camp, chopping down trees by day and then taking the 6:00 p.m. train to Zurich. He attended classes for three hours and then returned to Bonstetten. He usually fell asleep on the return trip, but the kindly conductor made sure he did not miss his stop.

~

Switzerland at the beginning of World War II was a small, land-locked country of just over 4 million people, wedged in between Germany to the north, Lichtenstein to the east, Italy to the south, and France to the west. Its government later claimed that its draconian refugee policy was dictated by fear of German reprisals: any evidence of softness toward Jews would lead to the mythical Operation Tannenbaum, the occupation of Switzerland. In fact, the evidence showed clearly there was no such risk, as the Swiss government was well aware.[11] The Nazi leadership was quite happy to trade coal for steel, to buy arms from Swiss manufacturers, and, above all, to deposit vast amounts of currency and gold in Swiss banks. They sent roughly 15 billion *Reichsmarks* to Switzerland for safekeeping, including large sums stolen from European Jews.

The Swiss policy toward refugees in general and Jews in particular dated back to the 1880s, became well entrenched during the interwar period, and received its finishing touches in the 1940s.[12] At the time of the first wave of emigration from eastern Europe in the 1880s, Switzerland was at pains to prevent any refugees from the Russian pogroms from staying in Switzerland rather than continuing on to America. A popular referendum in 1893 prohibited kosher slaughtering, a law that remained on the books until 1978. The intent was to deter observant Jews from staying in Switzerland by making kosher meat unavailable—just as the Nazis made kosher butchery illegal in Germany in April 1933.

In the wake of the Russian civil war and renewed outbreaks of anti-Semitic violence in the 1920s, Jews again began streaming westward. This time the Swiss government came up with a new justification for excluding Jewish refugees, an argument that they would repeat in the 1940s: an influx of eastern European Jews would exacerbate Swiss anti-Semitism, thereby imperiling Switzerland's small, well-integrated Jewish population.

The defining law governing Swiss policy toward refugees was the Law on Foreigners' Stay and Settlement, enacted in stages between 1931 and 1933. This law was designed to prevent the *Überfremdung* (foreign infiltration) as well as the *Verjudung* (Judaization) of Switzerland. The means to this end was the policy of "transmigration," which required that any stay in Switzerland by refugees be temporary, for the exclusive purpose of organizing immigration to a third country. Ostensibly to protect the Swiss labor market, the law prohibited refugees from being paid laborers. Transmigration remained the basis of Swiss refugee law until Switzerland signed the Geneva Refugee Convention in 1954.

The behavior and decrees of Swiss officials after 1938 were merely a continuation of the anti-Jewish immigration policy already in effect. It was the head of the Federal Department of Justice and Police, Heinrich Rothmund (holder of this office from 1919 to 1955), who proposed in 1938 that the German regime stamp the passports of all Jews with a large J. This measure, adopted with alacrity by the Nazi regime, helped Swiss border guards turn away the large number of Austrian Jews who sought asylum after the Anschluss suddenly added another 200,000 Jews to the population of the Third Reich.

Most notorious of all the Swiss anti-Semitic measures was the decision in the summer of 1942 to seal the borders. Despite the prevailing regulations, Jewish refugees had continued to cross into Switzerland. As of late 1941 and early 1942, it became clear that the Jews of France, Belgium, and Holland were being rounded up and "resettled" in the east. By the summer of 1942, government authorities knew that deportation meant death. It was then that the Swiss parliament passed legislation clamping down on refugees. Public protests were widespread, but to no avail. Rothmund defended the policy, repeating the argument he had used in the 1920s that the arrival of Jewish refugees would give rise to a new wave of anti-Semitism, thus endangering Switzerland's existing population of 19,000 assimilated Jews. In the infamous words of the federal councilor Eduard von Steiger, the Swiss analog of a prime minister, "the lifeboat is full."

In case there was any uncertainty about how to interpret prevailing laws, a new set of instructions was issued on December 29, 1942, two days before Ilse set out from France for Geneva. These regulations clarified that "refugees who had fled for racial reasons did not have the right to political asylum" and ordered that all refugees over age sixteen be sent back. Refugees turned away at the border would not be allowed contact with aid organizations, relatives, or lawyers. Implicitly, the Swiss endorsed the Nazi definition of Jews as a distinctive "race."[13]

Despite the best efforts of Swiss officialdom to turn away would-be immigrants, 22,500 Jewish refugees did find shelter in Switzerland between 1938 and 1944, though at least 24,500 and probably considerably more were turned away at the border.[14] The government faced a dilemma—it could not enforce its policy of "transmigration" after the Nazi occupation of almost all of western Europe—there was simply no place for the "transient" arrivals to go. The Swiss then decided to "intern" all those who were unable to leave the country: the men were sent to labor camps; the women and young children were sent to "homes," where they lived in conditions only marginally better than the men's. The camps were used to alleviate labor shortages—the men built roads and cleared forests for farmland; the women repaired uniforms and equipment. In both cases, the intent was to prevent the refugees' integration into society, ensuring that eventually, when conditions permitted, they would "transmigrate."

The goal of Swiss policy, passed into law by the legislature and articulated and enforced by the Department of Justice and Police, was to prevent Jews from entering Switzerland. The Jews who made it in, because of laxity or deficiencies in the security system, were to be sent back where they came from, usually to face arrest and deportation to extermination camps. To understand the plight of Jews in Germany, the Swiss need not have looked any further than to Hans's parents.

Wulff family studio portrait, Stettin, circa 1930: Ilse, age five, with her grandfather Max Berndt and her parents, Lotte and Hermann Wulff. (United States Holocaust Memorial Museum, Courtesy of Hans and Ilse Garfunkel.)

Ilse and her mother, Lotte Berndt Wulff, Stettin, circa 1937. (United States Holocaust Memorial Museum, Courtesy of Hans and Ilse Garfunkel.)

Paula and Julius Garfunkel, Osterode, 1930s. (Courtesy of the author.)

Hans with his mother, Paula Lonky Garfunkel, East Prussia, circa 1930. (Courtesy of the author.)

Osterode Marktplatz: the Garfunkel-Lonky store is the tallest of the buildings on the left. (Courtesy of the author.)

Ilse in Belgium, 1939. (United States Holocaust Memorial Museum, Courtesy of Hans and Ilse Garfunkel.)

Château de la Hille. (United States Holocaust Memorial Museum, Courtesy of Walter Reed.)

Recreation time at the Château de la Hille, 1942. Hans (far right) is reading a newspaper. (United States Holocaust Memorial Museum, Courtesy of Leo Lewin.)

Some children of La Hille, circa 1942. *Front row (left–right):* Inge Helft, Adele Hochberger, Edith Moser, Ilse; *back row (left–right)*: Manfred Kamlet, Walter Kamlet, Kurt Moser. (United States Holocaust Memorial Museum, Courtesy of Leo Lewin.)

Ilse (*standing*) with Charles Brütsch and his family, (*left–right*) Marguerite, Mrs. Brütsch, Anneclaire, Charlotte. circa 1943.(United States Holocaust Memorial Museum, Courtesy of Hans and Ilse Garfunkel.)

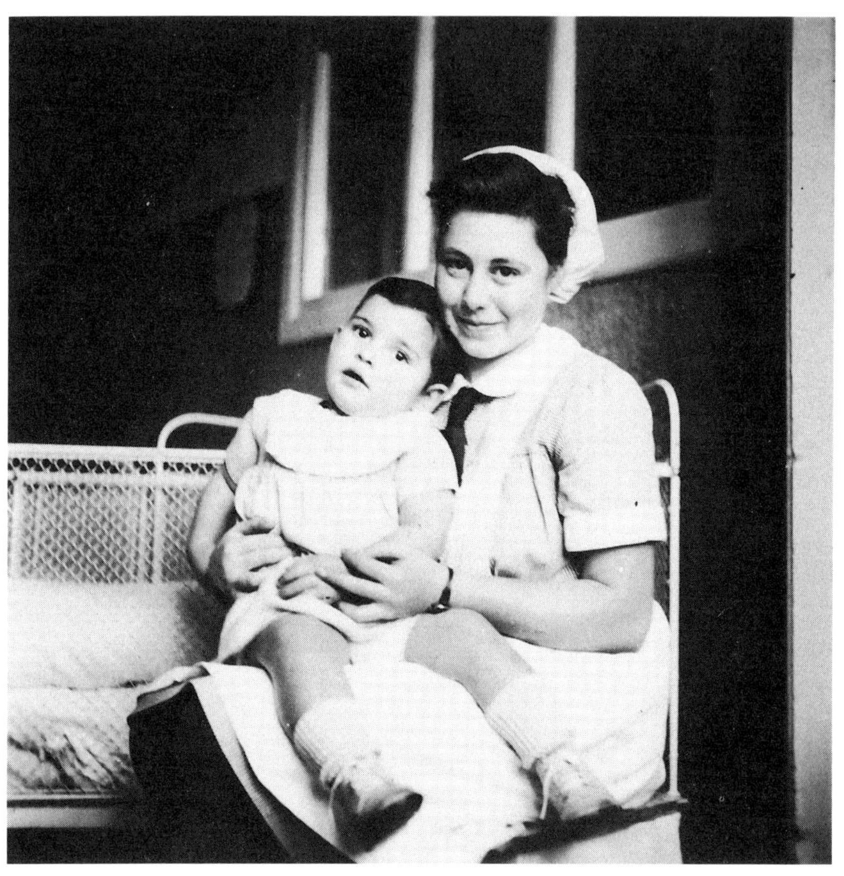

Ilse as a nurse in Switzerland, circa 1946. (United States Holocaust Memorial Museum, Courtesy of Hans and Ilse Garfunkel.)

Hans with Michael Dym in Switzerland, circa 1945. The Dyms were godparents of Peter Salz, one of Hans's friends from La Hille. (United States Holocaust Memorial Museum, Courtesy of Hans and Ilse Garfunkel.)

Hans in Sao Paulo, Brazil, 1947. (Courtesy of the author.)

Günther Garfunkel in Sao Paulo, Brazil, 1947. (Courtesy of the author.)

Ilse and Hans on their wedding day, September 18, 1948, with Herbert Strauss and Liselotte Rosenberg in New York City. (Courtesy of the author.)

7
What They Were Running From

> No one shall be subject to torture or to cruel, inhuman or degrading treatment or punishment.
>
> —Universal Declaration of Human Rights, Article 5, 1948

When Julius Garfunkel moved his family from the oppressive confines of Osterode to the comparative freedom of Berlin, he left all his furniture behind. In a bold testment to his belief in a prosperous future, he spent a fortune on a plush new sofa, a majestic dining room table of fine German wood, and elegant headboards for the brand new beds. Within months of Hans's departure on the Kindertransport, Julius would have to move out of the airy, spacious apartment on Kufsteiner Strasse to smaller quarters. In the spring of 1939, all Jews were forced out of their homes and either had to live in designated *Judenhäuser* (Jews' houses) or in shared apartments. Often they had to move repeatedly, typically into progressively smaller quarters where they might have to share a room with others.[1] Paula Garfunkel referred to one of their moves in a letter to her son in April 1941: "I have a lot of work because we have to move again. Our landlady is giving up her larger apartment. I am very sorry that we have to give up this lovely room. I felt very comfortable there. Also, the people we lived with were very nice."

What she did not explain was that Jews had a mere five days' notice before being evicted from their apartment—and that they had already moved twice when she wrote this note. They had to scurry about looking for a new residence, a room in one of the few remaining houses owned by Jews. They not only had to find a place to live but also had to dispose of much of their furniture as they moved to a smaller home. Although the phrase had not yet been invented, they were effectively internally displaced persons—refugees in their own homeland.[2]

In the two and a half months between Kristallnacht and the day Hans and Ilse left Germany on the Kindertransport, the vise that had been squeezing German Jews tightened a few more notches. Immediately after the November pogrom, Jews were banned from German movie houses, theaters, concert halls, and cabarets. The only available entertainment was performances put on by the Jewish Cultural League. With so many Jewish musicians and actors out of work, the league developed a diverse repertoire—notable for the absence of "Aryan" music—in major cultural centers such as Berlin. On November 12, 1938, the German government issued its Decree on the Exclusion of Jews from German Economic Life, which banned Jews from the few occupations they could still practice. In early December, the Decree on the Utilization of Jewish Assets ordered the "Aryanization" of any businesses that remained in Jewish hands. And as of January 1, 1939, Jews either had to have a recognizably Jewish first name or they had to add "Israel" or "Sarah" to their name.[3]

Those Jews who still lived in Germany at the beginning of 1939 became increasingly frantic in their search for a country to which they could immigrate. They lined up daily at foreign consulates, seeking to immigrate anywhere—Peru, Australia, the United States. Ilse's parents left for China—not a moment too soon, for the Jews of Stettin were the first German Jews to be deported. In February 1940, a full year and a half before the systematic and virtually complete expulsion of Germany's Jews began, the Jews of Stettin were sent to the Lublin region of Poland. The *New York Times* reported on the event on February 14:

> It was reported reliably today that all Jews in Stettin, totaling between 800 and 900, were rounded up early today and were being transported by railroad to an unknown destination, possibly the Lublin district of Poland. This was the first reported mass transport of Jews from the old Reich. . . . Nazi party officials and policemen appeared yesterday at the doors of Jews in Stettin and nearby towns and told each one to pack a single suitcase with clothes, take a bundle of food and cooking utensils and prepare to leave within eight hours. Before dawn buses picked them up and took them to trains. They were not allowed to take money.[4]

Despite all their efforts, the Garfunkels were not able to leave Berlin. Hans could not have imagined how desperate their situation would become. At first, they were able to write to him weekly although they told him little about their lives. Julius had not had steady work since he had been forced to sell his business for a pittance in 1935, when he moved from Osterode to Berlin. He presumably lived off his savings, spending the last of his dwindling resources helping his son Günther flee to Brazil. Already poor, Julius and Paula would become literally penniless in February 1939 when all Jews were required to deposit whatever cash and valuables they still had, including jewelry, in a "blocked account." Official permission was required for making withdrawals. Eventually, the authorities abandoned the pretense that these were true accounts and confiscated the assets.

The situation for the Garfunkels worsened considerably after the start of the war in September 1939. An 8:00 p.m. curfew was imposed on Jews. Major limits on shopping followed: Jews could only buy in selected stores, usually only during an hour or hour and a half time slot, typically right before closing, when all the best produce had been sold. Communication with the outside world was severely restricted—the weekly letters to Hans turned into monthly postcards. Listening to foreign radio broadcasts was outlawed—and punishable by imprisonment. That fall, all Jews had to hand over their radios. The day for the collection was deliberately set for Yom Kippur, the holiest day of the Jewish calendar. Observant Jews were prevented from attending services and forced to violate the proscription against working by lugging their eminently nonportable radios to the collection offices for surrender.[5]

With the German invasion of Belgium, Holland, and France in the spring of 1940 came a flurry of new decrees. Most alarming was the requirement that all Jewish women age eighteen to fifty and men eighteen to fifty-five register with the Jewish Community's Division of Labor in preparation for conscription into a forced labor brigade. The jobs involved heavy labor and long hours. Paula and Julius were mercifully exempt on grounds of age: Julius was fifty-nine; Paula, fifty-four.

The transformation of the phony war into a real war meant more restrictions. Starting in 1940, Jews were no longer allowed to buy shoes or clothing. They could not even buy the materials necessary to mend the clothes they had. Only a handful of Jewish shoemakers were authorized to repair their shoes, and public laundries were off limits.

The opportunities for recreation and relaxation also became increasingly limited. As of July 1940, Jews were forbidden to go to public parks. A month later they were no longer allowed to have a telephone.[6] The anti-Semitic propaganda film *Jud Süss* made its debut in September 1940, further poisoning the atmosphere. Screened in cinemas throughout Germany and occupied Europe and required viewing for the SS, the movie depicted a physically repulsive "ghetto Jew," along with a slimy "court Jew" who stopped at nothing in his quest for money and power.

In August 1940 the British began nightly bombing raids on Berlin. They did not inflict much physical damage, but they made up in psychological damage what they lacked in physical destruction. The reporter William Shirer noted in his diary on August 26: "We had our first big air raid of the war last night. . . . The Berliners are stunned. They did not think it could happen." On August 29 he wrote: "The British came in force again last night and for the first time killed Germans in the capital of the Reich. . . . I think the populace of Berlin is more affected by the fact that the British planes have been able to penetrate to the centre of Berlin than they are by the first casualties. For the first time the war has been brought home to them. If the British keep this up, it will have a tremendous effect upon the morale of the people here."[7]

Paula and Julius must have been simultaneously overjoyed that the British had finally begun to fight and anxious that their home might be destroyed. The residents of Berlin were expected to descend into bomb shelters whenever there was an air raid, but not all the Jews had a shelter to go to. "Aryans" and Jews were assigned separate shelters—the former spacious, in many instances accommodating couches and beds, the latter cramped and outfitted only with chairs. Some of the apartment buildings where Jews were permitted to live provided no air raid shelter. As Shirer put it: "If Hitler has the best air-raid cellar in Berlin, the Jews have the worst. In many cases they have none at all."[8]

Germans were cut off from news about the war, news about the rest of the world, and news about the goings on in their own country. They were fed a diet of propaganda in their newspapers and on the officially sanctioned radio stations. The German newspapers lambasted the "crimes" and "barbarism" of the British pilots who bombed Berlin, never divulging that German attacks on English cities were far deadlier, killing more than 1,000 London civilians in August alone.[9]

Food was still widely available in Germany, though the Allied blockade led to shortages of meat, butter, and fruit as well as coffee, tea, and chocolate. The average German diet consisted largely of potatoes, cabbage, and bread, but Jewish rations were significantly smaller than "Aryan" rations. The list of foods forbidden to Jews kept growing: along with restrictions on fruit and meat came prohibitions on buying milk, canned goods, and some vegetables. Hunger and malnutrition became commonplace among Jews during that bitterly cold winter.

As late as January 1941, the Garfunkels still hoped to be able to emigrate. Because Julius had been born in Lithuania, he and his wife were registered on the Lithuanian quota for the United States. Paula wrote to Cousin Bessie: "The Lithuanian quota is rather good—there are about a hundred numbers before us." But by October, the prospects for leaving the country were dim. In a letter to Hans written in October, Julius reported: "We got a letter from

Günther. The letter gives the impression that Günther cannot bring you and us over and also does not want to. Only the USA remains." Then, on October 23, 1941, Himmler banned further Jewish emigration.

~

In the spring of 1941, letters flowed back and forth between Berlin and La Hille, mediated by Otto Grädel, Hans's Swiss godfather. As Hans busily readied the château for occupation by the rest of the group, he discovered that some of the parents whose children were together in Seyre and then La Hille were in touch with each other. When one family learned something about their child, they shared it with the others, and conversely. In a letter from his father, written on March 2, 1941, Hans learned that "Hanni's parents are well; she shouldn't worry." But in the same letter, his father told him "it is no longer possible to send you packages or books." He offered no explanation.

A week later, Julius wrote to Otto Grädel, his paternal anguish evident underneath the formality and correctness of the lines: "My son, Hans Garfunkel, shared with me that you have taken over as godfather for him. I wish to be sure to thank you, together with my wife, from the bottom of my heart, for your enormous kindness. I gather that Hans is in contact with you by letter. It is now just over 2 years since he left us and I am sure you will appreciate that we miss him terribly, especially since he is the younger of our two children. We would be delighted if you could give us some news of him."

Typically Julius and Paula each wrote a few lines which they mailed in a single brief letter to their son. In early April, they each wished Hans a happy birthday. Julius expressed regret that he could not send a present: "With empty hands I send you heartfelt good wishes on your birthday. I hope you will always stay healthy and that you will never lose your courage and good temper." He said nothing about himself, but was clearly distraught at not being allowed to send a package, however small.

Then, abruptly, communication ceased. Aunt Cecilia sent a letter to Otto Grädel in early May 1941, volunteering to serve as the contact instead of Julius and Paula: "Since Hans's parents cannot write to him, I beg you cordially to continue to look after him. Hans's parents are doing well and are healthy—there is no need to worry about them. I would be very happy if you could send me news that Hans is doing well. Thank you for your kindness."

Cecilia provided no explanation for the new state of affairs. Hans believed the ban on sending mail out of the country was a punishment meted out to his parents for some petty infraction. He also thought that some of the letters that were sent to him by his aunt were in fact written by his mother. They were of course addressed to "my dear nephew" and signed "Aunt Cecilia," but they were typewritten, and the erratic key strokes bore a striking similarity to his parents' typewriter in Berlin. Hans speculated that his mother wrote the letters and sent them from Berlin to Tilsit (which apparently was permitted), then his aunt forwarded them to Otto Grädel in Switzerland, who in turn sent them to Hans in France.

In early October, Cecilia again wrote to Otto Grädel, indicating that she was in contact by letter with her relatives in Berlin and that they were well. Later that month, the ban on Julius and Paula's sending mail abroad was evidently lifted. But the fall of 1941 brought several new and ominous developments. First, Jews were required to wear a yellow armband. Then they were required to wear a yellow star with the word "Jude" in black, pseudo-Hebrew characters over the left breast. As an added indignity, they were required to buy the patches for ten pfennigs a piece and sew them securely to any item of clothing worn in public.[10] And then the Nazis began shipping the Jews of Germany to Poland.

Julius and Paula knew what was happening—one after another, their friends received deportation notices giving them a week to pack a fifty-five-pound bag, vacate their rooms, and report to the *Sammellager,* the point of assembly. Once the quota was filled, typically 1,000 people, they would be herded onto a train for deportation. Paula and Julius understood that it would soon be their turn. In the last three months of 1941, 50,000 German Jews were deported, most to ghettoes in the cities of Lodz, Warsaw, Minsk, Kovno, and Riga.

In October, Rabbi Leo Baeck conducted what would be the last wartime Yom Kippur service in Berlin.[11] The Garfunkels probably did not attend the service, which was held at the Levetzowstrasse synagogue, one of the few to survive Kristallnacht. They had never been very religious, and their synagogue, Prinzregentenstrasse, where Hans had had his bar mitzvah, had been burned down on Kristallnacht. At the end of the service, the Gestapo arrived to announce that the remaining Jews of Berlin were to be resettled in the East. The Levetzowstrasse synagogue was to be converted into an assembly point. Religious services continued to be held in Berlin surreptitiously. Some German Jews became more religious after the advent of Nazi rule. Ilse learned, years later, that her Onkel Erich retreated into his home after his release from Buchenwald and studied Torah. But in October 1941 the Garfunkels were preoccupied with their material survival.

House searches were commonplace as 1941 drew to a close—the Garfunkels may well have experienced one of these terrifying events. The SS would show up at the door and go through everything: opening drawers and closets, dumping out their contents, rummaging through what few personal possessions the occupants still had, in search of some unspecified contraband. If they found whatever they were looking for, or anything else that was illegal—

Jews were supposed to have turned in typewriters and toasters, combs and cash—they were likely to arrest the residents. If they didn't find anything illegal, they used the opportunity to insult the residents and simply steal from them. The searches were also the occasion for mistreatment of the inhabitants with beatings or sadistic humiliation.[12]

The only good news that the Garfunkels heard that fall was that the United States had entered the war in Europe. Prompted by the Japanese attack on Pearl Harbor, Germany declared war on America. For at least a fleeting moment, Paula and Julius entertained the hope that Germany would be defeated militarily in the near future, ending their oppression.

The deportations continued relentlessly during the winter of 1942. German Jews increasingly suspected that "resettlement in the East" did not, contrary to Nazi propaganda, entail moving to another country to find work. More and more people had friends who were taken to a concentration camp and died within days. "Concentration camp is now evidently identified with a death sentence," Klemperer wrote in his diary on March 1.[13]

By March 1942, Julius Garfunkel was a sick man. Every letter he wrote to Hans had included the claim that "we are in good health." It was no longer true. Getting medical attention was not a trivial matter, however, since as early as July 1938, Jewish doctors lost their licenses to practice medicine. A few were allowed to treat Jewish patients, though they were compelled to call themselves *Krankenbehändler,* roughly translated as practitioners for the sick, rather than physicians. The decree that deprived doctors of the ability to practice was extended to dentists and pharmacists in January 1939. But despite the thorough destruction of Jewish institutions in Germany, one medical facility remained. The Jewish Hospital of Berlin (Krankenhaus der Jüdischer Gemeinde) still functioned in the spring of 1942, and it continued to operate as a Jewish hospital, staffed by Jewish doctors and nurses and caring for Jewish patients, throughout the war. When the Soviets liberated Berlin in April 1945, they found 800 Jews living in the Jewish Hospital. Some were staff members who took up residence there; others were slave laborers assigned to work there. Many were patients; a few had been protected by prominent Nazis. The residents of the hospital comprised a large fraction of the Jews who survived the war in Berlin.[14]

The hospital opened at the Iranischestrasse location in 1913, across the street from a Jewish old age home. At its peak, it consisted of a seven-building complex, including a dormitory for nurses, operating rooms, and medical wards. As the only available employer for those Jewish physicians who had not succeeded in emigrating, the Jewish Hospital continued to attract a distinguished staff of physicians in the 1930s. When Julius became ill and needed a bladder operation, the Jewish Hospital was able to care for him, as it did for a select group over the next three years. The rate of surgery was at an all-time high in 1941, leading some to suggest that Jewish doctors may have performed unnecessary surgery to allow patients to avoid or postpone deportation. Julius, according to his friends the Lewins, had a "painful condition" and was operated on but did not survive the hospitalization, dying in early April 1942.

Years later, Hans was convinced that the surgeons at the hospital euthanized his father to spare him the deportation, torment, and probable death that awaited him. Hans believed that he had undergone a simple procedure for an enlarged prostate and never woke up. While others have speculated as well that euthanasia might have taken place at the Jewish Hospital, there is no compelling evidence for such claims. The Jewish physicians and nurses who worked at the hospitals labored under difficult circumstances, with inadequate supplies, to care for their Jewish patients. Occasionally they were faced with a moral dilemma—as when patients were admitted who had tried to commit suicide. Should they try to revive them or should they let them die peacefully? The evidence is murky, but physicians may not have pumped out the stomachs of some of the patients brought to them after an overdose.[15]

The suicide rate soared among German Jews, with about one-fourth of all Jewish deaths in Berlin attributable to suicide. In most cases, the individual swallowed cyanide or Veronal, a barbiturate sedative, sometimes procured on the black market at tremendous cost.[16] There were also suicides among the hospital staff, particularly when they were asked to participate in Nazi-mandated "selections" at the hospital—choosing which patients would be deported to their deaths and which would be able to remain at the hospital.

Paula was devastated by her husband's death. She was entirely alone. Her brother Max had died during the First World War; her other brother, Siegfried, had been deported to the Baltic States in November 1941. Her parents were long gone. Her sister-in-law and mother-in-law lived in Tilsit and she had no way of reaching them. Her older son was in Brazil: she had last heard from him in October 1941. Her younger son was in a castle in the southern part of France, safe, or so she thought, thanks to the protection of the Swiss Red Cross. She was fifty-six years old and had no means of support. She was a cultured bourgeois *Hausfrau,* with no marketable skills.

Paula's last four and a half months in Berlin were extraordinarily difficult. She could not even put flowers on her husband's grave; since March, there had been a ban on Jews buying flowers. Every day, new decrees were issued against the Jewish population: hair clippers and combs were forbidden; electrical appliances were banned. Rations were cut.[17] Along with the decrees came random acts of cruelty: the SS marched into a Jewish old age home and lined up women age seventy to eighty-five against the wall. They spat on them, poured cold water on them, took away their food, and bombarded them with abusive language.[18] To a remarkable extent, however, the Jews of Germany adapted. Klemperer wrote on May 30, 1942: "Today over breakfast we talked about the extraordinary capacity of human beings to bear and become accustomed to things. The fantastic hideousness of our existence, fear of every ring at the door, of ill-treatment, insults, fear for one's life, of hunger (real hunger), ever new bans, more cruel enslavement . . . absolute helplessness."[19]

Paula must have been completely dependent on the Reichsvereinigung der Deutschen Juden, the Jewish council that supported the Jews of Germany to the best of its ability, relying to a great extent on foreign donations. By the summer, she knew her deportation was imminent. One of her roommates in the apartment at Rheinstrasse 35, a woman who was almost exactly Paula's age and whose last name, coincidentally, was Lonky (Paula's maiden name), had received her deportation notice in May and was sent to Lublin, Poland, on June 2.[20] Paula never heard from her again. She warned her son that it would be her turn soon; whenever Hans did not hear from his mother for more than a couple of weeks, he wrote to Bessie that she might have already left for Poland. Perhaps she convinced herself that she would be taken some place that was more secure and comfortable than her room in a Berlin apartment, perhaps somewhere like Theresienstadt, which had gained an undeserved reputation as "a relatively humane place."[21] But Paula Garfunkel was not sent to Theresienstadt, the camp for "privileged" Jews, for the elderly, and for functionaries from the Jewish community. On August 15, 1942, she left on a transport bound for Riga.[22]

The first transport from Berlin to Riga had reached its destination in November 1941.[23] The new arrivals were immediately taken to the nearby forest of Rumbula and shot, along with 25,000 Jews who had been rounded up from the Riga ghetto. More Berlin Jews were sent to the Riga ghetto in 1941, replenishing the empty spots left by the murdered Latvian Jews who had lived there previously. In the ghetto they faced inadequate sanitation, insufficient food, contaminated water, rampant disease, and a bitter cold winter.[24]

From March to July 1942, the transports were put on hold. But in August they resumed, sweeping up Hans's mother, Paula, as they sought to make Germany *Judenrein* (free of Jews). The plan had been to bring Berlin's Jews to Auschwitz-Birkenau, but this camp had temporarily reached its "killing capacity," according to high-ranking Nazi officials, thanks to the successful campaign to rid Holland, Belgium, and France of their Jews. Reluctantly, the leadership decided to resort to the less efficient killing methods of the *Einsatzgruppen* instead.

Most deportees on the transports reaching Riga from August through the arrival of the last transport in the fall of 1942, and including the one that brought Paula Garfunkel, were taken by bus to a nearby forest and shot. A total of eight transports brought approximately 7,500 people from Berlin to Riga. Eight of them survived the war.[25]

At least Julius had a grave—in the Jewish cemetery of Berlin. Paula Garfunkel would have no tombstone to acknowledge her life or her death.

8

Transmigrants

> The Contracting States shall accord to refugees lawfully staying in their territory the same treatment as is accorded to nationals in respect to . . . remuneration, hours of work, overtime arrangements, holidays with pay.
>
> —Convention Relating to the Status of Refugees, Article 24, 1951

In the fall of 1943, Hans finally had a lucky break. He received permission to be a full-time high school student, to leave the work camp, and to live with a family in Zurich. This change reflected a moderation in the policy of the Swiss Department of Justice and Police toward refugees. Eager to make up for lost time, Hans decided to take a double load, both day and evening classes. He would complete the four-year high school curriculum in a record two years. His report card from the Juventus Institute, where he attended high school, indicates that he excelled in chemistry (receiving a grade of 6 out of a possible 6), math (with a grade of 5), and, not surprisingly for someone addicted to the news, geography (another 5).

His living arrangements had improved considerably since his work camp days: initially, he lived with the Dym family, godparents of Peter Salz, a friend from La Hille. Later he moved into another apartment, where he had his own room tucked under the roof. The father was a barber; the mother, a housewife; and the daughter worked as an office supervisor in Zurich. They were originally from Germany, and when Hans began dating the daughter, Lydia, he felt he was "the conqueror of the Germans."

Hans had reason for optimism. His social situation had improved; his educational prospects were good; and in a fireside chat broadcast the previous summer, President Roosevelt had told the people of the free world that "the massed, angered forces of common humanity are on the march. They are going forward—on the Russian front, in the vast Pacific area, and in to Europe—converging upon their ultimate objectives, Berlin and Tokyo. . . .The first crack in the Axis has come. The criminal, corrupt fascist regime in Italy is going to pieces."[1]

The summer of 1943 also ushered in an intensification of Allied bombing of German targets. The bombing of Hamburg in July was the first of what would become frequent and morally controversial fire bombings—culminating in the horrific and devastating fire bombings of Japanese cities. In a single night, 42,000 civilians died in the port city of Hamburg and 35,000 residential buildings were destroyed, leaving countless people homeless.[2] Later that summer, American and British warplanes bombed Berlin, causing less loss of life than they had in Hamburg or would later in Dresden, but inflicting psychic wounds, deeper and more painful than those caused by the blitz of London. On August 23 alone, more than seven hundred bombers flew missions over Berlin. In a raid that had great significance to the politically aware Hans, the Allies bombed the munitions factories of Peenemünde. This effort had little impact on overall German war production but was of great symbolic importance: increasingly, German citizens and German soldiers alike were becoming convinced that their country was far from invincible. Many of the bombers crossed over Switzerland on their way to their targets and Hans learned to recognize the British and American planes. He considered the sound they made as they headed for German cities on bombing missions "the most beautiful music in the world."

For Ilse, too, the fall of 1943 was a turning point. She continued to do household chores for the Brütsch family, but also began helping Pastor Brütsch with his work. In the course of assisting him with his French and German correspondence and proofreading the biblical commentaries he wrote, she came to respect and admire him deeply. Charles Brütsch was a man of integrity and strong opinions who regarded the Swiss policy toward refugees as immoral and preached that Switzerland's responsibility as a Christian nation was to help those who were suffering and in need.

Just as Ilse was beginning to feel settled with the Brütsch family, she received an official notice from the Swiss Department of Justice and Police. Dated August 25, 1943, the letter informed her: "You are commanded to appear at the Tivoli home to be interned on August 30, 1943. You will need to arrive that afternoon." Pastor Brütsch was outraged. He had arranged for Ilse to stay with him and not to be interned at one of the girls' homes. He stormed into the police department and indicated in no uncertain terms that Ilse was not going to Tivoli. In a letter dated September 1, the police rescinded their decree.

The government authorities also tried to prevent Ilse from going with the Brütsch family on vacation in the Swiss mountains. Because she was not allowed to leave Geneva without permission, she dutifully applied to accompany the family over the summer holidays. Her request was denied. Furious, Pastor Brütsch sent a series of nominally respectful letters to the bureaucrats who were determined to enforce their policy of restricting the movements of refugees. At one point, the police suggested that there was no need for Ilse to travel as far as the mountains; surely the air in the city of Lausanne was clean enough to be salubrious. In another exchange of letters, the police indicated that Ilse could not travel to the destination requested because it was near a highly secure military fortification. Presumably they were concerned that Ilse might be a German spy. As it turned out, the ultrasecret facility was a facade—it was merely an empty building. Whatever the reason for the Swiss authorities' reluctance, the police prevailed: Ilse was not allowed to go to the mountains with the Brütsch family.

~

In the fall of October 1943 the responsibility for monitoring Ilse's activities passed from the military authorities to the civilian government of Geneva. She had to sign a new declaration, promising to stay indoors between 10:00 p.m. and 7:00 a.m. and swearing that she would not publish any articles or attend any conferences. Ilse agreed to be paid only for household chores or agricultural activities. She promised to "do everything possible to leave Switzerland as soon as possible." In case that was insufficiently clear, she also had to agree that "I recognize that I will in no case be allowed to remain indefinitely in Switzerland." In addition, she said she would "adopt the discreet and correct behavior suitable to a refugee enjoying Swiss hospitality."

As an added indignity, refugees were required to maintain a blocked bank account. Ilse was paid fifty francs a month, of which she received thirty in cash. The rest went into an account at the Swiss People's Bank in Bern. If Ilse wanted to withdraw money from her account, she had to petition the bank authorities. On December 1, 1943, she wrote: "My dear sirs; since I need to pay taxes and buy clothing, I am requesting that you be so kind as to send me 20 francs."

Ilse could have visitors if they were able to travel to Geneva to visit her; that is, if they were Swiss citizens who did not need to apply to the police to go from one city to another. While she was living with the Brütsch family in Geneva, she met with Rösli Näf, the former director of the children's home at La Hille.

Rösli, who had been stern, almost militaristic when Ilse was in France, had mellowed. Ilse had of course changed too, forced by circumstances to mature quickly. For the first time in many years, she had a modicum of independence. Bizarre as it may seem to consider the orphanage in Brussels or the children's colony in Seyre or its successor at La Hille as protected environments, they were highly structured, quasi-institutional settings. In Geneva, Ilse had her own room and could organize her time. Rösli had been changed by her interactions with her own people. Seeing the children under her care carted off by the French police to a concentration camp, observing the conditions of the camp, and witnessing the indifference of the higher-ups in the Red Cross to their fate had profoundly affected Rösli. She told Ilse that she had been summoned to Red Cross headquarters in Bern for questioning after the group of five La Hille children had been caught at the Swiss border. The children had admitted they were German Jewish refugees who had been living under the protection of the Secours Suisse at La Hille. They had confessed that their escape route had been planned by Rösli Näf, who had given them money and provisions for the trip. After their confession, Rösli was interrogated by her superiors, who confirmed the story and then summarily fired the intrepid young woman. Thoroughly disillusioned, Rösli returned to her home in Switzerland. Her career with the Red Cross destroyed, she would move to Denmark after the war. More than forty years after the war's end, in 1986, she would be awarded the "Righteous among the Nations" medal at Yad Vashem, the Holocaust memorial in Jerusalem. Her colleague and co-conspirator Renée Farny received the same medal posthumously in 1992.

While Ilse was living with the Brütsch family, she received permission to visit her *Patin,* the godmother who had faithfully served as an intermediary between Ilse and her parents in Shanghai. During the long years in France, when mail could only be sent via a neutral country, she had been the conduit that enabled Ilse to have some contact, however erratic, with her mother. Now that Ilse was in Switzerland, her *Patin* wanted to meet her.

She set off on a Sunday to visit Miss Luise Keller and her sister, both of whom taught home economics in the local village school. They were simple, poorly educated, and very religious people. Ill at ease and eager to keep occupied, Ilse took out her knitting. Her *Patin* clucked at her reprovingly—knitting was not permitted in her home on Sundays. Ilse felt decidedly uncomfortable, wondering what gaffe she would commit next. She thanked her godmother for all her help and returned to Geneva.

By the beginning of 1944 it was becoming clear that the Allies would win the war. Roosevelt, Churchill, and Stalin had met in Teheran at the end of November 1943 to discuss Operation Overlord, the invasion of Europe that would commence with the landing of massive numbers of British and American troops on the beaches of Normandy, under cover of Allied warplanes and destroyers. At the end of January, the 900-day siege of Leningrad finally came to an end.

Hans was encouraged by the Allies' progress, but a pall lay over him personally: he was worried that at the end of the semester at Juventus he would have to reenter a work camp. Mrs. Dym, with whom he was staying, sent an impassioned plea to the authorities in February 1944. She reported that Hans was doing well in school but that his progress was limited "by his terror at having to go back to work camp." She urged that he be allowed instead to work on the farm belonging to his *Pate*'s father-in-law. She concluded, presciently: "As his foster parent, I am concerned about his emotional development, and don't want to see him fall back into depression." A letter from Hans follows, echoing her plea, along with a supportive letter from the farm owner himself. But on June 17, Hans received the verdict: "You will have to work like all other able-bodied student refugees."

That same month, the Allies arrived in Europe, first entering Rome and then moving into France on D-Day, June 6. The invasion of Normandy was a major turning point in the war. For the first time, when Ilse listened to the radio along with Pastor Brütsch, as she did regularly, she felt there was some hope that the nightmare would soon come to an end. By the time the residents of Switzerland awoke on the morning of June 6, a total of 18,000 British and American soldiers had already parachuted into Normandy, capturing essential bridges and destroying German lines of communication. By the following morning, more than 150,000 Allied troops were ashore. The Supreme Headquarters of the Allied Expeditionary Force issued a terse communiqué: "Under the command of General Eisenhower, Allied naval forces, supported by strong air forces, began landing Allied arms this morning on the northern coast of France." The *New York Times* supplied a few rhetorical flourishes: "The invasion of Europe from the west has begun. In the gray light of a summer dawn, Gen. Dwight D. Eisenhower threw his great Anglo-American force into action today for the liberation of the Continent."[3]

Benefiting from their ability to decrypt German military messages, the coordinated military plan, and the infusion of fresh American troops, the Allies finally began to wrest western Europe from German control. The liberation took time—the Allies did not enter Paris until the end of August—and there would be some backsliding. German troops mounted a counteroffensive and were not decisively repulsed from Belgium and France until the Battle of the Bulge at the very end of 1944.

As the battle for France raged, Hans vowed to return there and join the Resistance. He wanted desperately to fight the Nazis. Four of his friends from La Hille had joined the Resistance; one sixteen-year-old boy had died fighting for the underground group, the Maquis. Hans sought to join a Resistance group in Switzerland, but to his dismay, he was rejected. "Not," he recalled, "because of physical, psychiatric or emotional problems, of which I had none, but for being Jewish." He wrote to Bessie in veiled terms: "At first I wanted to return to France as fast as ever possible: but there are far more difficulties than one would like to acknowledge. So I have to wait and see." He would have to rely on the Allies to complete the job of liberating Europe from the Nazi yoke without his help.

Additional developments gave Hans cause for further hope. Athens was freed in October. General Rommel, Germany's fabled "desert fox," reeling from the loss of North Africa, committed suicide. Hans admitted how discouraged he had been, and presumably how much more optimistic he had become, in a letter to Cousin Bessie on October 15, 1944: "Today I can confess that I was not far away from giving up all hope as many of my friends had done. Unfortunately, the big change has come too late for so many of our parents and friends."

When he got back to Zurich after his stint clearing the land of rocks, he found a letter waiting for him bearing bad news. He resumed his correspondence with his cousin, which had been forbidden in the camp, explaining: "I am quite well, only that I feel so terribly alone. When I returned from the camp a month ago I found there a letter from the Jewish Counsel in [Prague] telling me that mother has been taken to Majdanek in August, 1942. That says everything indeed."

Hans was devastated. He was so shaken that he didn't think to ask how his mother, who had been transported to Riga in Latvia, could have ended up in Majdanek, outside Lublin in Poland. Nor did it occur to him to question what kind of "Jewish Counsel" could still exist in Prague in 1944.

A Jewish council did exist, though the original Jewish Council of Prague had been disbanded by the Nazis in 1943, its leaders deported. But a small, beleaguered organization known as the Council of Jewish Elders and comprised of half Jews and Jews married to "Aryans," took over in the summer of 1943. Its director and his deputy remained in charge for the duration of the war. The rump council worked closely with the Jewish underground, sending information to Jewish organizations in Geneva about the conditions under which the Jews lived in Prague and in Theresienstadt, both in Czechoslovakia.[4] The council may also have transmitted information learned by Soviet troops when they liberated the Majdanek concentration camp at the end of July 1944.

The Russian army found hundreds of unburied corpses, seven gas chambers, and records indicating that tens of thousands of people had been murdered at Majdanek since the spring of 1942. Photographs of the corpses formed the first visual evidence of the horrors of the camp, leading Hitler to rail at the "incompetence" of the SS for their failure to destroy all the evidence.[5] But if the council thought Paula Garfunkel was one of those killed at Majdanek, it was mistaken. All except one of the 1,004 German Jews deported to Riga from Berlin on August 15, 1942, had been shot on arrival.[6]

Among those murdered at Majdanek, however, was Minna Lonky—the woman who had lived in the same Jews' house as the Garfunkels before her deportation, who like Paula was in her mid-fifties, and who shared Paula's maiden name.[7] It was almost certainly Minna whose death the Jewish Council of Elders reported to Hans.

The specifics contained in the letter were inaccurate, but the conclusion Hans drew was correct: Paula Lonky Garfunkel was dead. As long as Hans had not received any notification of his mother's death, he had retained some hope she might be alive. Hans was enough of a realist to know that no news was in general bad news; now wishful thinking was impossible.

~

Hans was already beginning to imagine what he would do when the war was over. After abandoning the idea of joining the Resistance in France, he broached the possibility, once again, of trying to obtain a visa for the United States, writing to his faithful Cousin Bessie: "I don't know if you are still willing to make the necessary [arrangements] in order to get me to the United States. There are just six years passed since the famous November 1938 when you made your first demarches [efforts] for my American visa. Of course I should be most happy to arrive at last at my destination. Please, will you be so kind as to inform me about your further intensions. I am waiting impatiently for your answer."

As an aside, he explained that a charitable organization was subsidizing him in Switzerland: "On next Christmas, I shall be just two years in Switzerland, a little bit more than half of the time I spent in different camps. For the moment I have the opportunity to prepare myself for the matric [university entrance examination]. I am living with a family I didn't know at all before, the money is given by a socialist organization." He closed with the comment: "Let us hope together that New Year will see Europe at last in peace!"

Hans also enclosed a letter to his first love, Hanni Schlimmer, which he asked Bessie to mail to her. Apparently she did not as the message to Hanni was with Bessie's documents. To Hanni, he wrote about politics, commenting that there are "many allied military persons interned" in Switzerland, mainly escapees from Italian prisoner of war camps after Italy's surrender in September 1943. He added, "It is really astonishing how a small country just in the heart of Europe could manage to stay out of this terrible war." He mentioned that he had sent her at least a dozen letters since her birthday and signed the letter, "I am yours ever, Hans."

Another letter to Bessie followed a month later. Hans reported that he had met with the beloved teacher from La Hille, Eugene Lyrer, whom he described as "a friend to all the children at La Hille." Lyrer was Swiss and had returned home once all the children had left the château. Hans told Bessie that one of his friends was now a guard at Vernet—the same camp where the children of La Hille had been taken by the French police in August 1942. But this time the prisoners were Germans, captured during the liberation of France. He asked about his brother, Günther: "Did you ever hear anything from my brother? I haven't got any sign of life from him in many a year."

A week after the 1944 American presidential election, Hans commented to Bessie: "We have been all very happy when Mr. Roosevelt was reelected president of the United States. He is surely the right man for America and the world in the present and coming time." He closed on a wistful note, saying that he dreamed of a beautiful future. "Dreaming is a wonderful thing, isn't it? Without it life would be quite unbearable for me very often."

~

Ilse had been with the Brütsch family for nearly a year and a half when Mr. Brütsch began discussing her future with her. For the first time in several years, it was clear that she would *have* a future. She was not going to be sent back to France to be arrested and deported. Switzerland, unlike the countries where she had previously sought refuge, looked as though it was not going to be occupied by the Germans. Ilse would survive, but she had not had any formal schooling for more than four years. She had not been trained for any occupation. Much as Pastor Brütsch enjoyed having Ilse's help around the house and pleased as he was with the assistance she provided with his research, he realized she needed to acquire skills that would make her self-sufficient. He had a proposal: she should go into nursing, a good profession that offered the possibility of employment wherever she lived. Since she had shown she was good with children, pediatric nursing seemed like an excellent fit.

Pastor Brütsch contacted the Swiss Committee to Aid Emigrant Children (Comité Suisse d'Aide aux Enfants d'Émigrés) of Geneva, which in turn appealed to the office in charge of refugee activities to allow Ilse to go to school. The petitioner explained how Ilse had been placed with the Brütsch family after her arrival in Switzerland: "Pastor Brütsch, who has dedicated himself to taking care of the young girl, is concerned with her future and it seemed essential to him that Ilse be able to learn a trade that corresponds to her aptitudes and that will allow her, later on, to support herself and her mother, who is currently destitute in Shanghai; her father is dead."

In conclusion, the letter stated, "We have therefore decided to place the young Miss Wulff at the Protestant Pouponnière at Petit-Lancy . . . so that she can study the nursing profession. The course lasts two semesters, at the end of which the young girl will obtain a diploma." Key to the success of the petition was the promise of financial support: "Her upkeep at the Pouponnière will be guaranteed by our organization, with the assistance of other organizations, including tuition, expenses, pocket money, taxes, etc. We assume the responsibility for the duration of the training, lasting one year. On the basis of this commitment, we ask whether you would be disposed to authorize the young Ilse Wulff to stay in Geneva in the capacity of a student, and no longer as a maid."

Permission was granted by the police, but a follow-up letter added the proviso that "passing the exams at the end of the course will not grant the refugee the right to work in her profession without our formal approval."

In October 1944 Ilse left the security of the Brütsch household to become a residential student at the Pouponnière, a program to train pediatric practical nurses. The combination school and foundling hospital, situated on the outskirts of Geneva, was close enough for Ilse to visit the Brütsch family on the one afternoon and every other Sunday that she had time off. The rest of the week she worked or studied from 6:00 a.m. to 10:00 p.m. and then fell asleep in her dormitory, exhausted. The work was hard: Ilse took care of multiple babies and toddlers who had been abandoned by their mothers or whose parents visited regularly but were unable to support them. Most of the thirty girls in the training program were lower-middle-class girls preparing for a low status job in Swiss society.

Much of the course involved tedious practical labor. The girls had to adhere to a complicated process for preparing formula for the babies—Ilse would regard the American system of simply adding powder to water and warming the bottle as a revolutionary technology. Several times a week, two physicians lectured on nutrition, disease, and normal child development. Ilse found the didactic component of her program stimulating. She also enjoyed working with the children, especially the two- and three-year-olds. But some of the deaconesses who ran the Pouponnière were nasty and abusive, including one who regularly beat babies who soiled themselves.

Ilse's social life was almost nonexistent. She was prohibited from traveling to see her friends from La Hille who lived elsewhere in Switzerland and was too tired to make new friends. She remained under the auspices of the police department, which severely restricted her freedom. Ilse was so chronically fatigued that once, when she was visiting the Brütsch family on her afternoon off in the spring of 1944, she fell asleep in the garden for several hours.

Upon returning to the Pouponnière, she developed a high fever and became quite ill, drifting in and out of consciousness. During a fleeting moment of lucidity, she heard the staff debating whether to keep her at the school or to send her to a hospital—they kept her—and whether to telegraph her mother in Shanghai—they didn't. She had heat stroke, perhaps precipitated by lack of sleep and overwork, but she was young and fundamentally healthy, so she recovered and was able to continue her work-study program.

Ilse made friends with one Swiss-German student, a girl named Liesl, whose father owned a pharmacy. Better educated and more affluent than most of the other students, she was a bit of a misfit. Perhaps her parents thought she should have a career and not just become a good *Hausfrau,* but professions such as law and medicine were largely closed to Swiss girls. She was the one student with whom Ilse could have conversations about subjects other than how to mix formula. Occasionally, Liesl's parents picked up the two girls to take them to a movie. The girls who had crossed into Switzerland with Ilse, Ruth and Else, were living in the Tivoli "home" for refugees and were also prevented by the police from traveling.

Ilse kept in touch by mail with several former La Hillers, including one young man with whom she had never been particularly friendly but who seemed increasingly interested in her—Hans Garfunkel.

~

The year 1945 brought further auspicious developments. Hans raced to graduate from high school and take the matriculation exam for the university in April, just as the Soviet and American armies raced to retake control of Europe. Soviet troops captured Warsaw in January, liberating Auschwitz the same month. In early February, Roosevelt, Churchill, and Stalin met in Yalta to make plans for postwar Europe.

Shortly after the Yalta conference took place, on February 15, 1945, Hans wrote to Alex Frank, who had been head of the children's colony until the winter of 1942. Frank had escaped over the Pyrenees to Spain and remained in touch with some of the older members of the group. Knowing that Frank was one of those who had tried hard to make a difference, Hans lashed out against all those who had remained indifferent to the plight of so many: "Finally things are turning out well, though unfortunately too late for many people. I can't get over my anger when I think about it, that so many could have been saved if only someone had wanted to help."[8]

Hans commented in his letter on the remarkable good fortune of 1,000 survivors from Theresienstadt who were brought by a private organization to Switzerland. They arrived in February. Unfortunately, his Aunt Cecilia, his

Grandmother Rahel, and Ilse's grandfather were not among them. They were long dead. Cecilia had been transported from Theresienstadt to Auschwitz in May 1944, where she was killed; Rahel had survived in Theresienstadt from the time of her deportation on August 27, 1942, until her death on August 13, 1943, at age eighty-five. Max Berndt, Ilse's grandfather, had been deported from the Jewish old age home in Berlin two weeks before Rahel Garfunkel. Records from Theresienstadt show that he perished in the camp a mere two weeks later, on August 29, 1942.

Spring brought a stream of news, some encouraging, much tragic; death and destruction reigned even as the end of the war in Europe was in sight. Hans read in the *Neue Züricher Zeitung* and Ilse in the *Tribune de Genève* that President Roosevelt, hero of the free world, died of a stroke on April 12, 1945. Hans had been so pleased with FDR's victory the previous fall; he mourned along with so many others throughout war-ravished Europe. The *New York Times* editorialized the following day: "Men will thank God on their knees a hundred years from now that Franklin Roosevelt was in the White House . . . in that dark hour when a powerful and ruthless barbarism threatened to overrun civilization. It was his hand, more than that of any other single man, that built the great coalition of the United Nations."

The article continued, articulating what Hans felt about Roosevelt: "It was his leadership which inspired free men in every part of the world to fight with greater hope and courage. Gone is the fresh and spontaneous interest which this man took, as naturally as he breathed air, in the troubles and hardships and the disappointments and the hopes of little men and humble people."[9] The Nazis thought that American resolve to fight to the finish would die with Roosevelt. Instead, the war rolled relentlessly to its long-awaited conclusion.

Three days after Roosevelt's death, British tanks entered the concentration camp of Belsen, where they found 10,000 unburied bodies, most of them dead from starvation. The following day, the Russian army opened its offensive against Berlin. The Allied forces were on the march and would take over a new German city almost daily: Leipzig on the nineteenth; Nuremberg, site of the huge, annual prewar Nazi rallies on the twentieth. April 20 was Hitler's birthday, which he celebrated with ever-more barbaric atrocities, hanging twenty Russian POWs, as well as twenty Jewish children who had been the subjects of medical experimentation at Auschwitz.

On April 29 American troops liberated the concentration camp Dachau, finding 33,000 survivors. Of the 2,533 Jewish survivors, almost all were dead within a few months, succumbing to disease and profound malnutrition. And then, on April 30, hidden in his bunker under the streets of Berlin, Adolf Hitler killed himself. Goebbels, minister of propaganda, followed his lead, first ordering lethal injections for his six children and then commanding his subordinates to shoot him and his wife.

The war in Europe raged for another eight days. Berlin surrendered to the Russian army on May 2. American troops liberated the concentration camp Mauthausen on May 5, encountering further evidence of unfathomable brutality. At last, on May 8, 1945, the war in Europe was over. The *New York Times* headline screamed, "Germany Capitulates on All Fronts: American, Russian and French Generals Accept Surrender in Eisenhower Headquarters, a Reims School." The reporter continued: "Germany surrendered unconditionally to the Western Allies and the Soviet Union at 2:40 a.m. French time today. The surrender took place at a little red schoolhouse that is the headquarters of Gen. Dwight D. Eisenhower."[10] For the Americans, the war had lasted exactly five years, eight months, and six days.

Just two weeks after V-E day, Hans wrote to his Cousin Bessie: "War is over in Europe! I can't still believe it! The day we have been waiting for so impatiently so many a year has really come at last. For millions of people this big day has come unfortunately too late. Really, there have been long months—even years—when I didn't hope to live to see these better times." Whether he meant he expected to die young or that he believed the Germans might triumph, maintaining their rule of terror and bestiality throughout Europe and perhaps beyond, is not clear.

~

The end of the war in Europe ushered in a new phase of life for Hans and Ilse. Ilse completed the course at the Pouponnière and started her internship in pediatric nursing at a Geneva hospital. Hans enrolled at the University of Bern. College admissions in Switzerland followed one of two routes: either the student took a set of exams at the end of high school, earning him a diploma that served as an admission ticket to any Swiss university, or he sat for a special examination to be admitted to a particular school. Hans chose the second path, preferring to be tested in the subjects required by the University of Bern. The entrance exams, both written and oral, were held over a five-day period in April 1945. After taking the test in chemistry—a subject in which he had excelled in high school—Hans was convinced he had done poorly. He summoned up the courage to ask whether he could retake the exam, explaining he had been very tired and nervous. The official looked at him, incredulous. "You got a grade of 6 out of 6. You can't do any better than that," he told an astonished Hans. As soon as the tests were over, the students received the results. The minimum grade required for admission was an overall score of 3.5. Hans's grade was 5.4.

He was told that his score was the highest any student had ever received on the exams. Fortunately, there was no tuition at Swiss universities. He received a modest living stipend from a local refugee aid organization. Hans moved out of the apartment in Zurich where he had been living and found a room in Bern near the university campus. The Swiss seemed to be trying to redeem themselves in their treatment of refugees. But in a letter to Bessie, Hans hinted that despite having completed high school and having been admitted to the university, he had not forgiven Switzerland for its treatment of refugees: "I have made my matric in April and actually I am going to the university in Bern. I am studying specifically Physics, but am taking Mathematics too. Though I enjoy my study very much I should rather leave today than tomorrow."

In reality, he may not have enjoyed his studies all that much. In high school, he had excelled, but at the university, his performance on the entrance examinations notwithstanding, he discovered he was not the best student. His preparation in some areas was weak—he had, after all, crammed four years of course work into two. And he found himself in a new city, where he knew nobody. Peter Salz was in Zurich. Addi Nussbaum would attend the University of Bern but had not started yet. Ilse Wulff was in Geneva.

Shortly after beginning classes at the university, Hans again had to report for work at a labor camp. Every summer he was contacted by the police and required to spend several months away from his studies and his friends, engaged in strenuous physical labor. In July 1945 his assignment was the Bemont Lager. But when he arrived, he discovered he was the only inmate. After two days, he simply left the camp, writing to the director of the labor camp program: "I think you will understand that under the circumstances, it is senseless for me to stay here any longer and I therefore hope that you will not be angry with me because I left the camp today."

Five days later, he was sent to a different camp, the Arbeitsgruppe Nanztal near the town of Brig. Incensed by what he felt was an arbitrary, punitive, and absurd incarceration, he appealed for release on the grounds that his studies would be in vain if he could not prepare over the summer. A week later, he received an official reply: "We acknowledge the receipt of your letter from August 10, 1945, and regret to inform you that we cannot accommodate your request. You will be released on September 30. Yours faithfully, A. Meroz, Chief of the Police Department."

Desperate, and with a sense of foreboding, he appealed to one of the higher-ups in the Department of Justice and Police:

> An explanation of the grounds for this decision, which is for me most regrettable, is unfortunately entirely absent. It would interest me greatly to learn the motivation that led to this refusal, especially since in the past there was no requirement to spend the entire vacation incarcerated. I take it that the issue is not a lack of workers. . . . There must be some general principle which states that a refugee student belongs in a camp from the first to the last day of his semester vacation. I would be very grateful, Dr. Kraft, if I received from you a *written* declaration of the grounds that led to the refusal of my request.

There is no record of a response.

~

The Arbeitsgruppe Nanztal camp was located near a monastery. Hans's sole pleasure while interned was walking in the countryside, where he could talk with the Jesuits from the monastery. With limited access to newspapers and radio, he relied on the monks for news about current events. He learned from them about the atomic bombs dropped on Hiroshima and Nagasaki and the end of the war with Japan. On August 31, 1945, the twenty-one-year-old Hans had this to say to Alex Frank, the former director of the children's colony in Seyre: "We are finally at peace! It is so new for me that I have trouble believing it. It is certain that these new and terrible weapons played a big part in Japan's surrender, but nevertheless, I am not too thrilled about their invention because they're really too dangerous to entrust to human hands."

For the first time, he put in writing his views about his life at the camp and expressed how much he despised the work, free at last to say what he thought because the mail was no longer censored: "I am in a work camp. We are really at the end of the world—the camp is at an 1800 meter elevation. It is an old army barracks. We have no electricity, no connection to the next town." He went on to describe his job, which was to cut down trees and then chop them into pieces. Every week a tractor arrived to pick up the wood and deliver food. Hans continued:

> You surely can't imagine how urgently I want to get away from here. Switzerland may be "God's own country" for tourists with a lot of money, but that's not how it has been for refugees. Outside the camp we are under police surveillance. We have to register with the police every week. It is forbidden to leave the city without special permission and between 10 p.m. and 7 a.m. we can't be outside. It goes without saying that we can't participate in political gatherings.[11]

For Ilse, the end of the war was also a bittersweet time. Shortly after V-E day, she received a letter dated May 26, 1945, from her mother in Shanghai. Lotte Wulff wrote how glad she was that Ilse, or "Illichen" as she called her, was learning something useful. She added that nursing was a good profession and hoped that this time her education would not be interrupted.

Ilse's mother was ignorant of events in Europe. She admitted as much, saying, "We are so cut off from the world. You learn much more news." Revealing that she knew nothing about concentration camps and gas chambers or other forms of mass murder employed by the Nazis, she wrote innocently, "Have you heard from Grandpa, Onkel Erich and Kurt?" Grandpa had died at Theresienstadt and Kurt Moser at Auschwitz. Ilse had had no news of Onkel Erich in years.

Her mother was pessimistic about her own prospects: "Hopefully we will also have peace here," she wrote, but added "it is all very hopeless. . . . Unfortunately we will have to stay here for a long time." She concluded her letter by remarking that "everything is terribly expensive and the prices rise higher and higher. We are waiting here for relief. God will protect and help us. This hope keeps us going."

Ilse was not sympathetic to her mother's faith in divine providence. She had little use for religion and none for a God, if one existed, who took a hands-off attitude while human beings set about destroying each other in the cruelest and most painful ways they could devise. She had technically converted to Protestantism, not out of any heartfelt conviction, nor in response to pressure from Pastor Brütsch, but simply out of a desire to belong. She had believed that if she were baptized, she would more unequivocally fit in with the Brütsch family. In fact, long before the baptism, Charles Brütsch had taken to introducing Ilse as his oldest daughter.

And then, just as Ilse was studying for her final exams at nursing school, she received a telegram that her mother was very ill. The war was winding down in the Pacific, but Lotte Wulff had contracted typhus during an epidemic. Malnourished and prematurely aged, she did not have the resilience to fight this debilitating infectious disease. On August 28, 1945, with the prospects for being reunited with her daughter after six and a half years finally in sight, Lotte died in a Shanghai hospital. An acquaintance of Lotte's wrote to a friend in Switzerland: "Her daughter will be glad to know that her dear mother did not suffer. She had no pain and died peacefully. . . ." The letter continued: "Doctors brought her the most expensive medications and the nurses were also very attentive [as she lay in the isolation ward]. . . . The funeral was held August 30 and there was a memorial service at the Chaufoong Heim, attended by over 50 people. . . . Rabbi Kantorowsky gave a beautiful, long speech in which he lauded the many good deeds of the dead woman."

Ilse was devastated. She had crying fits. She felt that the cocoon of stability in which she had been living had been destroyed. Her friend Edith Moser managed to come and stay with her for a week. Gradually, Ilse's sadness began to lift. More slowly still, the psychic wounds inflicted by the accumulated traumas would begin to heal: the fear she had felt when she wriggled under the barbed wire fence between France and Switzerland, the agony she felt when the mothers at the Vernet camp tried to thrust their children on her as they themselves were dragged away, the anxiety she felt when her parents brought her to the Kindertransport train in Berlin gradually began to dissipate.

Even after she had largely recovered her emotional equilibrium, Ilse would have scars that were easy to rip open. A quarter of a century after the end of the war, as she emerged from the twilight of general anesthesia following a routine surgical procedure, she began to cry out, "No! no! Don't let them in!" Only after she was repeatedly told that she was in New York and there were no Nazis present did the fear begin to recede.

Lotte Wulff, née Berndt, had spent six years as a refugee in China, only to die just when she anticipated returning to Europe and being reunited with her daughter. Ilse could scarcely imagine what the experience in Shanghai had been like.

9
Refuge in Shanghai

> The Contracting States shall accord to refugees lawfully staying in their territory the same treatment with respect to public relief and assistance as is accorded to their nationals.
>
> —Convention Relating to the Status of Refugees, Article 23, 1951

In April 1939 Lotte and Hermann Wulff set sail for Shanghai, the "city above the sea," as the two Chinese characters spelling its name denote. The port stands on mudflats, barely above sea level. Known variously as the Paris of the Far East and the opium capital of the world, Shanghai in the 1930s had a population of 4 million, allegedly including the highest number of prostitutes per capita of any city in the world.[1]

China was already at war. Skirmishes with the Japanese had begun in 1932, finally erupting into a full-fledged conflict in 1937. Among the early casualties of the war were the people of Nanking, the capital city of China. The Japanese attacked Nanking in December 1937, demonstrating their military superiority, racist ideology, and merciless brutality as they murdered as many as 300,000 Chinese citizens, often after gang raping or otherwise tormenting them. By 1939 the Japanese were also the masters of Shanghai, though the International Settlement, initially established in 1854 as an independent base of operations for European and American traders, remained quasi-independent. Another casualty of the Sino-Japanese War was the Nationalist government's passport office. It simply ceased to exist. None of the other countries represented in Shanghai were empowered to exercise passport control. What this meant in practice was that while British ships often required visas for passengers and the Nationalist Chinese government consulates in Europe continued to issue visas, anyone could go ashore in Shanghai.[2] As a result, Shanghai was known in German and Austrian circles in 1938 and 1939 as one of the only remaining sites for immigration.

The Wulffs' voyage to Shanghai was alternately frightening and exhilarating, an occasion for anxiety about the future but also for rejoicing in the present. It began with a train trip to Italy. After selling most of their worldly possessions to buy tickets—the passenger ships leaving for Shanghai were usually luxury liners—and having already used their savings to pay the steep exit taxes imposed by the Nazis, they set off. At the Brenner Pass, marking the boundary between Austria (which was part of the Reich) and Italy, everyone had to get off the train. Michael Blumenthal, future U.S. secretary of the treasury, made the trip to Shanghai with his parents when he was fourteen years old. He left Berlin on April 6, 1939, arriving in Genoa the following day, possibly leaving on the same ship as the Wulffs. Blumenthal recalled the border crossing as the final humiliation inflicted by the Nazis: the passengers were strip-searched, their baggage torn apart with "sadistic delight."[3]

The ship from Italy to Shanghai took four weeks to reach its final destination. Passengers debarked at many ports along the way, but the bulk of the travelers were German or Austrian Jews seeking refuge in Shanghai. They were treated respectfully by the ship's crew, as befit their status as passengers on a luxury liner. For the first time in years, they could relax and enjoy the excellent and abundant cuisine.

From Genoa, the ship sailed across the Mediterranean to Port Said, leaving Europe behind, and then traversed the Suez Canal. The passengers at that point were a stone's throw from Palestine. But the Holy Land was off-limits to all but a few immigrants each year, thanks to British policy, so the passengers continued on through the Red Sea. Passing alongside the coast of Saudi Arabia, a country that had just concluded an arms deal with the Third Reich and a friendship and trade treaty with Japan, they made their way into the Arabian Sea. From there they entered the Indian Ocean, circumnavigating India, whose troops would fight alongside the British in Japan and North Africa, halting in both Bombay and Ceylon. The ship then dipped farther south toward Malaysia, dropping anchor in Singapore. People in both areas would live peacefully under British rule until occupied by the Japanese in early 1942. From Singapore, the ship traveled through the South China Sea, docking in Hong Kong, where some passengers disembarked and then headed up the coast of China to the Yangtze River. From there it steamed up the Whangpoo River, where the remaining passengers could not fail to notice "the smell of death and destruction in the air."[4]

Upon their arrival in Shanghai, the refugees were met by representatives of a relief organization set up by the leaders of the Shanghai Jewish community—primarily Baghdadi Jews, merchants who had established themselves in Shanghai a hundred years earlier. The immigrants were taken to the Embankment Building, a huge apartment complex owned by Victor Sassoon, patriarch of the established Sephardic Jewish community, one floor of which had been converted into a reception center for refugees. Every new arrival received a blanket, sheets, a tin cup, a dish, and a spoon. Soon the women in their stylish European clothes and fashionable hats would find themselves standing in line with their tin dish for a handout of food.[5]

From the reception center, the refugees entered one of several types of accommodation. Those who had money were able to rent an apartment in the French part of the city, the French Concession. Those with nothing moved into one of the Heime (homes) in Hongkew, the Japanese part of the international section of Shanghai. These were barracks, warehouses, or schools that had been converted to refugee housing.[6] Penniless, having been allowed to take only ten *Reichsmarks* with them when they left Germany, Lotte and Hermann Wulff moved directly into the large dormitories that constituted the Heim.

The Chaoufoong Road Heim had just opened when the Wulffs arrived in May and its newly established isolation ward was already in use to quarantine residents with scarlet fever. Scarlet fever was one of many epidemic diseases the refugees would face: typhus and typhoid fever frequently swept through the population, as did malaria and tuberculosis. Situated near the Whangpoo River, the Chaoufoong Road flooded when the typhoons hit in August. Later, the Chaoufoong Heim would also serve as the site for performances of comedies and operettas put on by talented residents, and would host competing community soccer teams on its regulation playing field.[7]

The Wulffs reached Shanghai just in time for summer. Lotte wrote in a postcard to her daughter in August: "Here it is very hot—unbearably hot, and we suffer a great deal. The climate is unhealthy." She was not exaggerating: the temperature hovered between ninety-five and one hundred degrees Fahrenheit with unrelenting humidity.[8] There was little ventilation in the Heim. War had not yet broken out in Europe and Ilse was in civilized Belgium. Much as she missed her daughter, Lotte was confident that sending her on the Kindertransport had been a wise decision.

~

The Shanghai that Lotte and Hermann Wulff found upon their arrival in 1939 was overpopulated, dirty, congested, and wracked by crime. After sunset, everyone was at risk. Burglaries, political assassinations, and holdups were everyday occurrences thanks to rampant corruption in the city's administration. Hongkew, where the Wulffs lived, was the poorest area of the city, a section fully under Japanese control. Much of Shanghai's trade and most of its industry had been destroyed by the Sino-Japanese war. It was still possible to get from the Japanese section into the other parts of the International Settlement by crossing the Garden Bridge. But each day on the bridge, a bizarre scene played itself out, emblematic of Sino-Japanese relations: "Two cheerful-looking soldiers of the British Seaforth Highlanders in their almost theatrical costumes patrol the southern entrance of the iron bridge as the living outposts of Western influence and power." Just a few hundred feet away, "well-armed Japanese sentries guard the entrance into the vital sections of Hongkew and Yangtzepoo, on whose factories and warehouses depends Shanghai's importance as an industrial and commercial metropolis. Dark uniforms and the inevitable antiseptic leather masks give these sentries a sinister look." Then, one at a time, "The Chinese file past them on their way into the northern section, and the rule that each of them has to remove his hat and to bow deeply when he presents his pass is rigidly enforced." "Rigid enforcement" meant that violators were beaten or even thrown into the polluted waters of the Whangpoo River.[9]

Lotte and Hermann spent most of their time in Hongkew, seldom finding the opportunity to enter other parts of the International Settlement, where a brisk global trade still flourished. Ostentatious buildings housed banks, fur trade companies, and department stores. The Bund, the main thoroughfare of the International Settlement, looked more like Fifth Avenue in New York City or the Kurfürstendamm in Berlin than a Chinese street. Nor did Lotte and Hermann spend much time in the traditionally Chinese section of the city, now controlled by the Japanese, where laborers bustled along the banks of the river, pushing rickshaws and carrying heavy loads on bamboo poles.[10]

The Wulffs had a few acquaintances in the French Concession, but they were in no position to enjoy the vibrant social life of that area. With their worn workaday clothes, German manners, and empty wallets, they were not welcome clients at the Cercle Sportif Français, the French club that boasted a roof terrace, indoor pool, tennis courts, and fancy ballroom. They were too tired after a day's work and too poor to contemplate spending the evening in one of the Concession's fancy nightclubs frequented by the well-heeled Americans, Belgians, British, and other foreigners who were part of Chinese high society.

The refugees built their own insular community in which everyone spoke German. With loans from wealthy Sephardic Jews who were already established in Shanghai, some enterprising German and Austrian Jews set up their own businesses: a watch repair shop, a margarine factory, a butcher shop. The Café Louis, modeled on an Austrian *Konditorei,* was a popular meeting place for refugees throughout the war, featuring *Sachertorte, Apfelstrudel,* and other central European favorites. Those establishments that took root in the elite French Concession catered to more affluent refugees. At the Fiaker Restaurant on the Avenue Joffre, the cuisine was said to rival that of the best Viennese restaurants, and the Black Cat on the Roi Albert Avenue was a typical German cabaret.[11] Hongkew was the shabbiest and most depressing part of town. As Michael Blumenthal recalled, "If you didn't know how to live by your wits and had no money, it was one of the most miserable places in the world."[12]

The Wulffs arrived in Shanghai in the nick of time. Reeling under the impact of 15,000 refugees arriving in less than a year, many of whom were destitute and dependent on local charity to survive, the doors to further immigration were all but closed in August 1939. Already the previous December, the Municipal Council of Shanghai, the governing body of the International Settlement, had cabled the Joint Distribution Committee, the major New York–based refugee aid organization: "Shanghai is gravely perturbed by abnormal influx of Jewish refugees. Shanghai is already facing most serious refugee problem due to Sino-Japanese hostilities. It is quite impossible to absorb any large number of foreign refugees." Then came what would have been a death knell, had it been heeded: "Council earnestly requests your assistance in preventing any further refugees coming to Shanghai. Council may be compelled to prevent further refugees landing in International Settlement."[13] The Joint Distribution Committee relayed the message to German authorities and to the German Jewish community, which wisely ignored the warning.

At the urging of Jewish community leaders, the Shanghai Municipal Council next adopted a strategy of prohibiting refugees from landing in Shanghai. After further negotiations, an agreement was reached allowing those with at least four hundred dollars to enter, as well as individuals who had a contract in hand for a job in Shanghai or had a spouse already residing in the city.[14] With the new regulations in place, immigration slowed dramatically. It was cut off almost entirely in June 1940 with Italy's entry into the war, which closed the sea route to China.

The only remaining access to Shanghai from Europe was overland, across the entire six-thousand-mile span of the Soviet Union. The last of the European Jewish refugees to find some semblance of safety in China followed this route. Two thousand Polish Jews, including the entire student body and faculty of the Mirrer Yeshiva, one of the many Talmudic academies of Poland, reached Kobe, Japan, in the spring of 1941. About half of them continued on to Australia and other countries in the western hemisphere; the remaining 1,000 departed for Shanghai. Just as the group reached Japan, Germany invaded the Soviet Union, sealing off the last escape route from Europe.

Hermann Wulff had made a living in Stettin in the last years before he immigrated by repairing typewriters and making primitive photocopies of documents. He may well have done the same in Shanghai. As long as Hermann could work, he and his wife were poor but not destitute. Lotte mended clothes on the side to bring in a little extra money. Her situation would deteriorate radically after her husband died in September 1940.

Hermann's death left Lotte lonely, alone, and with no obvious means of support. She had known for some time that he was dying, as she implied in her letter to Ilse written in March 1941: "You must have received the sad news that your dear father died after a serious illness. He would never have gotten well because he had liver cancer."

The loss was overwhelming. Lotte, who rarely alluded to her feelings in her letters, wrote in May 1941: "Everything is so sad," adding "actually, there is no future here and we don't know how long we'll be able to stay here." With no training other than as *Hausfrau,* Lotte was reduced to doing menial work to survive. In June 1941 she wrote to Ilse: "I help with cleaning and peeling vegetables. I start at 6:30 a.m., work until mid-day, and am busy in the afternoon. We sit outdoors [because it is intolerably hot inside]. I am careful with my clothes. I don't have much, but I make do. . . . I also go to the cemetery where I see dear Daddy. It's far away. Some people have a room outside the Heim. They are lucky to have a job where they earn some money—or get money from relatives abroad." The letter ends with her characteristic exhortation to be "my well-behaved little girl."

Dependent on charity, Lotte turned to the International Committee for Granting Relief to European Refugees. Financed by Victor Sassoon, the IC, as it was known, was soon overwhelmed by the needs of the new arrivals and was largely supplanted by a second relief organization, the Committee for the Assistance of European Jewish Refugees in Shanghai, or CFA. The IC continued to provide some services: it sponsored English classes—English was the lingua franca of the Shanghai business world, and anyone who hoped to find employment had to speak English. Lotte wrote to Ilse that she had been taking English but had to stop when she could no longer afford the classes. The CFA, on the other hand, established the Heim on Chaoufoong Road where Lotte lived, along with four other homes, and provided two meals a day to Heim residents. The CFA also started a Kitchen Fund to serve meals to several thousand refugees who eked out enough of a living to rent a room in one of Hongkew's lane houses but who were far from self-sufficient. In addition, the CFA organized medical care for the refugees.[15] The Joint Distribution Committee based in New York provided some financial aid—a paltry $5,000 in 1938, and a somewhat more substantial contribution of $100,000 in 1939, when the refugee population had tripled.[16]

What Lotte needed desperately, beyond food and shelter, was community. She had a few contacts from Stettin: Ilse's former teacher and her husband, a physician, had also immigrated to Shanghai. Lotte saw them periodically, but indicated in her letters, with considerable bitterness, that they did not have much time for her. She failed to appreciate that Walter Cohn was tremendously busy, making house calls on his bicycle and treating patients free of charge. One contemporary described him as "a kindly young man with a beard who had been affectionately nicknamed Jesus of Stettin." Dr. Cohn, who suffered from malnutrition and perhaps tuberculosis, died in the summer of 1943.[17]

A small Jewish community had existed in Shanghai before the arrival of the central European refugees. Comprised of two distinct groups, it included both a tight-knit group of about 700 Jews who had emigrated from Baghdad in the second half of the nineteenth century and a contingent of Russian Jews, numbering somewhere between 4,000 and 6,000, who had fled Russia after the 1917 Revolution.[18] For assimilated Jews like Lotte Wulff, who thought of herself as more German than Jewish, the Baghdadi and the Russian cultures were only slightly less alien than that of the Chinese.

The Sephardic community traced its roots to David Sassoon, who had left Baghdad to set up shop in Bombay in the early nineteenth century. With the opening of the treaty ports in China after the First Opium War (1839–42), Sassoon sent representatives to explore commercial possibilities in Canton and Shanghai. In short order, David and his five sons became highly successful merchants, trading in cotton and opium.[19]

The Sassoon patriarch most in evidence when Lotte lived in Shanghai was Sir Victor. Known as a bon vivant and a womanizer, Sir Victor was a builder, and he liked his buildings to be large.[20] He commissioned the Broadway Mansion, a twenty story apartment building, and the Embankment House, a massive gray edifice that stretched for a quarter of a mile along Shanghai's Songpoo Creek and contained 114 apartments and a swimming pool. Victor Sassoon also put up Grosvenor Gardens, a luxury apartment complex in the French Concession, and the Metropole Hotel in the International Settlement. The wealthy Sassoons spent their time conducting business transactions and partying in the fanciest clubs and hotels of the International Settlement. They had no time for and no personal contact with the poorest of the poor European refugees.

Other Baghdadi Jews had also made their fortunes in the International Settlement of Shanghai. Silas Hardoon was a successful businessman who had started out as an employee of David Sassoon and later ventured out on his own, finding sufficient opportunities in flourishing Shanghai for him, too, to become a millionaire.[21] Sir Elly Kadoorie—many of the Sephardic Jews had British citizenship and the most distinguished among them achieved knighthood—also initially worked for the Sassoons. When he left their employ, he went on to make his fortune in banking, rubber, and utilities. Kadoorie, who owned a Shanghai hotel chain that featured names like the Majestic and the Royal, lived in a private mansion on Bubbling Well Road where he was known for the extravagant parties he held in his larger-than-life eighty by fifty foot ballroom.[22]

The Sephardic community had built two synagogues—Ohel Rachel and Beth Sharon—both of which were Orthodox. They looked and felt different from the very liberal congregations familiar to most German Jews. The prayer books were entirely in Hebrew (Reform synagogues in Germany had long ago adopted the vernacular for their services); the men and women were strictly separated; and even the dress code was foreign. Lotte Wulff, who became more observant during her time in China, felt out of place in the Sephardic synagogues. She was drawn to a new, liberal congregation, where services were conducted in German, that opened its doors in 1941.

The other Jews already living in Shanghai, Russian émigrés, were newer arrivals and less financially successful than the Baghdadis. They tended to be small businessmen in the export-import business, dealing in commodities such as wool and fur. Some were professionals; a number were musicians. Barely able to make a living themselves, they were not enthusiastic about the flood of new arrivals from Germany and Austria, with whom they would have to compete for jobs. They also remained insular, socializing with each other or with wealthy foreigners who patronized their clubs and tea houses; in any case showing little interest in befriending the likes of Lotte Wulff.[23]

~

If Lotte was poor and lonely after her husband died, she found herself substantially worse off after Pearl Harbor. For Ilse, Pearl Harbor marked America's entry into the war, a sign that the tide was turning and Germany might ultimately be defeated. For her mother, December 8, 1941, was a day of infamy: Japan was at war not just with China but also with the Allies. The internationalization of the conflict had profound consequences for the Jewish refugees in Shanghai.

The first repercussion was an attack by Japan on the British and American presence in the International Settlement. Two journalists, among the few Americans posted in Shanghai on Pearl Harbor Day, described the events on the day after Pearl Harbor was bombed: "Without the slightest warning the city of Shanghai was wakened at dawn on Dec. 8 by the uproar of Japanese guns destroying the sole British gunboat remaining in the Whangpoo River—the *Petrel*. The vessel refused to surrender promptly and sank in a roaring mass of flames. . . . One British seaman died. The American gunboat *Wake* surrendered and its crew was interned with the *Petrel*'s."[24]

The Japanese military commandeered various venerable institutions such as the American Country Club and the British Shanghai Club to serve as headquarters for their operations. Allied personnel—as well as assorted reporters and businessmen—were interned in camps in primitive conditions. Stores and factories were taken over by the Japanese.

Foreigners had to register as "enemy aliens" and were required to wear four-inch red armbands, labeled B for British or A for American. They were banned from hotels and restaurants, and their bank accounts were frozen. Two shiploads of foreigners were repatriated; the 8,000 individuals who were left behind were sent to Japanese concentration camps for the duration of the war.

The result, from the point of view of the Jewish refugees, was that basic supplies became even scarcer and prices even higher as trade ground to a halt. In addition, communication with the West, which had never been reliable, became increasingly erratic. Lotte received letters from her daughter that had been mailed four months earlier. Once she went for nine months without any correspondence getting through. Sometimes only postcards were allowed.

Two days before Ilse was arrested by the French police and taken to the French concentration camp Vernet, she wrote to her mother. Lotte responded on December 8, knowing nothing of her daughter's experience in the interim: "Your last letter was 25 words from the Red Cross on 8/24/42. You shared with me that dear Grandpa was sent to Poland. I didn't know that. Hopefully it will be bearable for him. I pray to God that He will protect you. Be brave. Hopefully better times will come."

The painfully long delays between letters continued. Lotte's next letter to Ilse was written on January 21, 1943, in response to the note she received dated October 4, in which Ilse mentioned in passing that she had been to an internment camp and back. Lotte sensed that her daughter had kept some crucial details from her and yearned for better communication, writing: "You didn't share with me that you had a different residence [Vernet]. How was it? You can write me everything that's on your mind. I will also tell you everything. We have to have patience." Lotte, like so many parents separated by time and space from their children, continued to think of Ilse as the immature, thirteen-year-old girl she had said good-bye to at the train station in Berlin, exactly four years earlier. She wrote to her as though she were still a child, asking "How are your teeth? Your feet?" and failing utterly to grasp that, both by dint of her experiences and by the passage of time, Ilse had grown up.

Isolated, impoverished, and feeling increasingly distant from her only child, Lotte Wulff did not think her life could get much worse. Then, in February 1943, the Japanese announced that all stateless residents of Shanghai—which effectively meant the Jewish refugees—would be confined to a ghetto.

Japan's German allies had argued for some time that the Jews were a pernicious people who needed at the very least to be segregated from the rest of society and at best eliminated altogether. The chief SS officer in China, Colonel Josef Meisinger, had previously distinguished himself by establishing the Warsaw ghetto and ordering the murder of many of its residents, winning him the sobriquet "the Butcher of Warsaw."[25] Rumors of plans to kill the Jews of Shanghai by such unsavory means as forcing them onto small boats without food and water or by working them to death in the salt mines circulated through Hongkew. They proved to be baseless. But in February an ominous announcement was read over the radio and printed to circulars throughout the International Settlement:

> Due to military necessity, places of residence and business of the stateless refugees in the Shanghai area shall hereafter be resettled in the undermentioned area in the International Settlement. . . .
>
> The stateless refugees at present residing and/or carrying on business in the district other than the above area shall remove their places of residence and/or business into the area designated above by May 18, 1943. . . .
>
> Persons who will have violated this proclamation or obstructed its enforcement shall be liable to severe punishment.[26]

Lotte lived in the Chaoufoong Heim, on the edge of the designated ghetto. She would not have to move. But the one-square-mile area of Hongkew, which had housed some 6,000 refugees, would henceforth be home to close to 18,000. What this meant for Lotte was, as she wrote to Ilse in August 1943, that she now lived with twelve other people in a single room. The oppressive heat and crowding would sap what little energy she had: "I don't have much stamina and can only do light work. There's also terrible humidity. Butter, milk, meat, and sugar are not available. We get a small ration."

Just a month after the deadline for moving into the Hongkew ghetto, Lotte wrote to Ilse telling her how overjoyed she was to learn that her daughter, living with the Brütsch family in Geneva, was satisfied with her lot: "That at least gives me some solace in my loneliness. Our life is not so good. The economic situation gets harder all the time." Lotte then commented on a rumor that international mail would soon be discontinued: "That would be a heavy blow for me because your letters are my only joy."

The crowding in the Hongkew ghetto got even worse. In a letter dated September 28, 1943, Lotte said she was living with twenty-three people in a small room. Secure in the knowledge that Ilse was safe, she let down her guard and revealed the discouraging truth about her daily life:

> Every day I clean my bed to prevent the bedbugs from multiplying. The worst months are July to September. The humidity is so bad we can hardly breathe. The mosquitoes are also bad. There has been no milk or butter for the past year. I have bread and syrup with tea [for breakfast]. We get a small loaf at a reduced rate. At lunch we get warm soup or rice with sauce. In the evening we have to fend for ourselves. The midday meal is not very satisfying. Shoe soles, soap, etc. are unbelievably expensive. I cannot work as much as previously. I have to sell some of my things to make ends meet. I even had to sell some of my underwear. But don't worry about me—things will work out.

Lotte wished her daughter a healthy and happy New Year, referring to the Jewish New Year, Rosh Hashanah, which fell on September 22–23 that year. As Jewish observance became more important to her, she became a regular at the congregation where Rabbi Georg Kantorowsky presided.

Born in 1883 in Upper Silesia, Kantorowsky had been arrested during the November pogrom and taken to Sachsenhausen for six weeks. He reached Shanghai by traversing the Soviet Union, then going by ship to Japan and from there to China. He was hired by a congregation that had split off from the established Orthodox synagogues in Hongkew, establishing itself as a liberal alternative. He delivered his first sermon in Shanghai for Rosh Hashanah in 1941.[27]

On top of the crowding and the shortages, the refugees had to endure new Japanese leadership. The relatively benign figures who had previously been in charge were replaced by unsympathetic and sometimes downright vicious individuals. The Japanese appointed Kano Ghoya to head the Bureau of Foreign Affairs in Shanghai; he became known for his volatility and his capricious, often abusive behavior. Responsible for distributing day passes that permitted Hongkew residents to leave the ghetto, he insisted that the supplicants line up, sometimes for hours, to request a pass, which he would arbitrarily grant or deny.[28]

Few Western journalists filed reports from China during the Japanese occupation. A rare article datelined February 15, 1944, dramatically described the predicament of Shanghai:

> There is now no cotton to be bought anywhere. On November 11 the Japanese requisitioned all cotton for shipment to Japan and North China. There is a lack of raw materials, they cannot get electric power and the Japanese buy products at fixed prices which are less than the cost of production. Even the most luxurious hotels like the Cathay

> have been without heat most of the winter and have had hot water only a few hours in the morning. Electric cars stop running at 8 p.m.[29]

Just when Lotte believed her existence had reached rock bottom, the Allied bombing of Shanghai began. As with British and American bombing of Berlin, this was simultaneously encouraging and frightening to the Jewish inhabitants. The bombing raids—which began in the skies over Shanghai in June 1944, picked up in July, and became a regular occurrence in November—portended Allied victory. But they were disruptive and destructive: American B-29s, which, by July 1945, could be heard almost daily, often sent Shanghailanders scurrying for safety in a city with no bomb shelters and only ramshackle dwellings that offered minimal protection.[30] In July 1945 Hongkew itself was bombed for the first time. Targeting Japanese military installations, the Americans inadvertently killed 31 refugees and 250 Chinese, wounding many others.[31]

As the German army was collapsing and the Soviets liberated the death camps of Auschwitz and Treblinka, news of the Nazis' barbarism trickled in to the Jews of Shanghai. Much of the news came from Russian broadcasts that seemed so extreme and so incredible that the refugees in China attributed them to Soviet hyperbole.[32]

The bombing of Hiroshima was followed four days later by a second atomic bomb being dropped on Nagasaki, resulting in Japan's unconditional surrender. The people of Shanghai danced in the streets when they heard the voice of Emperor Hirohito on the radio and on public loudspeakers, announcing the surrender. U.S. Marines arrived on September 3, liberating the ghetto, followed by the U.S. Navy 7th Fleet and the U.S. Army Air Corps, which airlifted much-needed supplies into the Shanghai ghetto.[33]

Lotte did not dance in the streets. She lay in a hospital bed, stricken by typhus, which she had contracted in one of the city's periodic epidemics. She died on August 28, 1945, and was buried in the Hung-giao Cemetery. The graveyard, along with Shanghai's three other Jewish cemeteries, was destroyed during China's Cultural Revolution.[34]

10

Post-Traumatic Stress

> The Contracting States shall as far as possible facilitate the assimilation and naturalization of refugees. They shall in particular make every effort to expedite naturalization proceedings and to reduce as far as possible the charges and costs of such proceedings.
>
> —Convention Relating to the Status of Refugees, Article 34, 1951

A week after pleading with the authorities to release him from the work camp, Hans woke up to find that he could not get out of bed. He was unable to walk. The camp staff carried Hans down the mountain on a stretcher to the town of Brig. No trains or buses traveled to the camp and evidently no one had a truck available. In town, he was taken to a community hospital where the young intern on duty pronounced solemnly that Hans had an enlarged heart, which he attributed to "excess sports activity." Though a more senior physician examined Hans the next day and concluded there was nothing wrong with his heart, it was too late. Hans would remain convinced—emotionally if not intellectually—that he had heart disease. Whenever he had one of his anxiety attacks, and he would have them regularly over the years, he would get palpitations. And whenever his heart began to race, he would be convinced he was having a heart attack.

Hans stayed in the hospital for two days. When he could walk again, he was sent back to the work camp, which then discharged him for medical reasons. He returned to his room in Bern, but he had terrifying nightmares from which he woke up crying out loud, his heart pounding, convinced the Nazis would burst into the room any moment. He took to locking the door from the inside and putting the key under his pillow, a routine that allowed him to sleep. Hans discovered that he could be walking down a peaceful Bern street and suddenly feel faint and dizzy. He often developed a tightness in his chest and found himself screaming, asking complete strangers for help. They did not know how to help him.

A math professor at the University of Bern who had taken an interest in the young refugee student arranged for him to see a physician at the university health clinic. In a letter addressed to the Department of Justice and Police on November 12, 1945, the physician asserted: "I diagnosed a severe anxiety neurosis. Psychoanalytic care is urgently indicated and has a good prognosis." Hans appealed for assistance to the Swiss Jewish Refugee Help, which urged the police to facilitate a referral for treatment, asserting that they needed to "address this case promptly" if a "catastrophe" was to be avoided.

Hans saw a psychiatrist on November 27 who concurred that he had severe anxiety and also "suffered from the feeling his heart would stop." The physician continued, "The case is one of psychically induced anxiety in an arrogant young man who is prone to intellectualization." Hypnosis was tried unsuccessfully. The psychiatrist concluded that "because of the severity of his condition," Hans could not be treated as an outpatient. He sent him to another psychiatrist who hospitalized him in his clinic the following day.

At the psychiatric facility in Muri, about fifteen miles outside Bern, Hans received state-of-the-art psychiatric therapy, which in 1945 began with insulin shock treatment. In this now-discredited treatment, a nondiabetic patient is given insulin to drive down his blood sugar so low that he falls into a coma. He is sustained by intravenous fluids while his sugar is allowed to return to normal; then he wakes up. The treatment was widely used for depression, but it had no proven benefit. It certainly did nothing for Hans.

While at the clinic in Muri, Hans wrote to his Cousin Bessie. The penmanship is shaky, the lines not absolutely parallel as in his earlier letters, but he was coherent and quickly launched into his usual talk about immigration: "First of all I wish you a very happy and good new year 1946! Then I have to thank you a lot for the money you sent me a short time ago which I was only handed over these last few days and then I specially thank you for all the trouble you take to draw up new papers." He continued, "I hope at last it will be successful now and it won't take a long time any more until I can go off. You will surely know that I am not quite well presently and I am in a hospital since the end of November."

Hans added that the International Rescue and Relief Committee (IRRC) had or would soon be in touch with the Silvermans about all the necessary arrangements—affidavits, visas, transportation—to facilitate his immigration to the United States.

At the clinic, the doctor next tried electroconvulsive therapy (ECT) on Hans. Electric shock treatment has proved to be an effective treatment for depression, but Hans did not have conventional depression. The technique used at the time involved giving shocks to both sides of the brain. Typically, numerous patients were brought to a single large room and the ECT machine was wheeled on a cart from bed to bed. Patients were not sedated in advance; they watched in terror as each person in turn jerked and writhed from the electric shock.[1]

Today, patients are anesthetized so they do not experience any discomfort during the procedure. Ordinarily only one side of the brain is shocked, which vastly reduces the risk of inducing memory problems. At the time Hans was hospitalized, "physical methods" such as insulin coma and shock treatments were very much in vogue at the most modern psychiatric facilities. And Swiss psychiatry was on the cutting edge—the Burghölzli clinic, fifty miles away in Zurich, was one of the earliest and most sophisticated university-affiliated mental institutions. The Zurich School of Psychiatry laid the foundation for the field of dynamic psychiatry, and such distinguished physicians as Carl Jung (student of dreams and mysticism), Paul Eugen Bleuler (who coined the term "schizophrenia"), and Hermann Rorschach (of inkblot fame) were all Swiss.[2]

Hans refused further shock treatments. He expected to be discharged from the clinic, but his psychiatrist, the director of the clinic, wrote to the Department of Justice and Police on January 26, 1946: "This patient, whom we hoped to release from the clinic in the middle of January, unfortunately continues to have such severe symptoms that a release is not possible. . . . He suffers from such severe agoraphobia that he is in no condition to go out alone." Hans stayed at the clinic until the end of February, with the Department of Justice and Police paying 10 francs per day for his treatment. The balance of the cost, roughly 200 francs a month, was underwritten by the IRRC.

When Hans finally left the clinic, he returned to Bern, better but far from cured. He does not appear to have been referred to an outpatient physician for ongoing treatment. But Hans was *débrouillard,* a French word that is usually translated as "resourceful" but means more than that. He was brilliantly resourceful. He was ingenious. He could not have successfully crossed the Swiss border in 1942 or found a way to go to high school while living in a work camp, without being resourceful. Many years later, Ilse would say that if Hans were stranded in the Sahara desert he would find a telephone booth. Despite his repeated claims that he had heart troubles, Hans knew that he needed ongoing psychiatric care. He knew that electroshock treatment, as practiced at the time, was barbaric and unhelpful. He ended up on a psychoanalyst's couch.

Elisabeth Rothen was a classical Freudian analyst—if any kind of psychiatry could be called classical when the field was only decades old. When Hans began seeing her, she made house calls. Then she met him halfway between her office and his home. Finally, he was able to walk all the way to her office. After a short time, Dr. Rothen felt he was ready to return to the university.

Hans went back to school, only to discover that he could no longer follow what was going on in his math classes. His friend Addi Nussbaum, one of the other "mathematicians" from La Hille, who by then was also enrolled at the University of Bern, remembers an incident in which Hans was called on in class but did not know the answer. Mortified, Hans abruptly left the classroom. Addi found his behavior puzzling. He did not know that the twenty-one-year-old Hans had sustained memory impairment from the shock treatments.

Dr. Rothen did not want Hans to give up his studies and strongly encouraged him to transfer from math and science to liberal arts. Hans arranged the switch, all the while continuing to see Dr. Rothen in therapy. Very gradually, he improved, even finding a new girlfriend.

~

Post-traumatic stress disorder (PTSD) was not officially recognized as a distinct psychiatric disorder until 1980.[3] Physicians and family members of affected individuals had long been aware that traumatic events sometimes produced dramatic symptoms in their victims. Immediately after the Civil War, soldiers manifested nightmares, intense anxiety, and other symptoms of severe distress.[4] In the 1890s the French physician Pierre Janet wrote about "hysteria" characterized by physical symptoms like Hans's in which the patient could not walk despite normally functioning nerves and muscles. Janet hypothesized that hysterical symptoms were "disguised representations of intensely distressing events that had been banished from memory" and offered examples of symptomatic improvement that occurred when the "traumatic memories and the intense feelings that accompanied them were recovered and put into words."[5]

Interest in the syndrome increased after World War I with the introduction of the term "shell shock." Psychiatrists came to recognize that the stress of prolonged exposure to violent death could produce a "neurotic syndrome" in men that resembled hysteria in women. But interest faded as the trench warfare of World War I receded into the past, only to be revived with the reappearance of what was called "combat neurosis" during World War II. Once again, the number of studies of the phenomenon rose and then fell, in large measure because of a failure to realize that "combat neurosis" could have enduring effects.

Descriptions and analysis were rekindled with the Vietnam War. This time, the Veterans Administration, the major source of medical care for America's ex-soldiers, commissioned a study of the effect of wartime experiences. The result was a five-volume study that definitively delineated the syndrome of post-traumatic stress disorder and demonstrated beyond any reasonable doubt that it was directly related to combat exposure. After the publication of this massive report, PTSD finally entered the *Diagnostic and Statistical Manual of the American Psychiatric Association*—the psychiatrist's bible, which names and describes all medically recognized psychological disorders.

Treatment of the disorder has evolved markedly since it was first described. Today the mainstay of treatment is medication, and the drug of choice is an antidepressant.[6] But many authorities believe that recovery is never complete. Especially among Holocaust survivors, the traumatic events continue to exert their effects throughout the life of the victims.

What is far from clear is why some people fare better than others after exposure to very similar traumas. Differential responses result to some extent from the inherent resilience or, conversely, the built-in psychological vulnerability of the individual.[7] Interestingly, social support during or after the traumatic events can mitigate against the onset of symptoms.[8] Perhaps Hans's crossing the border to Switzerland alone set him up for PTSD; Ilse's undertaking the same trip with two other girls attenuated the effects of the trauma. And Hans's subsequent experiences—incarceration in Swiss work camps that were structured to promote isolation and alienation—increased his susceptibility to PTSD. Ilse's experiences in the sheltering and nurturing environment of the Brütsch family, by contrast, aided her recovery.

~

Hans remained enrolled at the University of Bern while reporting weekly to the police as was required of all refugees. He continued to see a psychiatrist, with the cost of his treatment borne by a refugee committee, one of the many predominantly Jewish organizations that had contributed to the support of refugees in Switzerland during the war. And then, out of the blue, he heard from his brother, Günther, with whom he had not been in touch since October 1941. Stimulated by the news from his brother, he typed a letter to Cousin Bessie which began with a request for more help: "I hope you will have got my letter from last week in the meantime. You may believe me when I tell you that it does cost me a big effort to send you these lines because I'm being obliged to ask you for something. I have been thinking over the whole matter for a good time but I really can't find another issue from the present difficulties."

At last he got to the point:

> You know that I'm being ill for a rather long time and even when I feel quite better today than only a few months ago, I still need the treatment and help of a doctor. You will understand that this treatment and my long stay in a hospital near Berne as well as the fact that I am obliged to take much care of me today have caused a lot of ex-

> penses depassing [surpassing] by far the amount which is accorded by the International Rescue and Relief Committee. Moreover the situation has become such that the financial possibilities of the Int. Rescue and Relief Committee are restricted and the Committee has even difficulties to find the necessary sums to continue its work in Switzerland. Therefore I beg you to see if you can't make it possible to send *once* a sum of 30 or 40 dollars. . . . I simply like that this money may be regarded as a contribution to the work of the IRRC and specially as a contribution to the help they have given me.

Next he reported on his current activities: "I'm going again to the university in Berne and I have much pleasure with my studies. There is a good number of English students in Berne now and I should awfully much like to get in touch with them as I think it would be a good refreshment for my bad English."

Finally, in closing, he repeated news he evidently had shared with Bessie earlier, in a letter that either never reached her or was not preserved: "I[n] my last letter I told you that I have fine news from my brother Günther and I'm so happy about it." He ended with a rhetorical flourish: "With all my love and a lot of good wishes and kind regards, I'm your very grateful cousin, Hans."

Hans continued to work on immigrating, writing Bessie during his summer break, in July 1946: "On Monday I got your kind letter of June 17 containing the new set of affidavits. I was really very happy when your letter and the papers arrived. Many, many thinks for it, dear cousin Bessie! I had the affidavits sent to the Consulate General in Zurich immediately."

He then responded to her comments about her own son, Leslie, who had interrupted his studies to join the army, expressing the hope that Leslie would return home soon. He used the news about Leslie as a segue to his own university experience: "I had a rather difficult time at university as my health is making only little progress. I have been ill for almost one year and the convalescence is so slow, so terribly slow that I'm often quite despaired."

Shortly afterward, when Hans next reported to the police, he received a new shock. The official had some news for him. He sat Hans down, gave him a cup of coffee, and then expounded on the policy of his boss, Heinrich Rothmund. "We Swiss," Hans recalls him saying, "do not want to have any anti-Semitism in our country. The best way to prevent the rise of anti-Semitism is to keep down the number of Jews. Now that the war is over," he said to Hans, whose file he had in front of him, "you will have no problem leaving the country. You already have applied for visas to Brazil and the U.S. You have sixty days to arrange to emigrate."

Suddenly immigration, long a dream, became a pressing necessity. Hans had to move quickly. He went to Geneva to obtain a special passport issued by the Swiss for stateless individuals, meeting up with his old friends Peter Salz, a student at the University of Geneva, and Werner Rindsberg, an American soldier, while he was there. The three of them made a surprise visit to another La Hille friend who lived in Geneva, the young pediatric nurse Ilse Wulff. When Hans traveled to Geneva a second time to apply to the Brazilian Consulate for a visa, he again paid a call on Ilse. He promised to write to her regularly.

A few weeks later, Hans made a momentous decision. On August 26, 1946, he announced to Bessie: "Please excuse me that I should write you only a few lines, but things are *very* urgent. Today I have got the visa for Brazil and I have made up my mind definitely to join my brother for the present moment, specially as I am not always in the best of health so I have the wish to be with my nearest family and people I know from before. I think you will understand these feelings, but I always hope that one day I shall come to the United States, and I think it will be quite easy to do this when being in South America."

He implied that he viewed South America merely as a way station along his route to the United States. He also indicated that he had little choice: he had a visa for Brazil in hand; the visa for the United States was still being processed; and he had a deadline to meet: "In any case I could not wait for the visa for the US, as I shall not get a permission for a longer stay here in Switzerland. Unfortunately your affidavits have come too late."

Hans then asked Bessie to wire him two hundred dollars toward the cost of transportation. His brother, Günther, and the International Relief and Rescue Committee would provide the balance of the money. "There is a possibility to leave on October 5th and I must try to catch this opportunity."

As late as mid-September, various agencies continued to argue about who would contribute to the cost of Hans's emigration. He received support for his visa, a suitcase, and partial payment for his passage. But he had a letter from a psychiatrist indicating he was in no condition to take the long boat trip to Brazil and, for mental health reasons, would have to fly. Finally, on September 11, the Department of Justice and Police acknowledged that "out of consideration of Mr. Garfunkel's health condition, we are prepared to make an exception and contribute 600 francs to the cost of his airfare to Brazil." Two days later, Hans signed a statement that he had "received from the Swiss Division of Police a sum of 600 francs for passage to Brazil and is willing to pay back the above mentioned amount at a later date."

Eager to be sure they would finally be rid of this troublesome refugee, the Swiss sent Hans a thick envelope with a train ticket to Paris and a Pan American airways ticket that would take him from Paris to Lisbon, from Lisbon to Dakkar, then to Recife, Rio de Janeiro, and finally Sao Paulo. In early October 1946, Hans set off for the New World.

~

The same month in which she learned of her mother's illness and then her death, Ilse also received a questionnaire from the Swiss government about her future plans. A copy of Ilse's polite and respectful answers remained on file, in her neat Germanic script. Only two of the questions were applicable to Ilse. To the first, "Do you want to return to Germany?" she replied "Not at the moment, as I wish to complete my training as a children's nurse in Switzerland." To the second question, "Insofar as you don't want to return to Germany, where do you plan to travel to?" she answered, "I don't have any specific travel destination."

Perhaps because she didn't answer firmly enough that she was not planning to return to Germany in the future, or perhaps because the authorities paid little attention to the replies on the questionnaires, Ilse received a very disturbing letter on November 30, 1945: "At the end of August 1945, we informed you by letter about the goal of the Allied officials to make it possible for German refugees to return to their homeland." The chief of the police section continued with the news that a transport to Germany had been organized for December 5 and that Ilse was expected to be on board. He added that "altering the transport is not possible." Ilse was required to present herself at the train station in Basel by 1:30 p.m. on December 15—he even indicated the track number. Arrangements had been made to allow her to clear out her otherwise blocked bank account.

The final paragraph was the most stunningly insensitive part of the letter: "Switzerland was honored to take you in when you were in danger. We are delighted to be able to help you to return to your homeland, and don't want to neglect to extend you our best wishes for the future." Ilse fired off a response immediately: "Yesterday I received your letter demanding that I appear in Basel on December 5 for the transport to Germany. There must be some mistake as I have absolutely no intention of returning to Germany at present, as I informed you in the questionnaire."

Her stay was extended to permit her to complete an internship at the Hôpital Gourgas for Sick Children in Geneva, which taught Ilse practical skills such as giving injections and dressing wounds. She also saw what the field of medicine was like by assisting in the operating room. And she gained an understanding of how people can behave under stress when she watched, appalled, as the father of a sick baby pointed a gun at his child's surgeon, his twisted mind leading him to believe that the threat of violence could save his baby's life.

At about the same time that Hans unexpectedly heard from his brother, Ilse received a surprise postcard from her Onkel Erich. She had assumed that her entire family was dead. Addressed to her in care of the Hôpital Gourgas, he wrote in May 1946: "After a long time it is now possible to send you a sign of life. We [Erich and his wife] survived the last year and are both still healthy. Today, exactly one year ago, we were liberated by the Russian army from Theresienstadt. We hope you are well and want news from you."

Because her Onkel Erich was married to an "Aryan" woman, he had not been deported until February 1945, just months before Allied and Soviet troops closed in on Berlin and the war came to an end. According to the perverse and arbitrary racial ideology of the Nazis, some intermarried couples were deemed specially "privileged," with "privilege" having been defined by regulations issued by Goering himself, at the direct insistence of Hitler, in December 1938. In a set of rules intended to appease "Aryan" relatives, the Reich announced that mixed marriages where the husband was Jewish and the children were brought up as Christians or where the wife was Jewish but there were no children were to receive special treatment. The Jewish partner in such cases was exempt from some of the discriminatory laws the state would subsequently put into effect.

Since Onkel Erich was Jewish and he and his wife were childless, their marriage did not meet Goering's definition of privileged. But even in supposedly nonprivileged marriages, a Jew was less likely to be arrested or deported as long as he remained married to an "Aryan." As a matter of course the Gestapo applied pressure to non-Jewish wives such as Trude to divorce their husbands, offering the women the opportunity to have their marriage annulled on "racial grounds."[9] But for those couples who stayed together, the odds of survival for the Jewish partner were greatly enhanced. Erich and Trude remained in Hohenstein-Ernstthal until, though the Germans were clearly losing the war and needed to devote all available manpower to the war effort, they sent Erich to Theresienstadt. He survived, was freed, and rejoined his wife in what was to become Soviet-controlled East Germany.

Ilse had never much cared for Onkel Erich; she did not want to return to Germany; and she particularly didn't want to live in the Russian sector of Germany. Thanks to the nursing shortage in Switzerland, she was able to continue working at the hospital for another year, though every three months she was required to apply for an extension. A letter from the Hôpital Gourgas, sent to the authorities on June 4, 1946, stated explicitly that "in view of the lack of personnel in the hospitals, we are asking you to please allow Miss

Wulff to prolong her stay." But each successive extension came with the comment: "We take the opportunity to remind you that you are obligated to take active steps to emigrate."

After Ilse graduated in the fall of 1946, similar requests were filed to allow her to work as a private nurse for a family. In October she got permission to work as a nurse caring for a newborn, but with the caveat that "the present authorization will cease to be valid the moment the opportunity presents itself for this refugee to leave our country." Her first job came to an abrupt end when her employer's previous request for a nurse from Italy was fulfilled. The Italian woman arrived in Switzerland and Ilse was out of a job. The Swiss were so determined to deny employment to refugees that they preferred importing foreign workers to giving a job to a refugee already living in the country.

Luckily, Ilse found a second job—her final job in Switzerland. She served as a live-in for another family. The mother, a music critic for the *Journal de Genève,* sometimes brought Ilse with her to concerts. The baby's grandfather was also a musician, a violinist with the Orchestre de la Suisse Romande. He liked Ilse and thought she was a superb nanny for his granddaughter.

The job was satisfactory and it paid 180 francs per month. But Ilse realized she had no future in Switzerland. Just as she was mulling over her options, she received a letter from Tante Friedel, the same Tante Friedel who had persuaded Ilse's parents to send her to Belgium, had ultimately placed her in the orphanage, and had succeeded in leaving the country when the Germans invaded. Friedel and her husband, a physician, had initially made their way to Chile but had since immigrated to the United States. They urged Ilse to come to New York and promised to sponsor her, providing the necessary affidavit.

Ilse was skeptical. America was an ocean away. Apart from Tante Friedel, who had been a friend of her mother's and whom she had not seen in seven years, she knew hardly anyone in America. A few of the La Hille group had immigrated to the United States, including Hans's first flame, Hanni Schlimmer, and Werner Rindsberg, who had joined relatives in the States in 1942. But Ilse did not speak English and she didn't want to leave Europe. The only other possibility, aside from joining her Onkel Erich, an option she had already vehemently rejected, was Palestine.

The two girls who had escaped to Switzerland with Ilse, Else Rosenblatt and Ruth Klonover, would both immigrate to Palestine. Ruth had begun her life in Switzerland in a labor camp, or "children's home" as the girls' version was euphemistically called, and was later taken in by her *Pate* (godfather). She took a course in social work along with evening high school classes in Zurich, subsequently working for the Red Cross and then in a Jewish children's home. Ruth was in touch with members of the Zionist movement, and in 1948 she crossed into France and sailed from Marseilles to Palestine just as the State of Israel came into existence.

Else had also spent the war years in various Swiss "homes" and was later placed with several families. Like Ilse, she studied nursing and then worked as a nurse. She was one of the last refugees to leave Switzerland: in 1950, she made her way to a kibbutz in Israel.

Ilse says that going to Palestine never crossed her mind. Maybe living in the family of a Protestant minister had something to do with her perspective—she had, after all, been baptized, though she viewed that as a symbol of belonging, of blending in, rather than as a theological statement. More likely, she had never strongly identified with the Jewish people. Her only exposure to Jewish culture and religion took place during her brief stint attending the Jewish school in Stettin. She had found it interesting—much as she found languages and nursing interesting—but not something she was passionate about or even excited by. While Judaism may have had a certain intellectual appeal, it also had a tremendous downside. More than anything else, to Ilse being Jewish meant being mocked, expelled, murdered. The Swiss, while not barbaric in the way the Germans had been, had done little to dispel Ilse's deep-seated view, instilled in early childhood, that nothing good could come of being Jewish. Going to Palestine meant living as a Jew among Jews. Ilse would not consider such a possibility. She would become a universalist—a philosophy she would teach her daughter and convey to her grandchildren as well.

Ilse continued working and periodically applying to extend her stay in Switzerland until she finally agreed with Charles Brütsch that immigration to the United States would afford her the greatest opportunity. Responding enthusiastically to this decision, the Department of Justice and Police in May 1947 granted one final extension after acknowledging that "Miss Wulff has already taken steps to immigrate to the United States." By June she had the papers necessary to go to the United States but lacked a passport.

In July 1947 Ilse filled out the application for a "certificate of identification," popularly known as a Nansen passport, named after Fridtjof Nansen, the first administrator of the League of Nations' High Commission for Refugees and a tireless advocate for the rights of stateless refugees. This passport enabled the bearer to leave Switzerland—but not to return. It was not a true passport and stated very clearly that the bearer was not a Swiss citizen. But together with the visa for immigration to the United States, it was a major step in ensuring her departure. The final step was procuring money for the ticket. Friedel Brandenstein, her mother's longtime friend, had supplied an affidavit but no travel expenses. Ilse appealed to the Swiss authorities for financial assistance and received a stinging rebuke from the chief of police on September 8: "Miss Wulff has worked since September 1946 as a nurse in Geneva and earns 150 francs per month. Her departure for the USA should take place in December 1947. Miss Wulff will thus have earned a total of 2250 francs in wages during the period September 1946 through December 1947. Had she used these funds frugally, she would be in a position to finance her own departure." They concluded, "We regret that under the circumstances we cannot contribute to the travel expenses of Miss Wulff."

Pastor Brütsch was furious. In a letter oozing with politeness but simmering with contempt, he asked the director of the federal police to reconsider:

> The undersigned, pastor in Geneva and secretary of the Swiss Federation of Protestant Churches, certifies that Miss Ilse Wulff, who arrived in Switzerland as a refugee on the first of January 1943, and has been living in our family since February 8, 1943, had no possessions on her arrival in our country. After a year taking a course at the Pouponnière at Petit-Lancy and then a necessary internship at a hospital, there were only 9 months during which she was employed at a salary of 150 francs per month. It is evident that she needed to acquire all sorts of clothes and critically important items. I can certify that Miss Wulff is economical. Her trip will necessitate all sorts of other expenses aside from the ticket itself, the cost of travel equipment that I cannot contribute to. During her stay in Switzerland, there have been no complaints lodged against Miss Wulff. I would be obliged if, in consideration of her true situation, the federal police could pay the most important part, the entire cost of the voyage to America.

The Emigrant Aid Society added their plea to that of Pastor Brütsch, clarifying that Ilse had actually earned only 90 francs a month for some time and that she had led an extremely frugal life, spending money only on the most urgently necessary clothes, laundry, and shoes. The organization also noted that after repeated requests on their part, the Evangelical Refugees Aid Society had agreed to make a small donation of about 150 francs, and beseeched the Department of Justice and Police to contribute 880 francs, so that "Miss Wulff does not run the risk of losing her reservation on the ship and also the possibility of immigrating to the United States before her visa expires."

Letters went back and forth, finally resulting in a 300-franc contribution from the Swiss authorities, who continued to insist that with appropriate frugality, Ilse could have paid the full travel costs. Moreover, they argued, she would soon be gainfully employed in America and on her nanny's salary would surely be able to put aside money to repay her debt. On December 12, 1947, the Department of Justice and Police of Bern closed her case, writing to their subordinates in Geneva that "we have the honor of informing you that the refugee, Ilse Wulff, German, born December 25 1925, has left Switzerland for the United States, in accordance with the law, on December 1, 1947."

In January 1949 she repaid her debt to the Swiss Department of Justice and Police.

~

Hans and Ilse were among the lucky ones who succeeded in immigrating to the Americas. There was never any serious doubt that they would have to leave Switzerland; the only question was where they would go.

As early as 1944 the Swiss government had begun asking refugees where they wanted to go after the war was over. The children who responded to the government questionnaire expressed preferences different from those of the adults, with far more of them hoping to go to Palestine. Among the children, 23 percent wanted to return to France, Belgium, or Holland; 17 percent, to the United States; and 28 percent, to Palestine. A few, 7 percent, dreamed of staying in Switzerland. Within days of the liberation of France, Belgium, and Holland in the summer of 1944, the Swiss authorities began organizing the return of large groups of refugees to these countries.[10]

"Transmigration," the official Swiss policy toward refugees, remained nonnegotiable and would stay in effect until 1954, when Switzerland ratified the Geneva Refugee Convention. Twelve hundred refugees were sent via several transports to Palestine. Survivors of the Buchenwald and Theresienstadt concentration camps who had entered Switzerland thanks to a dramatic rescue in early 1945 were also sent to Palestine. Despite the best efforts of the Swiss to force refugees to leave, more than 15,000 still lived in Switzerland in 1946. This number the authorities regarded as intolerable. They applied increasing pressure on the refugees to leave, requiring them to report regularly on their efforts to obtain travel documents. Ultimately, only 896 refugees received permanent asylum in Switzerland.[11]

~

Despite Hans's conviction that he would finally make his way to the United States, there was no guarantee he would be any more successful in 1946 than he had been during the previous seven years. The war had created an unprecedented number of refugees. Stalin and Hitler had between them expelled, deported, or otherwise displaced an estimated 30 million people, all of whom, at the conclusion of the war, were desperate to return home or to find a new home.[12] Included among them was the traumatized, malnourished, and impoverished remnant of European Jewry. Most of the western and central European refugees would find themselves in displaced person (DP) camps. These camps were created by the Allied forces, in some instances using the same sites, even the same barracks, that had previously been used by the Nazis as concentration camps. The Allies converted Dachau and Buchenwald into DP camps, and in a misguided effort to avoid any semblance of racism, initially housed Jews alongside Ukrainian and Polish prisoners, who had themselves tormented and murdered Jews.[13] Administered first by the Allied forces and then handed over to the United Nations Relief and Rehabilitation Administration, the camps at their peak housed just under 7 million people.[14]

The conditions for Jews in the DP camps were abominable. Only after Secretary of the Treasury Henry Morgenthau persuaded President Truman to investigate did conditions improve.[15] The inquiry led to a report that confirmed that Jews were being treated as virtual prisoners of war: they were confined, forced to wear uniforms, given prison rations, and subjected to intimidation by non-Jewish DPs. Truman sent a directive to Eisenhower on August 31, 1945, to revamp the camps, commenting that the army was treating the Jews much as the Nazis had except that "we don't exterminate them."[16]

Change came and the Jews in the DP camps received more food, moved in some cases into requisitioned German homes, and gained access to recreational facilities and rehabilitation programs. But just as conditions were improving, there was an influx of 120,000 Polish Jews into the U.S.-occupied zone of Germany.[17] In the summer of 1946, Polish Jews who had fled to the USSR after the German invasion of Poland were repatriated to Poland. What they found when they returned to their towns and villages was hatred and resentment. Sometimes the inhabitants turned murderous, as in the Kielce pogrom of July 1946, in which forty-two Jews were killed and another sixty injured.[18] The returnees' families had vanished and their homes had been occupied by non-Jewish Poles. A small number of Polish Jews, unwanted in the towns of their birth, settled in Sczcezin, formerly Stettin, only to face a pogrom in their new home. Despondent, they made their way west, where they were soon joined by Jews from Hungary and Rumania who faced similar, though seldom lethal, rejection.

The United States was initially not much more hospitable than Switzerland toward the Jewish refugees of Europe. A Gallup poll conducted in December 1945 found that 37 percent of Americans wanted to admit *fewer* immigrants than before World War II, and 32 percent were willing to maintain prewar levels.[19] Reluctantly, President Truman agreed simply to meet the existing annual quota in full. Of the 39,000 quota numbers available, 25,957 were allocated to Germany and Austria. Both Hans and Ilse entered the United States under the German quota. But for most of the 250,000 Jews in DP camps at the end of 1946, the quota system was a farce—two-thirds of the refugees were originally from Poland and the Polish quota was a mere 6,514 per year.

Congress considered amending the immigration laws. A vigorous campaign began under the direction of Lessing Rosenwald, founder of the Citizens Committee for Displaced Persons. The committee recommended that the United States use both current and unfilled wartime quotas, without reference to national origin, to admit 400,000 immigrants over four years. Truman submitted a bill with this proposal to the House, where it passed. But the bill soon encountered a roadblock in the form of the chairman of the Senate's Immigration Subcommittee, William Chapman Revercomb, who had publicly held the Jews responsible for their persecution in Europe. He introduced his own counterlegislation, which had the diabolical feature of limiting the designation DP to refugees who reached the American zone by December 22, 1945, effectively excluding a huge number of Jews. Other provisos, such as a requirement that half of the German quota go to those of "German ethnic origin" and an insistence that 30 percent of visas be reserved for individuals with experience in agriculture, excluded even more of the people who needed the bill the most.

Truman signed the legislation, the Displaced Persons Act of 1948, declaring that a bad bill was better than no bill. He added, however, that "the bill discriminates in callous fashion against displaced persons of the Jewish faith. This brutal fact cannot be obscured by the many technicalities in the bill." Proposed amendments to the legislation, changes that would have eliminated its most egregious provisions, were stonewalled by further Senate opposition. A second Displaced Persons Act was passed in June 1950, authorizing the admission of 341,000 refugees—including 150,000 who had already immigrated.[20]

Between 1945 and 1952, a total of 83,000 European Jews found safe haven in the United States. Hans and Ilse were among them.

11

Brazilian Detour

> Everyone has the right to a standard of living adequate for . . . health and well-being . . . including food, clothing, housing and medical care.
> —Universal Declaration of Human Rights, Article 25, 1948

Hans's tickets arrived in the mail in September 1946. The distance from Bern, Switzerland, to Sao Paulo, Brazil, is six thousand miles as the crow flies, but given the need to refuel and the limited demand for international travel, airplanes followed a more circuitous route than the hypothetical crow. Hans's itinerary called for him to take a train to Paris, fly from there to Lisbon, then fly to Dakar, the capital of Senegal. The next leg of the journey was the longest, crossing the Atlantic. He traveled to Recife, Brazil, in what he considered to be a very large airplane—it accommodated a total of 48 passengers. From Recife he took a second plane to Rio de Janeiro. For a young man who had never been out of Europe and who had never flown, it was an intimidating undertaking. It was very nearly subverted before the first flight.

Hans set off for Paris, alone and anxious. At the border, the French police boarded the train to check papers. There was a problem. According to their records, an arrest warrant had been issued for Hans Garfunkel. Though he suffered from panic attacks and became terrified by sounds in the night, under stress, Hans was remarkable. He assured the policeman there must be some mistake and promised to sort matters out at the police station in Paris. He must have had astonishing powers of persuasion—they let him proceed.

Instead of a few delightful days as a tourist in Paris, a city he had never visited, Hans spent the time before his flight left for Dakar dealing with the French bureaucracy. The charge proved to be that he had left France illegally in 1942. Through the bizarre machinations of the Vichy and Swiss bureaucracies, the Swiss Department of Justice and Police, after apprehending him on the Swiss side of the border on Christmas Day 1942 and taking him to a reception camp and then a labor camp, had reported his arrival to the French police. The French then issued a warrant for his arrest—though why they cared that this unwelcome refugee had left the country without their permission, particularly given that he had been accepted, albeit reluctantly, by another country, is obscure. Moreover, Ilse, when she left Switzerland via

France a year later, did not encounter a similar obstacle. But four years after Hans's unsanctioned flight from La Hille via Toulouse, Annecy, and Annemasse into Switzerland, the French were eager to compensate for their oversight. No matter that the puppet government in Vichy had fallen in 1944 and the military leader of the Free French Resistance forces, the charismatic Charles de Gaulle, had until recently been president of the Provisional Government of France. The twenty-three-year-old stateless and nearly penniless refugee Hans Garfunkel was persona non grata in France.

Hans already had substantial experience with the police. He remembered all too well the gendarmes who had arrested him at La Hille, along with forty other teenagers, and taken him to Vernet; he had had extensive dealings with the Swiss military police who ran the labor camps; and he had reported regularly to the Swiss cantonal police when he was not confined to a labor camp. He also spoke French, which helped, though he was a bit rusty after three years in the German part of Switzerland. After conversing with a supervisor and then the supervisor's superior, Hans finally made the French understand that he was not a criminal but a refugee. They also realized that they had a chance to be rid of him forever if they let him board the plane to Lisbon. The alternative was to be stuck with him indefinitely since his passport was a "Nansen passport" that allowed him to leave Switzerland but not to return. Germany had revoked his citizenship years earlier. The French authorities released Hans just in time to catch his plane.

After many hours in the air, Hans finally arrived in Rio de Janeiro, at the time the capital of Brazil. He then performed what his brother would refer to as his first miracle: he reached Günther by telephone. Telecommunication in Brazil, epitomizing the country's general level of modernity, was erratic at best. Many of Brazil's industries and services worked smoothly only if oiled by bribes; others were very badly designed and poorly maintained. But on that magnificent spring day—situated in the southern hemisphere, Brazil's seasons are the reverse of Europe's—Hans heard the voice of a family member for the first time since leaving Berlin on January 30, 1939. He told his brother he was on his way; he spent the night in a hotel in Rio; and the following day he flew the remaining two hundred miles to Sao Paulo.

The reunion between the brothers was one of the most emotional experiences of Hans's life. But eager as they were to be together, the two were strangers to each other. Hans had been twelve years old when Günther, himself only twenty, left Germany to seek security halfway around the world. Now Hans was an adult, and in the intervening nine years he had lost both his parents, experienced several brushes with death, spent a total of eighteen months in labor camps, and suffered a mental breakdown. All the two young men shared was half of their genes and a few fading memories of their parents and a childhood in Nazi Germany.

Günther brought Hans to his home, a small house in the predominantly German Jewish section of Sao Paulo, where Hans would live for the next year. He reintroduced him to Friedel, now Günther's wife. Hans thought his brother was embarrassed to be seen with a woman who was almost old enough to be his mother, though perhaps that was sheer projection. What he did not know was that the cancer that would kill Friedel in less than a year was already beginning to eat away at her body, aging her prematurely.

Hans felt safe but not at home in Sao Paulo. Most of the neighbors were transplanted German or Austrian Jews. They spoke German and they had done their utmost to re-create the environment they had left behind, establishing an *Apotheke* (drugstore) and a *Konditorei* (bakery), much as the German Jewish refugees had done in Shanghai. People brought their groceries at the *Markt* (market) and conducted their business at the *Büro* (office). Hans was glad to have left German culture behind him and had no desire to live in its Latin American reincarnation.

The two brothers soon discovered that the emotional distance that had always separated them had if anything grown greater. Hans could not overcome the anger and resentment he felt toward his brother for having failed to bring their parents to Brazil. Günther had left on a tourist visa and simply stayed on in Brazil, but once he arrived in Sao Paulo, he had sent for Friedel Kitkowski, Tante Änne's sister. Paula and Julius Garfunkel had not approved of the match: not only was Friedel fifteen years older than Günther, but as an "Aryan," she had had no compelling need to leave the country. According to family lore, Günther squandered his family's money on Friedel's passage to Brazil, depleting the remaining resources that could, in theory, have helped his parents and his younger brother escape the clutches of the Nazis.

Günther's perspective on the prospects for his parents' immigrating to Brazil in 1937 differed substantially from the view that Hans held. In October 1937 Günther recapitulated for his Cousin Bessie what he had told his father in a previous correspondence about the situation in Brazil: "To my greatest regret I was compelled to relate him that I can't see a good chance for him in this country as it is very hard—if not impossible—for a man of his age [fifty-six] to find a new existence here except he would be able to bring a certain sum of money with him. But as you know the latter is almost impossible. Hans is, of course, not lucky [happy] about this reply, but I could not give another one by good concious [*sic*]."

Günther went on to say that he knew it was hard for Jews in Germany but: "It is very difficult to come to Brasil, as there are here the same difficulties as with the USA, i.e. that people here does not wish more immigrants. For the last weeks they are not give more visas for Brasil."

Hans believed that his brother could have gotten his parents out of Germany if he had exerted himself sufficiently. After all, one of his old friends from the Luise Zickels Höhere Privatschule in Berlin had immigrated to Brazil with his parents, and they now owned a coffee plantation. The truth about immigration was more complicated.

Brazil had had neither immigration quotas nor appreciable anti-Semitism until 1930, when the small-time rancher, lawyer, and professional soldier Getulio Vargas seized power in a bloodless coup. A mercurial dictator whose ideology has been called a cross between fascism and New Deal reformism, Vargas promoted modernization and industrialization.[1] He wanted Brazil to become a player on the international stage but he was a man of contradictions: he came from Rio Grande do Sol, home of many of Brazil's coffee and sugar plantations, but stood for the industrialists not the landowners. He sided with Germany in the late thirties, even sending Hitler a telegram on his birthday in 1941 with "best wishes for your personal happiness and the prosperity of the German nation," but he hoped to win the economic support of the United States.[2]

Vargas came to power in the wake of the great crash of 1929, which affected Brazil by driving down the demand for coffee. Brazil's fortunes, still dependent primarily on a one-crop economy, followed the coffee market. In response to the Depression, nativism and nationalism developed a strong following in Brazil. And both nativists and nationalists found immigration policy a convenient vehicle for putting their beliefs into practice.

A mere month and a half after Vargas carried out his coup d'état, he introduced measures limiting immigration.[3] Only current residents of Brazil, farmers with special government permission, or agricultural immigrant families brought to the country by an approved organization were to be admitted. The new regulations were not uniformly enforced and could still be circumvented with a little ingenuity or a large bribe to the appropriate official. But in 1934 Vargas introduced a new constitution that made immigration restrictions the law of the land. It sought to guarantee the "ethnic integrity of Brazil" by setting strict annual quotas.

During the years between 1933 and 1937, a small number of German Jews nonetheless found their way to Brazil. For a brief period in the mid-1930s, the high commissioner for refugees from Germany, James McDonald, who had been appointed by the League of Nations, even cherished the hope that Brazil would serve as a home for the Jews of Germany.[4] Vargas responded enthusiastically to the commissioner's proposal that Brazil take in 500 Jews per month, but as was often the case with Vargas, his official pronouncements were intended solely for public relations purposes. Vargas never made good on the promise and most likely never had any intention of doing so. As a result, only 363 of the 37,000 German Jews leaving Germany in 1933 immigrated to Brazil. Discouraged, McDonald resigned his post in 1935. And in 1937, shortly after Günther Garfunkel's arrival in Brazil, the Vargas regime began to crack down further on Jewish immigration.

In 1938 Vargas established the Novo Estado do Brasil, with himself as dictator. One of his first acts after this coup was to prohibit entry into Brazil of anyone of "Semitic" origin. Simultaneously, the minister of justice, founder of one of Brazil's fascist-inspired movements, began laying out a comprehensive anti-Jewish policy. He announced that 90-day temporary visas—the kind Günther had used to enter the country—would not be extended. Moreover, anyone in Brazil with an expired visa would be deported to his country of origin. This was a problem for at least half of the 4,400 Jews who had arrived since 1933. The United States put pressure on Vargas to rescind the decree and, eager to enhance Brazil's standing in the eyes of America, he called off the planned expulsion. Refugees who were in Brazil illegally, such as Günther, were no longer harassed, but the barriers to further immigration mounted.[5] Henceforth, Brazil invoked economic rather than racial grounds for excluding refugees: only scientists or other professionals with needed technical expertise, or those with savings of $29,000, a small fortune, would be admitted. As a result, in 1938 a mere 500 German Jews entered Brazil out of the 40,000 who emigrated from Germany, compared to 1,315 out of 23,000 the year before.[6]

In May 1939 Julius Garfunkel sent a telegram to his Cousin Bessie, acknowledging that the prospects for immigrating to America were fading fast. Perhaps unaware of the comparable situation in Brazil, or perhaps simply wanting to help Günther, he wrote: "Impossible to come to USA. Send desired support to Günther, San Paulo by telegraph. Julius."

Between 1940 and 1942, Brazil issued further decrees effectively limiting Jewish immigration to Brazil to a trickle.[7] Only foreigners who were married to a native-born Brazilian or who had children born in Brazil were allowed in. But Julius still clung to the belief that with sufficient effort, Günther would be able to bring his parents and brother to Sao Paulo. In a postscript to one of the last letters that Hans received from his father, Julius penned the bitter words that would echo in Hans's head for years to come: "We got a letter from Günther. The letter gives the impression that Günther cannot bring you and us over and also does not want to. Only the USA remains. That must be energetically pursued."

~

Within days after Julius sent that letter to Hans at the Château de La Hille in southern France, the Nazis banned all further emigration of German Jews.

German Jews continued to immigrate to Brazil in small numbers until 1941: 2,899 arrived in 1939 (3.7 percent of the 78,000 Jews who left Germany); another 1,033, in 1940 (6.9 percent of the mere 15,000 who got out); and 408 arrived in 1941 (5.1 percent of the 8,000 who escaped from the Third Reich that year).[8] The money spent on Friedel Kitkowski's passage would not have been nearly enough for the elder Garfunkels to qualify. Günther's inability to rescue his parents, which would mar his relationship with his brother, Hans, forever, was not so much a personal failure as a reflection of rapidly dwindling opportunities.

Far more inexplicable than his inability to save his parents is Günther's lack of communication with any family members between October 1941 and the end of the war. Hans repeatedly asked Cousin Bessie, the one relative whose address did not change for the duration of the war, whether she had heard from Günther. He still has no idea why Günther stopped corresponding with his family. Perhaps Julius sent him an accusatory letter in October 1941, at the same time that he wrote those painful lines to Hans, alleging that Günther "cannot bring you and us over and also does not want to." Perhaps he had psychological problems of the kind Hans would develop. But what led him to reestablish contact at the end of the war? Whatever was going on in Günther's mind during the war years, once he was back in touch with his younger brother, he did his best to help him. He provided the necessary affidavit for Hans to obtain a Brazilian visa; he let him live in his small Sao Paulo home; and he found him a job. Hans worked for a company that imported paper goods, owned by a German Jewish refugee. His job, translating correspondence from English into German, was tedious and paid poorly, but it afforded Hans a modicum of independence.

Günther and Friedel socialized mainly with other members of the refugee community, playing the card game Skat with another German Jewish couple. Hans wanted to integrate himself into Brazilian society. The greatest barrier to assimilation was Hans's complete ignorance of the Portuguese language. To overcome this obstacle, he proposed teaching German or English in exchange for Portuguese lessons, advertising in the local newspaper. He soon had a response from a wealthy young Brazilian, Isolde, who proved to be an astonishingly beautiful woman. Distracted by her looks and her outgoing personality, Hans did not accomplish much in the way of teaching or learning a foreign language over the next few months.

The Brazil Hans found in October 1946 was a relatively young nation. The country had become independent in 1822, following more than three hundred years of Portuguese colonial rule that had been interrupted only by a brief period of Spanish rule and a short period of "co-equality" with Portugal (the two kingdoms were supposedly separate but equal under a single ruler). In a strange historical twist, Brazil remained an "empire" after declaring its independence, ruled over by the same Portuguese royal scion who had been regent before independence.[9]

Brazil did not abolish slavery until 1888, and in 1830 it was the largest slave economy in the world, with more slaves than free people. Not until 1889 did Brazil become a republic. Its new constitution guaranteed religious freedom and abandoned Catholicism as the state religion, thus paving the way for the arrival of Jews. The ban on slavery stimulated immigration as a source of labor. First came the Italians, then the Japanese, and then the Jews, primarily eastern European victims of Russian pogroms.

The Jews initially arrived as prospective farmers in an inspired but quirky scheme concocted by the Bavarian-born Jewish philanthropist Baron Maurice de Hirsch. Operating out of his headquarters in Brussels in the first decades of the twentieth century, de Hirsch aimed to find refuge for persecuted European Jews and hit upon the strategy of creating farming colonies in South America. He realized that although Brazil aspired to industrialize, it was still primarily an agricultural economy. Brazil had always relied heavily on a single export—first sugar, using African slaves as laborers; then, until the mines were exhausted, gold and diamonds; for a time rubber, until England and Holland planted rubber trees in the East Indies; and finally coffee. By bringing Jewish families to Brazil as coffee farmers, de Hirsch cleverly undercut the stereotype of Jews as bankers and as city dwellers. His efforts were strongly supported by Britain, Brazil's principal ally and trading partner, in no small measure because the British government was delighted to promote a plan that provided refuge for Russian Jews in a country other than England.[10]

But the largest number of immigrants, Jewish and otherwise, flocked to Brazil after World War I. The United States, Canada, and Argentina all passed restrictive, nativist legislation in the 1920s, leaving Brazil one of the few destinations available for displaced and persecuted eastern Europeans. Brazil had not previously been especially appealing to Europeans, particularly not to Polish Jews who thought of Brazil as "the country of the monkeys."[11] The new head of the Jewish Colonization Association, de Hirsch's organization, vigorously sought to dispel the negative image. His pamphlet praising Brazil, "Brazilye: A Tsukunfland far Idisher Emigratsye" (Brazil: Land of the Future for Jewish Emigration), was widely distributed in Poland. As growing numbers of European Jews arrived—bringing the Jewish population in Brazil to

30,000 in the 1920s—the immigrants built their own communal institutions. Synagogues, old age homes, schools, burial societies, libraries, and newspapers rapidly proliferated. Centered in the major cities of Rio de Janeiro and Sao Paulo, despite the early efforts to turn Jews into farmers, the Jewish community of Brazil was substantial and thriving by the time the Vargas regime took over in 1930.[12]

Brazil under Vargas became increasingly centralized and industrialized. The government fought off challenges from the Communist Party and flirted with fascism. It continued to demonstrate a strong nativist bent, manifesting a hostile attitude toward "nonwhites," the "unassimilables" that included Jews, Japanese, and blacks. But most of the resulting anti-Semitism was theoretical rather than actual, directed against the hordes of foreigners who *might* descend on Brazil rather than those who had already made Brazil their home.[13]

One refugee from Hitler's Third Reich, the eminent writer Stefan Zweig, had nothing but praise to lavish on Brazil. Zweig may have seen only what he wanted to see, or he may have received unusually beneficent treatment as a distinguished author. His first impression on arriving in Brazil from his temporary refuge in England in August 1941 was extraordinary: "One who has just escaped the crazy destructiveness of Europe first greets the total absence of any hatred in public and private life as something unbelievable. . . . As soon as one enters this country, it is one's first pleasant and ever-recurring surprise to find . . . how friendly and peaceful a way people live with each other in this immense space."[14] Based on his own experience, he claimed that "every foreigner is received with the utmost courtesy, and everything possible is done for him." But what impressed Zweig most was the sense that Brazilians were race-blind: "Whether in the army, in business, in the market, shops, or factories, [an] individual never considers separating himself from others on account of colour or background, they all work in peace and friendliness together."[15]

Zweig had great hopes for what Brazil might become, going so far as to predict that Brazil would be the great new civilization of the future. He reassured himself with the thought that if "the Old World should destroy itself in its suicidal struggle," Brazil would surely rise to take its place as the pinnacle of enlightenment.

Unfortunately Zweig was subject to periods of deep depression. His moments of despair increased in frequency and duration until he and his wife took their own lives in Petropolis, Brazil, on February 23, 1942. Even in his suicide note, Zweig was at pains to "give heartfelt thanks to this wonderful land of Brazil which afforded me and my work such kind and hospitable repose."[16] He was an exact contemporary of Hans's father, Julius, who was also born in 1881 and would die less than six weeks after Stefan Zweig, in the Jewish Hospital of Berlin.

~

When Hans lived in Brazil, it was a poor country, ravaged by disease. It offered minimal medical care and few social services to its citizens. Life expectancy was a mere forty-six years.[17] Malaria and tuberculosis were rampant and psychiatric care was virtually nonexistent, which was a major problem for Hans. The panic attacks that had plagued him in Switzerland returned in Brazil. Even a trip to his brother's cottage in the countryside turned into a nightmare as Hans found himself miles from anyone he knew, with no means of communication or transportation. His palpitations were so severe that Hans thought he would die, alone in tropical Brazil. He consulted an internist who was mystified by his symptoms and prescribed sleeping pills.

His social life was almost as problematic as his mental health. At the same time that Hans was fantasizing about carrying on a torrid affair with his lovely language student Isolde, he found himself pursued by not one, but two other women. The wife of his brother's Skat partner, herself the mother of two young children, professed to be hopelessly in love with Hans. And Günther's wife, who had a history of being attracted to younger men, also made advances to the disoriented refugee. A photograph taken in Sao Paulo shows that Hans was handsome but hardly debonair with his wavy dark hair and aristocratic mien. Manifestly bright, serious, and ambitious, perhaps his wartime adventures made him seem exotic to the pedestrian Brazilians.

Less than five months after his arrival in Brazil, Hans began making plans to leave. While still in Switzerland, on receiving his visa for Brazil, he had written to Bessie that "I have made up my mind definitely to join my brother for the present moment. . . . But I always hope that one day I shall come to the United States." In February 1947 he wrote again, strongly suggesting that his psychiatric problems—over and above the lack of economic opportunities and his confusing social situation—fueled his wish to leave Brazil: "I am working at the above mentioned firm, but only for half a day as my health has been growing [worse and worse]. I desperately need some medical help and I cannot get along with it here, specially as the climate is undermining my health too."

He then implored Bessie to help him immigrate to the United States, in a reprise of all those letters he had sent from Europe between 1938 and 1945: "Please, let me know what you can do for me with regard to passage. I really cannot wait any longer and I should like to leave for the States as soon as ever possible."

Hans's wish to leave Brazil may also have been stimulated by the prevailing unrest. The country had just emerged from fifteen years of dictatorial rule by Getulio Vargas. General Enrico Gaspar Dutra, its new president, faced repeated challenges from labor, including a strong Communist movement.[18]

In January 1947, a few short months after his arrival, Hans witnessed his first free elections. The Communist Party had a strong showing, claiming 1 million votes throughout Brazil.[19] Labor unrest was evident in the streets as well as at the ballot box: taking a streetcar to work, Hans experienced frequent delays as student demonstrators burned buses to protest the working conditions. One of the demonstrations was dramatic enough to gain the attention of the foreign press. The *New York Times* reported on August 2, 1947, that the "city looked like a battlefield, with its streets and avenues strewn with the charred skeletons of street cars and buses that were wrecked yesterday by infuriated crowds of men and women refusing to pay the higher fares decreed by the city."[20] The toll was considerable, with 3 deaths, 30 injuries, 45 buses damaged or destroyed, and total losses to the city estimated at $1.5 million.

The economic situation was precarious as well. In April the market price of coffee plummeted in New York, triggering a near crisis situation in Brazil, which was largely dependent on the United States for coffee sales.[21] Reflecting the turmoil evident in the political and economic situations, the intellectual scene was also chaotic. An American visiting lecturer at the University of Brazil observed that life was confusing and disorienting; as a result many intellectuals were attracted to the structure and order of the Communist Party.[22]

~

Hans was painfully aware of the economic instability in Brazil, along with the ominous rumblings on the political scene. He summarized his personal situation and that of the country in a letter to Alex Frank, the former director of the children's home in Seyre: "In the meantime, I am working as an English, French, and German-speaking correspondent for an import firm. We import stationery goods especially from the US, but also from England and Switzerland. At the moment we have a severe economic crisis in Brazil. Even more, everyone is waiting for WW III in a short time (USA vs USSR)."[23]

Working for the import firm gave Hans a new link to the United States. In addition to corresponding with Bessie, whose help he continued to seek, and with Hanni Schild (née Schlimmer), whose husband sent him a shipment of ballpoint pens that he sold in Sao Paulo to help pay his passage to New York, he also wrote to a Philadelphia firm with which his employer did business. He received a prompt reply offering him a job in the company's paper factory upon arrival in the United States.

Job offer in hand, Hans was able in June to renew the visa to the United

States that he had finally received during his final weeks in Switzerland. All that remained was to procure a passport. He was still stateless and had traveled to Brazil on a one-way Nansen passport. In this instance the notorious corruption of Brazilian officialdom served him well. For the tidy sum of 500 cruzeiros (equal to about 27 U.S. dollars in 1947, or 300 of today's dollars), Hans persuaded a Brazilian police captain to issue the necessary document. He sent Ilse a letter announcing his planned departure, a letter she never received. Hans thinks the Brazilian postal carrier stole the stamps.

In September 1947, slightly less than a year after arriving in Brazil, Hans left for the United States. His brother could not bring him to the port city of Santos to say goodbye as he was at the hospital with his wife, who was seriously ill. While Hans was en route, Friedel passed away.

Shortly after reaching New York, Hans wrote to the inimitable Bessie: "I arrived here yesterday by SS *A. Mitchell Palmer* (a cargo boat of the Lampost and Holt Liner Ltd.) The trip took exactly 5 weeks. We stopped at Recife (Pernambuco), Fostaleza (Ceara), Belem (Para), Port of Spain (Trinidad), and Fort de France (Martinique). I think you already know that my sister-in-law died a month ago, on September 13. It has been a terrible shock to my brother—and to me too. Please, let me know kindly by return airmail if you want me to come to Chicago and if you think I will find a job within a very short time."

The ship, carrying twelve passengers, was supposed to have made the journey in four weeks. But the captain and the first mate were so distracted competing for the favors of the wife of one of the passengers that the ship got stuck on a sandbar. The ship remained stranded for several days. During that time Hans traveled with members of the crew to the jungle. It does not sound like the best expedition for someone suffering from claustrophobia and panic attacks, but perhaps the jungle was less confining than the SS *A. Mitchell Palmer*.

Almost nine years after he first appealed to Cousin Bessie for help in reaching the United States, Hans Garfunkel arrived at Pier 5, Staten Island, New York. He would remain in New York City for the next forty years.

12

"Give Me Your Tired, Your Poor"

> The United Nations High Commissioner for Refugees, acting under the authority of the General Assembly, shall assume the function of providing international protection, under the auspices of the United Nations, to refugees who fall under the scope of the present Statute and of seeking permanent solutions for the problems of refugees by assisting governments and, subject to the approval of the government concerned, private organizations, to facilitate the voluntary repatriation of such refugees, or their assimilation within new national communities.
>
> —Statute of the Office of the United Nations High Commissioner for Refugees, 1950

The SS *A. Mitchell Palmer* arrived from Brazil at the pier in Staten Island October 10, 1947, two days before Columbus Day. Waiting for Hans were Hanni Schlimmer (now married and going by the name Hannah Schild) and Herbert Strauss. Hans had known Hanni in Berlin, where they had both attended the Luise Schickels Höhere Privatschule, the Jewish private school that had been a haven for the two of them. Hanni had also been in the group in Seyre, in Southern France, where she had transformed a life of poverty and misery into a time of romance for sixteen-year-old Hans. When he saw the familiar face on that glorious day in New York City, memories almost overwhelmed him. He remembered being stranded outside the dilapidated barn that was their home, having gotten back from a berry-picking expedition after curfew. But it hadn't been so bad having to spend the night outdoors: he snuggled up to Hanni and they read books together in English until it was too dark to read.

Herbert Strauss had also lived in Berlin, but Hans had not known him then. He was a few years older and had graduated from high school in his native Wurzburg, a small Bavarian city, moving to Berlin to attend divinity school. The Hochschule für die Wissenschaft des Judentums was virtually the only institution of higher education still open to Jews after the November pogrom. Remarkably, Herbert had been able to continue his education, which included a strong classical curriculum as well as Jewish studies, until the Gestapo finally closed the school in 1942. Herbert remained in Berlin another year; then he and his future wife, Lotte, escaped across the Swiss border. He enrolled in a doctoral program in history at the University of Bern, where he met and befriended Hans in 1945.[1]

Hans had been in touch with Hanni since she left with her parents for the United States in the spring of 1942. His letters to Cousin Bessie often included a letter for Hanni, which he asked his cousin to forward. They had been adolescents when they had last seen each other; five years later, they had matured and grown apart. Hanni had evolved a new identity as a married American woman. She would soon move with her husband to San Francisco and become only a small, remote part of Hans's life.

After a celebratory cup of coffee together, Herbert took Hans to his apartment in northern Manhattan where he lived with his wife and infant daughter. The baby took up what seemed like an inordinate amount of space in the one-bedroom apartment, but Hans was grateful to have a couch to sleep on and a friend to guide him.

Hans's plan had been to get a job in Philadelphia, as promised by the firm with whom he had corresponded in Brazil. He took a train to Philadelphia—courtesy of the firm—and was met by the two owners at Thirtieth Street station. They took him out to Longchamps Restaurant for lunch, impressing Hans greatly. But then they told him that they had had to lay off workers in their paper factory and were not hiring any new employees. Apart from the lunch, the trip to Philadelphia had been a waste of time. Hans returned to New York and asked Herbert Strauss for advice.

Herbert, whose academic specialty was German Jewish emigration, was an instructor in history at City College. He had contacts with refugee organizations and was able to help Hans find a job with a firm that had a government contract as part of what would become the Marshall Plan. President Truman would not sign the European Recovery Act until April 1948. But as early as June 1947, Secretary of State George Marshall had given a speech at Harvard University outlining the plans for a European recovery program.[2] A month later, the Marshall Plan, which would authorize the United States to spend $17 billion on economic development over four years, was unveiled at the Paris Economic Conference. In the meantime, Germany was receiving generous U.S. grants for rehabilitation through the Government and Relief in Occupied Areas program. The billions of dollars that flowed from the United States to the European nations devastated by six years of war and destruction not only helped revive Europe's economy but also stimulated U.S. economic growth. The infusion of capital created jobs, and one of those jobs went to an energetic and capable refugee named Hans Garfunkel.

The job at Ernst Seidelman and Company was neither interesting nor challenging, but it was a job. Hans was in charge of processing requisitions for basic supplies for the U.S. troops stationed in Germany. The job allowed him to improve his vocabulary as well as giving him experience in the world of business: he recalls learning the word "condom" because it was one of the supplies he ordered for the troops. His office was in the Woolworth Building, a magnificent tower modeled on the Gothic buildings of Europe. Known as the Cathedral of Commerce, it had been the world's tallest building when first erected in 1913. With its marble-floored lobby and dramatic spire rising above its fifty-eight stories, it had lost none of its grandeur. The job gave Hans a measure of independence: as soon has he got his first check, he moved out of the cramped quarters on Manhattan Avenue and rented a room in an apartment in Washington Heights.

The area of Manhattan north of 135th street known as Washington Heights was a hilly community, boarded on three sides by rivers. It included Fort Tryon Park, the home of the Cloisters, a medieval art museum housed in a castlelike edifice. Nestled inside Washington Heights, along with Yeshiva University and Columbia-Presbyterian Hospital, was a robust German Jewish community.[3] Most of the German Jews who lived there, making up about 10 percent of the population of Washington Heights, had come to the United States in the 1930s. They had arrived as refugees before the war broke out. Many had come before Kristallnacht. Most had experienced the loss of civil rights and economic opportunity but not the physical and emotional torments that their compatriots would later suffer. They had lived in safety in New York while Hans and Ilse moved from Belgium to France and then to Switzerland, unwanted refugees.

The German Jewish émigrés who resided in Washington Heights tended to come from small towns in southern Germany, rather than from large northern cities such as Berlin and Stettin, where Hans and Ilse grew up. They were, on average, more traditional, more observant, and somewhat less well-educated than German Jewish refugees in other parts of the country, including the Upper West Side of Manhattan.[4]

Max Frankel, who would become editorial page editor and then executive editor of the *New York Times,* had arrived with his mother from a small town near Leipzig in 1940, when he was ten. They moved to Washington Heights after a brief stay in Brooklyn. Frankel described Washington Heights as "a marvelous neighborhood." He remembered feeling very comfortable as long as he stayed away from the gangs in the Irish neighborhoods, but he had had no desire to remain in the area. Like most of his contemporaries, he sought to escape from its intensely German environment, seeing himself as an American and a citizen of the world. The German Jews in Washington Heights, by contrast, "were very German. I think many of them would have been loyal German citizens if they had been allowed to be. I think I would have been. . . . I felt greatly deprived when I couldn't march in the Hitler Youth parades at age six."[5] Henry Kissinger, another German Jewish refugee who grew up in Washington Heights, would put both his German and Jewish past behind him.

Rents were lower in Washington Heights than in much of the rest of Manhattan, and many of the apartments had five or six rooms, generous by New York standards. They could accommodate entire extended families and often allowed a struggling household to rent out a room to newcomers like Hans. A single subway ride from downtown Manhattan, Frankfurt on the Hudson, as it was sometimes called, or the Fourth Reich, as Hans and Ilse referred to the neighborhood, was a practical location for a poor refugee. It was a place where middle-aged couples took strolls along the river on weekends and lingered over a cup of coffee at a café—much as they had in small towns in Germany before 1933. Social life revolved around visiting friends for the inevitable *Kaffee und Kuchen* and around the synagogues, which flourished in the late 1940s. Hans Garfunkel was not interested in any of these pastimes. He was not nostalgic for life in Osterode, the town in East Prussia that he associated with provincialism and hooliganism. He was interested in becoming an American. He was also a political junkie. As soon as he started receiving a paycheck, even the meager thirty-five dollars per week that was his starting salary, he began forking out three cents a day for the *New York Times.*

Hans read the paper, he went to work, and he felt secure, but he was lonely. When he learned from a mutual friend in Switzerland that Ilse Wulff was living in New York City, it was natural for him to seek her out. She was working as a live-in nurse on the Upper West Side and had been in the United States for only a couple of months. She had barely made it to America at all.

~

Ilse did not want to leave Switzerland in 1947 any more than she had wanted to leave Germany in 1939. As on that earlier journey, she was accompanied to her departure point by someone very dear to her. Charles Brütsch, by now a surrogate parent and the person she trusted most in the world, went with Ilse by train from Geneva to Paris in December 1947. For two days, he showed her around Paris, a delightful adventure marred only by the uncertainty about when she would see the Brütsch family again.

Mr. Brütsch brought Ilse to the train station in Paris, much as her parents had brought her to the railroad station in Berlin nearly nine years earlier. She traveled the last leg of the European trip to Le Havre alone and then took the boat train to the ship itself, a good-size passenger liner, the SS *De Grasse.* Apprehensive but excited, Ilse settled into her cabin, all her possessions packed in one modest suitcase, and waited for the ship to leave.

Her departure was delayed, and then delayed further. Something was terribly wrong. Ilse was unaware that France was in a state of upheaval. Spurred on by the French Communist Party, increasing numbers of workers had gone on strike to demand higher wages. The disruption had begun in Marseilles on November 20 and by the time the *De Grasse* was scheduled to sail, 10 percent of the country's workforce, or 2 million people, had walked off their jobs. In parts of France, the conflict had turned violent, with the newspapers reporting that "mobs seized public buildings and fought the police and troops." Sabotage of trains was widespread; twenty people were killed and another forty injured in one incident alone.[6]

For five days the *De Grasse* sat in the harbor with all its passengers, waiting for word that the strike had been settled. The passengers ate in the ship's dining room where Ilse was actually able to enjoy the food: since the ship was docked, she was not seasick. On the fifth day, the public address system summoned everyone to a large common area. It looked as though the strike was not going to be settled any time soon. Everyone had to disembark. A French official came on board to extend transit visas, granting permission for Ilse and the other passengers to stay longer in France than they had anticipated. The cancellation of the voyage was sufficiently newsworthy to be reported by the *New York Times*.[7]

Ilse was caught in the crossfire of a major conflict, a situation far more momentous than a run of the mill labor-management dispute. The *Times* had editorialized while Ilse was innocently seeing the sights in Paris with Charles Brütsch:

> The struggle between the French Government and the French sector of the Communist International has assumed proportions which make France the first real battlefield in the "cold war" between Russia and the West. The outcome of this struggle will go far in determining the future course of events both at the London peace conference and in Europe. For, as our London dispatches reveal, the success of the Communist leaders in paralyzing France's economic life has been such as to raise Moscow's hope for detaching France from the West and making her another puppet.[8]

The survival of France as a free and democratic nation may have been at stake; for Ilse, so too were her prospects for immigrating to the United States. The Swiss had issued her a one-way passport that did not allow her to reenter the country. She knew nobody in France and she had hardly any money. Not knowing what else to do, Ilse tearfully told the official her plight. He listened sympathetically but said he could not help.

From behind Ilse in the line, a young woman suddenly stepped forward.

She couldn't help overhearing Ilse's story, she said. She had been in France visiting her parents, who lived in Paris, and was on her way to Chicago to rejoin her husband, an ex-GI. Would Ilse like to stay with her at her parents' apartment until they could make alternative travel arrangements?

Ilse was incredulous. She waited nervously while the woman—she introduced herself as Gaby Neely, a few years younger than Ilse—telephoned her parents to tell them she was stranded in France and to ask whether she could bring along a guest. Her parents, themselves Romanian Jews who had immigrated to France before the war and had escaped the roundups that sent most foreign-born Jews living in Nazi-controlled France to their deaths, readily agreed.

The war had been over in Europe for more than two and a half years, but France was still struggling economically. Food continued to be rationed, and Ilse, as a foreigner, had no food coupons. Staying with Gaby's parents was a considerable imposition on them. Finally, on the night of December 9, the Communist leaders within the Labor Confederation accepted the government's ultimatum, and the workers of France reported back to work.

Ilse's difficulties were not over. Thousands of stranded travelers needed to rebook their passage. Each morning, Ilse made the rounds of steamship lines and airlines, trying to find a seat. She sent a telegram to Charles Brütsch asking for money, which he wired her, so she could partially compensate her hosts for their trouble. She went to the Swiss consulate to ask to return to Switzerland, but permission was denied.

As Ilse remembers the story, it was Gaby's mother who found a solution. She bribed a steamship employee with two pounds of sugar and suddenly he found a ticket for Ilse on the SS *America*. The ship sailed on December 15, the same day her transit visa was due to expire.

As soon as the captain turned on the engines and the ship began to rumble and sway, Ilse was sick to her stomach. She had been prone to motion sickness ever since the train ride from Cologne to Brussels. She had been violently ill on the cattle car from Brussels to France, and she was sick again during the entire seven days of the ocean voyage to New York.

Ilse shared an inside cabin with two older women. Desperate for air, she turned on the fan in the cabin. The others protested that it was too cold and turned it off. Ilse threw up and had to call the ship's steward to clean up after her. She was embarrassed that she did not have any change with which to tip him.

Most of the trip Ilse spent on deck. To her surprise, she encountered a young woman who had been with her in the children's home in Brussels. Ursula, who was a few years younger than Ilse, had been reunited with her family, had spent the war years in Belgium, and was now immigrating to the United States. Ilse befriended another passenger who also spent most of the voyage on deck, a Vietnamese doctor on his way home to Saigon after attending a medical conference in Paris. The two walked the decks together, talking about their hopes and their worries while they marveled at the flying fish sailing through the air. On the last day of the voyage, Ilse's motion sickness was gone and they played ping-pong together. As they approached New York, the Statue of Liberty came into view. The passengers, most of whom were refugees from Europe, wept and sang.

While the SS *America* was steaming to the United States with a full complement of refugees, thousands of miles away, in the Mediterranean, a decrepit former fishing vessel called *Lo Tafhidunu* (You Shall Not Frighten Us) was carrying 800 Jews toward Palestine. The same day that Ilse's ship docked uneventfully in New York harbor, the British navy intercepted the small schooner, turning its passengers away from the Holy Land.[9]

The vessel was not the first that the British had prevented from reaching its destination, nor would it be the last. Since intercepting the *Exodus* in July 1947 and sending her 4,500 passengers to a displaced persons camp in Hamburg, the British had bowed to international pressure—interning the Jews trying to reach Palestine without a permit in Cyprus rather than in Europe. A total of 50,000 Jews were kept behind barbed wires in Cyprus until finally, after the establishment of the State of Israel, they were welcomed as new citizens rather than as criminals.[10]

Occasionally, a boat would get past the British. On November 17, 1947, for the first time since March, approximately 200 illegal Jewish immigrants managed to land in Palestine before dawn after eluding English naval patrols. Perhaps the British were too busy intercepting a second ship, the 250-ton *Kadimah* (Forward) carrying 714 refugees, to notice the smaller craft.[11]

~

Across the Atlantic, the SS *America* landed legally in New York. Ilse worried that she would not recognize Tante Friedel—she had not seen her since the Germans invaded Belgium in the spring of 1940. But while Ilse had grown up during those seven formative years, Friedel looked much the same and Ilse, with her formidable visual memory, recognized her immediately. Friedel brought her to stay at her daughter's Upper West Side apartment where she lived with her husband, Henry Teterka, a radiologist, and their little boy.

Ilse did not stay long with the Teterka family. She wanted to be independent and her course in nursing in Switzerland gave her the credentials to seek a position in New York. She found a job as a live-in nanny for a wealthy Belgian woman who was as arrogant as she was beautiful. But at least she spoke

French, so Ilse could communicate with her. Ilse also reconnected with an old acquaintance from La Hille and Switzerland, Hans Garfunkel.

Their first attempt to rendezvous was not auspicious. They planned to meet at 79th Street and Broadway, but there was a misunderstanding and they did not find each other. Hans was persistent, as he had demonstrated with his endless correspondence with Bessie Silverman. They rescheduled their meeting for 86th Street, near the Tip Top Inn. Hans arrived looking very distinguished in a salt and pepper suit and a raincoat. Ilse had considered him a snob in France; she decided he was not nearly as arrogant as she remembered him. At La Hille, the other children had looked up to him for what they viewed as his superior knowledge and intelligence, and he had not attempted to disabuse them of their beliefs. But when Ilse met Hans in New York, she discovered a soul mate, someone with whom she felt comfortable, someone she felt understood her.

They were so comfortable together that Hans periodically visited her at the apartment where she worked. On one occasion, the baby's grandparents stopped by for a surprise visit and were appalled to discover that Ilse had a gentleman caller. The indignant grandparents patronizingly cautioned Ilse against picking up strange men in the street. She assured them that she was not a call girl and that the dapper young man seated primly on the living room sofa was not a client. Determined to have visitors if she wished—the apartment was her home as well as her place of employment—and convinced that her employers would prohibit any socializing, Ilse submitted her resignation.

She needed a new job, which was not so easy to find for an immigrant with minimal English language skills. Ilse took English classes at a local high school but felt the pace was far too slow. She answered an advertisement for a nanny in the newspaper, which proved a near disaster. She was almost in tears by the time she reached her destination in Brooklyn: she found the subway system hopelessly confusing; she did not understand the directions she had been given; and when she finally arrived, she could not communicate with her prospective employer.

Fiercely independent, Ilse did not seek assistance from the relief organizations set up to help the 2,000 refugees arriving every month integrate into U.S. society. Most of the money raised by the National Council of Jewish Federations and Welfare Funds was earmarked to help the Jews who remained in displaced person camps in Europe and to support settlement in Palestine. But $13,664,000, or a little more than 5 percent of the total, went toward helping new arrivals in the United States.[12] Ilse was too proud to ask for assistance.

Most of the aid was devoted to those new arrivals who had no friends or family in the United States, youngsters like the 86 "children without a childhood" who were brought over from a displaced persons camp in Germany. On reaching New York, the children were taken by chartered buses to a reception center in the Bronx. From there, they were sent to foster homes and children's homes throughout the country. A year later, one of the teenagers in the group said of her new life in America: "For the first time we have become alive."[13] Contrary to the rosy picture presented by most journalists, many immigrants experienced enormous difficulty integrating into U.S. society, especially refugees from eastern Europe who had spent years in concentration camps. The reality was often concealed from public view by social workers and bureaucrats who were either naive or willfully blind to the situation.[14]

Ilse and Hans, too, felt very much alive. It was spring, they were young, and they were discovering each other. They probably did not notice an article buried on page 7 in the *New York Times* on April 9, 1948, with the headline "Conviction Due on SS Men Today." The subtitle elaborated: "U.S. Military Tribunal Starts Reading Judgment in Killing of 2,000,000 by Germans." Only 389 words long, the report acknowledged that the trial—the ninth of the eleven "subsequent trials" conducted by the United States after completion of the first and best-known Nuremberg tribunal, the "trial of the 39 major war criminals" in October 1946—was the biggest murder trial in history.[15]

The murders addressed by the trial had been carried out by the *Einsatzgruppen,* or mobile killing units. Their preferred mode of execution was by shooting, typically after herding their victims to mass graves, using whips to ensure cooperation. But the *Einsatzgruppen* had operated in eastern Europe, which must have seemed terribly far away. What Hans did not know at the time was that the SS officers on trial were responsible for the murder of both his mother outside Riga and his Uncle Siegfried in Kovno.

The verdict was announced the following day: fourteen of the SS officers were sentenced to die by hanging; two received life terms; three were given twenty years; and two received ten-year terms. The *Times* devoted a few paragraphs on page 9 to the judgment.[16] It did not report the comments of the presiding judge, Michael Musmanno of Pittsburgh, in the indictment: "The charge of purposeful homicide in this case reaches such fantastic proportions and surpasses such credible limits that believability must be bolstered with assurance a hundred times repeated." Relying on documentation by the defendants of their own crimes, including internal memoranda and reports to headquarters in Berlin, Musmanno and the other two judges were forced to conclude that "we have here participation in a crime of such unprecedented brutality and of such inconceivable savagery that the mind rebels . . . and the imagination staggers in the contemplation of a human degradation beyond the power of language to adequately portray."[17]

Only four of those convicted were actually hanged; the rest had their sentences commuted, were released, or died in other circumstances. Hans and Ilse were three thousand miles from the Palace of Justice in Nuremberg and had more mundane matters to deal with.

Ilse found a new job as a live-in nanny, but this job, too, turned sour. Ilse was fond of the baby in her care and she liked his mother, but the father was a different story. He came home drunk one evening while his wife and baby were staying at the couple's Connecticut summer home and Ilse was attending to a few chores in the city apartment. Disgusted, Ilse told him he needed to go to bed and sleep off his intoxication, which he took as an invitation to try to get her into bed with him. Ilse gave him a swift kick and retreated to her own room, locking the door.

The next day she reported the episode to Hans. He paced back and forth like a caged lion. He wanted her to tell the man's wife about his behavior and then quit, but if she resigned her position immediately, she would have no place to live. Hans suggested they move in to a hotel room together and, acknowledging that she could not remain with her current employer, Ilse agreed. For the next few months, they shared a room at the Hotel Harmony on the upper West Side. With no kitchen and just a small hot plate, they subsisted on little more than chocolate milk and fruit. Ilse found another job as a nanny—this time not as a live-in. She also found out about Hans's psychiatric problems.

Hans in the interim had also lost his job. He had been laid off when the company he worked for failed to renew its lucrative government contracts. He quickly found a new position, also in the import-export business. Just as he was getting used to his new job, the owner committed suicide. Distraught, Hans's own precariously balanced psyche became unhinged. After a period of relative emotional stability, he had a panic attack while walking downtown in the vicinity of city hall. With remarkable presence of mind, Hans found a policeman and told him he was having heart palpitations. Alarmed, the policeman offered to call an ambulance. Hans assured him he did not need to go to a hospital, but rather wanted to meet with the social worker who had been assigned to him some months earlier. What he really needed, Hans indicated, was someone to *take* him to the social worker's office. Would the policeman be willing to escort the young refugee to her office?

Remarkably, the policeman agreed. One of New York's finest saw fit to help a troubled young immigrant with emotional problems. Equally astonishing, in the midst of a panic attack, Hans was able to figure out what he needed. Despite his many negative experiences with the police in other countries, he implicitly trusted a New York City police officer. New York was not Bern or Berlin or Paris.

By the time Hans reached the social worker's office, his panic attack had abated. He explained his history, describing the psychiatrists he had seen in Switzerland, his time in the clinic, the shock treatments. Within an hour the social worker had set up an appointment for him to meet Rose Spiegel. She agreed to treat Hans for a nominal fee. A traditional Freudian psychoanalyst, Dr. Spiegel would remain his therapist for the next several years.

Ilse had never heard of panic attacks and she knew nothing of Freudian psychoanalysis. Her course in pediatric nursing had not prepared her for the screams that awakened her at night when Hans had nightmares. She was so wrapped up in her life and his that she scarcely noticed the momentous event that took place on May 14, 1948.

Hans and Ilse know where they were when John F. Kennedy was assassinated and they remember the devastation after Kristallnacht, but they have no specific recollection of the creation of the State of Israel. The *New York Times* reported the event in terse but dramatic prose:

> *In Tel Aviv* at 4:06 last Friday afternoon (Palestine time), in the Museum of Art on Rothschild Boulevard, the Jewish Provisional Government proclaimed the sovereign State of Israel.
>
> From the *Port of Haifa,* at the stroke of midnight, the British cruiser *Euryalus,* with High Commissioner Sir Alan Gordon Cunningham aboard, steamed out to sea. Great Britain's rule in Palestine had ceased to exist.
>
> *In Washington,* twenty-one minutes later (6:21 EDT), President Harry Truman announced that "the United States recognizes" the new State of Israel in Palestine.
>
> Over *Tel Aviv* at dawn yesterday Egyptian planes appeared: they dropped bombs on the heart of the Jewish state. Zero hour for the much-publicized Arab invasion of Palestine was at hand.

The actual declaration of independence was made in an art gallery in Tel Aviv, where more than a hundred Jewish officials gathered, some bearing tattoos from the concentration camps. Surrounded by pictures of Jewish life outside Palestine, the attendees listened to David Ben Gurion, Israel's new premier, read the proclamation of independence. They stood up and sang "Hatikvah," the national anthem, and the new state was born. Ben Gurion explained to the world that it was the Holocaust, which had "engulfed millions of Jews in Europe," that necessitated the reestablishment of a Jewish state, "which would solve the problem of Jewish homelessness by opening the gates to all Jews and lifting the Jewish people to equality in the family of nations."[18]

Skeptics questioned the viability of the plan to create two independent states joined in an economic union, a Jewish state and an Arab state. As the *New York Times* had editorialized after the UN General Assembly approved partition the previous fall, many political observers had doubts "concerning the wisdom of erecting a political state on a basis of religious faith."[19] The legitimacy of the Jewish state depended on viewing the Jews as a people, a perspective that to Hans smacked suspiciously of Nazi racial ideology. To him, America, not Palestine, was the promised land.

When Ilse and Hans thought about the nascent Israeli state, they were afraid the killing was going to start all over again. With the Arab armies of the surrounding states of Egypt, Syria, Iraq, Lebanon, and Transjordan preparing for war, aided by volunteers from Saudi Arabia and Libya, they worried about their friends who had immigrated to Palestine.

Ruth Klonover, who had escaped over the border from France to Switzerland with Ilse on New Year's Eve 1942, was aboard a ship to Palestine when Ben Gurion announced the birth of the State of Israel. Peter Salz, Hans's closest surviving friend from La Hille, was already in Palestine, living on a kibbutz. He, like Hans, had gone to the Juventus High School in Zurich, and then had matriculated at the University of Geneva. In 1947 he, like Hans, was forced to leave the country. With no surviving relatives anywhere in the world, he left for the one country that truly wanted him. All Hans could think of was that, despite having survived the war, Peter might meet his death as an Israeli soldier.

To Hans and Ilse, the precarious position of the State of Israel demonstrated once again, as though further proof were necessary, the dangers of being identified as Jewish. They had no interest in Judaism as a religion and little knowledge of Judaism as a civilization. They wanted simply to be treated as members of the human community, regardless of color or creed or national origin.

~

Ilse and Hans continued to live in the Hotel Harmony until one hot summer day, while riding the subway and clutching a pole for support, Hans suggested they get married. Ilse did not give him an answer on the subway. She thought about her own parents' unhappy marriage. She knew Hans was troubled and that he had been deeply scarred by his experiences in a way that she had not. She had no rescue fantasies. But she thought they made a good couple. She had also realized, after spending so much time taking care of other people's children, that she wanted a child of her own.

On a glorious fall day in 1948, Ilse Wulff and Hans Garfunkel were married. The ceremony was performed by a Protestant minister, an acquaintance of Pastor Charles Brütsch. It never occurred to them to be married by a rabbi. Herbert Strauss was in attendance, as was a girl Ilse had befriended in New York. They did not need a church or a synagogue or a hotel room to host the event: the city of New York provided the venue. They got married under the blue skies of America, against a backdrop of trees in Central Park.

Epilogue

> The Charter of the United Nations and the Universal Declaration of Human Rights . . . have affirmed the principle that human beings shall enjoy fundamental rights and freedoms without discrimination.
>
> The United Nations has . . . manifested its profound concern for refugees and endeavoured to assure refugees the widest possible exercise of these fundamental rights and freedoms.
>
> —Convention Relating to the Status of Refugees, Preamble, 1951

It has been over sixty years since my parents arrived in the United States to start new lives: sixty years since Ilse stood on the deck of the SS *America* while her fellow refugees sang and cried as they passed the Statute of Liberty steadfastly holding the torch of freedom high above her head; sixty years since Hans finally realized the goal first articulated in his schoolboy letter to Cousin Bessie when he naively—and prematurely—wrote from Berlin, shortly after the November pogrom, "You have no idea how grateful I am that you have made possible my emigration to America." By any objective measure, their lives over those six decades have been remarkably successful. They are the first to acknowledge that after nearly nine years as refugees, they finally arrived in the promised land.

The first years were not easy. My mother wanted desperately to fit in to American society, to feel that she belonged, but with her foreign accent and European manners, she was conspicuously different from native-born Americans. Nothing was more shocking and disturbing than to be taken for a German—the vanquished enemy. My father wanted to make something of himself and was tremendously disappointed when the job he had been promised in Philadelphia fell through. He was frustrated when his social worker arranged for him to take an aptitude test, concluded that he was college material, and then announced that the refugee relief organization for which she worked had no funds with which to help him attend school. For years he was exploited by greedy employers who paid him as little as they could get away with, knowing he was grateful to have a job of any kind. And his demons—the nightmares, the panic attacks, the hypervigilance, all hallmarks of post-traumatic stress disorder—never left him. His psychiatrist, like most of her profession who cared for survivors of the war in Europe, attributed his problems to developmental problems, not to his wartime experiences.[1] But despite the difficulties and the disappointments, my parents made it in America: they lived the American dream.

My father began as a clerk, earning scarcely more than minimum wage. But he had a knack for numbers; he had strong managerial and analytic skills; and he gradually taught himself the equivalent of a comprehensive business school course. He was promoted several times, and after ten years, he was hired by a British steel firm as a manager. He spent the rest of his career with that firm, rising in the ranks to become vice president and ultimately president of the corporation. He was well respected in the steel business, frequently traveling to headquarters in Britain as well as to meetings with important customers and associates across the United States.

My mother began as a nanny and then advanced to the marginally better respected position of nursery school teacher. She read constantly—chiefly novels in English, French, and German—but felt vastly inferior to college-educated Americans even though she was often more knowledgeable than they were about history and literature. After I graduated from college, I cajoled her, with considerable difficulty, into quitting her job as a nursery school teacher and pursuing her own higher education. Apart from the nine-month practical nursing course in Switzerland, her last formal schooling had been in Stettin when she was twelve. She was intimidated by the very idea of seeking a high school equivalency diploma, which typically entailed taking tests in multiple subjects, including math and science. But I found a program at New York University called "University without Walls" that allowed students to enroll in college classes and be retroactively awarded a general education diploma if they passed their college-level courses. Moreover, the program offered credit for "life experiences" that corresponded in content to courses in the NYU catalog. My mother and I pored over the course list and I helped her make the case that twenty years of teaching nursery school presupposed mastery of the contents of assorted courses in early childhood development. Gaining credits for mastery of French and German was a no-brainer. In the end, NYU awarded my mother nearly two years' worth of college credit based on her life experiences. She matriculated in 1973 and, three years later, graduated from college.

Once she started going to school, she did not want to stop. She decided to pursue a master's degree in social work and got her degree when she was fifty-three years old. One of her field placements when she was a student was at SelfHelp, the same organization that had provided assistance to German Jewish refugees in the Washington Heights area during the postwar period.

While in school, my mother switched her specialty from small children to older adults, specializing in geriatric psychiatric social work. She was a star: nursing home patients whose psychiatrists had given up on them would speak to her and no one else. The director of the Greenwich Village psychiatric clinic where she found her first job came to her for advice. She never stopped working in her chosen field, although most of her work today is as a volunteer therapist in a local nursing home. She also serves as an English language tutor for recent immigrants.

~

My father did not meet the venerable Cousin Bessie until after I was born, when she traveled to New York City to visit her son. Outgoing and generous, she gave me a gauze party dress lined with crinoline, so stiff that my mother says she could stand the dress up on the floor. Bessie was well intentioned, if a bit overbearing. Thanks to her, I later discovered that I had cousins close to my own age.

Bessie had two children. One of them, Leslie, had previously lived in New York and in fact had socialized with my parents before I was born. After he and his wife moved to the Washington, D.C., area, the couples lost track of each other. But after a long period of silence and the birth of his three children, Leslie got back in touch.

We traveled to Arlington, Virginia, in the early 1960s and I met my third cousins: Beth, a vivacious eight-year-old; Amy, at six, already showing signs of an imaginative and penetrating intellect; and Sara, a devilishly mischievous four-year-old. Knowing that I was connected to these three was tremendously important to me, even though what we had in common was principally a shared set of great-great-grandparents. I suddenly understood why it had mattered so much to my father, after being uprooted from all that was familiar and after losing so much, to travel across the Atlantic Ocean to be with his brother in Brazil.

My father was also in touch with his Tante Änne. She had been in communication with her sister Friedel, who had moved to Brazil to marry Günther Garfunkel. When my father showed up in Sao Paulo, Änne reestablished contact with him, too, and when he immigrated to the United States, she continued to write to him. I met Tante Änne when I was nine and traveled with my parents to Germany, and then again when I was a college student spending a semester studying in Germany. She was an elegant lady with snow-white hair and a smooth, wrinkle-free face. She complained of loneliness, of poverty, and of suffering. Since she was the only member of my father's family aside from Hans and his brother to survive the war and since both her husbands died before the war began, leaving her an untarnished "Aryan" and therefore not subject to persecution, I'm afraid I was not terribly sympathetic.

In one of her letters, Tante Änne casually revealed a well-kept family secret: Hans had a half brother, also named Hans. My grandfather Julius had had an illegitimate son, born to a Christian woman before he met his future wife, Paula. Julius provided support for his erstwhile girlfriend and her son as long as he was able to, keeping the boy's paternity a secret. The secret was guarded extraordinarily well and Hans Wagner grew up without the Nazis ever suspecting that, according to their definition, he was a *Mischling* of the first degree, a half Jew. After the war Tante Änne, who knew both the true identity and the whereabouts of the older Hans, told my father that he had a brother in Germany. Hans Garfunkel wrote to Hans Wagner and received a letter from him in June 1953:

> Dear Brother Hans, dear Sister-in-Law, dear Muriel,
>
> I was deeply moved by the warmth and cordiality of your lines. . . . That our father died April 1, 1942, I learned first from you. . . .
>
> Now I want to tell you about my life: in 1911, our father lived in the town of Eisleben with my grandparents and worked as a manager for the Goldstein company. Then he met my mother and a year later I was born. It is the song of love, right? According to my relatives, Julius would have been welcome to marry my mother. I don't know why it didn't happen.

He may have owed his life to Julius Garfunkel's decision not to marry his mother.

When my parents decided in 1961 to travel to Germany for the first time since they left as refugees in 1939, we visited the Wagner family. It was a cordial but not very successful visit. Hans Wagner was short with dark wavy hair, like my father. There the resemblance ended. Hans W., who was twelve years older than his newfound half brother, owned and operated a grocery store with his wife. Like many of his contemporaries, he had continued in school only until age fourteen, when he was apprenticed to a blacksmith. He had worked for a number of years in business, and then joined the army. He was a hard-working man, thoroughly Christian and entirely German. His father's greatest gift to him had been to stay hidden from view, allowing him to successfully conceal his Jewish parentage—surely an unsettling realization for Hans Wagner. Meeting his half brother, who lived in the United States and had spent the war years as a refugee, must have been equally unnerving. After a polite exchange of thank-yous, there was little further contact between Hans Garfunkel and Hans Wagner.

The only survivor on my mother's side of the family was her Onkel Erich. Onkel Erich survived Theresientstadt, the concentration camp to which he had been sent in February 1945, and at the end of the war he moved back to Hohenstein-Ernstthal, which became part of East Germany. In August 1960 I traveled with my parents to West Berlin, where we were joined by Erich and Trude. The rendezvous nearly didn't take place as the train was delayed by a lengthy police inspection of the passengers' papers. Evidently whoever the police were looking for, it wasn't an elderly couple—the Berndts were in their seventies—so they were left alone. A week later, the wall went up separating East and West Berlin.

During that visit, I remember walking in the *Tiergarten,* Berlin's zoo, content to watch the animals in their cages rather than my great-uncle. My German was limited and his English was nonexistent, which put a crimp in direct communication. He was portly and unsmiling; his wife was stocky, dressed in a white blouse, shapeless tweed skirt, and black "old lady" shoes. I was nine, the same age my mother had been when she visited Onkel Erich in his home, and even with the language barrier I could sense he was intimidating. I was glad I had my own parents to shield me from this gruff, no-nonsense man.

Starting with nothing, my parents became solidly upper middle class. They moved to the Boston area after my third child was born in 1987, trading their modest Upper East Side Manhattan cooperative apartment for a condominium in the Boston suburbs. They bought their first car that same year—my mother had learned to drive when she was forty, but they had never felt the need for a car in New York City.

My parents' quick adaptation to American life mirrored the experience of other refugees from Hitler's Europe. A reporter writing a story in 1948 about children who arrived in America from displaced person camps marveled, "I had expected some assimilation. What I had not guessed was the extent to which this could be accomplished in a few brief months." She attributed the successful integration, in part, to host receptivity, commenting on "the natural ease and simple friendliness with which Americans have warmed to the former DPs."[2]

The DPs who arrived as children or young adults, like my parents, were ambitious and hardworking and they were in a hurry to make up for lost time. Just as my father completed high school in Zurich in two years, a number of the DP teenagers raced through school, sometimes squeezing as much as two and a half years of classes into one year.

While many of the refugees forged a successful new life for themselves, the experience of the group as a whole was mixed. One contemporaneous report commented, "What tended to make for difficulties in adjustment was, first of all, the fact that many of the refugees had undergone indescribably horrible experiences, and hence arrived here filled with anxieties and fears."[3] But they were young and hopeful—the very young and the very old seldom survived the war—and were able to find jobs in America's booming postwar economy.

As a physician steeped in evidence-based medicine, taught to look for data rather than anecdotes to support practice, I was curious whether the observations made in the 1940s would hold up and whether my parents' experiences were typical. Were there any statistics describing the cohort who arrived in the United States as children or young adults, refugees from Hitler? When I searched for answers to these questions, I found numerous articles and books about the professors and scientists, writers and artists, who immigrated in the 1930s. But they already had established reputations; it was no surprise that these German and Austrian intellectuals including Hannah Arendt, Albert Einstein, and Enrico Fermi—predominantly but not exclusively Jews—were successful in America. Then, quite by accident, I found what I had been looking for: an analysis of immigrants who left Europe between the ages of three and eighteen.

An Internet search revealed that Gerald Holton, a distinguished Harvard professor of physics and of history of science, had presented a paper at an international symposium, Austria and National Socialism: Implications for Scientific and Humanistic Scholarship, at the University of Vienna in the spring of 2003. The title of his paper was "What Happened to the Austrian Refugee Children in America? A Report from Research Project 'Second Wave.'"[4] The preliminary results were so astonishing that Holton went on to gather more data and to write an entire book based on his findings; it was published while I was working on *Once They Had a Country.*[5]

Born in Vienna, Holton immigrated to the United States as a teenager—parenthetically graduating in 1941 from Wesleyan University, the school that all three of my sons would attend—and received a PhD in physics from Harvard in 1948. He morphed from a physicist into a historian of science, writing about many of the scientists who, as he discovered, had also spent their early years in Austria or Germany and then fled persecution. Together with his colleague Gerhard Sonnert, another central European refugee, Holton launched the project he called the Second Wave—by contrast with the First Wave, those immigrants from Nazi Germany or Austria who were already distinguished professionals and who were easily accepted into American intellectual and professional life. The pair chose to study what became of central European Jews who left their homelands, principally Germany or Austria, but including Czechoslovakia and Hungary, between the ages of three and eighteen, to start anew in America. The vast majority of the group of 28,000 that Holton and Sonnert studied reached the United States before World War II, a few continued to trickle in between 1939 and 1941, and a smaller number still arrived after 1945. They represented a significant fraction of the 100,000 children who survived—out of 1.6 million in Europe targeted by the Nazis for extermination.

The researchers were fortunate to have available to them two extraordinarily useful data sets, the 1970 U.S. Census and the National Jewish Population Survey conducted in the same year as the census. Holton and Sonnert also devised their own written survey and carried out face-to-face interviews with a small sample drawn from the larger group. When I mentioned this project to my mother, she said she already knew about it—she had been one of those interviewed.

Holton and Sonnert came to some fascinating conclusions. Most members of the group they studied had arrived before my parents and had spent little if any time in Nazi-occupied Europe. Nonetheless, they had all experienced some sort of trauma prior to their arrival. Most arrived without knowing English; with no money; separated from their parents for an indefinite period of time, sometimes forever; with little to sustain them; and afflicted with horrendous memories of persecution.

Gerald Holton had expected that the group might well "spiral into anomie and despair."[6] What he and his coinvestigator found instead was that the majority continued their education, often obtaining college or even postgraduate degrees, and ultimately pursuing successful careers. The group included four Nobel Prize winners in science, as well as such distinguished figures as the public servants Henry Kissinger and Felix Rohatyn and the academics Fritz Stern and Henry Rosovsky.

In the group of central Europeans who immigrated between 1935 and 1944, fully 48 percent of the men and 18.5 percent of the women completed at least four years of college, compared to only 15 percent of American-born men and 8 percent of American-born women. A more limited amount of information was collected about people like my parents who arrived after the war (1945–49). These statistics are only slightly less dramatic: 27 percent of men and 6.6 percent of women completed at least four years of college, an accomplishment, that was, as Holton realized, "nothing short of amazing."[7]

Income data were similarly impressive, reflecting in large measure the refugees' educational attainments. The incomes of central Europeans who arrived as children and teenagers between 1935 and 1944 were almost twice those of American-born individuals. They found careers as professionals (50 percent) or managers (23 percent), with a strikingly large number going into science.[8]

But comparing the refugees to the rest of the American population might be misleading. Suppose American Jews were generally better educated and earned higher incomes than the average citizen. What Holton and Sonnert really wanted to know was how the refugees compared to American-born Jews. The National Jewish Population Survey gave them the answer to this question: two-thirds of men who emigrated from central Europe in 1933–44 completed at least four years of higher education, compared to just over half of the American-born Jews. Fully 56 percent of the refugee men received postgraduate education, compared to 36 percent of those born in the United States. In terms of occupation, a stunning 60 percent of the central European 1933–44 immigrants became professionals, compared to only a third of the American-born Jews. Careers in science were especially popular among the refugees, with 22 percent of the central Europeans compared to only 4 percent of the American-born Jews going into science. Incomes of the two groups were statistically comparable.[9]

When Holton and Sonnert went beyond their analysis of the large databases of the U.S. Census and the National Jewish Population Survey, distributing their own survey to some of the immigrants and conducting in-depth interviews with others, they confirmed the findings of impressive educational attainment, overrepresentation in managerial and professional positions, and high income levels. They also discovered a strong allegiance to democratic institutions. The political sensibilities of the immigrants studied mirrored those of my parents exactly: because they had lived under a dictatorship, they developed a profound appreciation for American democracy. They felt obligated to become civically active, which often translated into writing letters to their legislators and engaging in volunteer work.

My father would fire off innumerable letters to his congressman. My mother, after she retired from her private social work practice, continued to volunteer in a local nursing home. She also volunteered as a teacher of English as a second language, working with adults who had recently immigrated to the United States and knowing all too well how difficult it was to thrive without mastery of a country's language.

Holton and Sonnert's study only hinted at the reasons for the extraordinary success of this group of immigrants. The researchers argue that while the refugees assimilated in numerous critical ways—they rapidly became proficient in English and took advantage of American educational opportunities—in other respects, they remained outsiders: "The former refugees' greater socioeconomic success, as a group, did not so much occur in spite of their often incomplete assimilation, as it occurred because of that incomplete assimilation."[10] The group maintained a cosmopolitan focus and a strong sense of internationalism, with only weak ties to religion. "Overall, they had a strong work ethic, a strong will to achieve, and an interest in high culture."[11]

My parents likewise subscribe to a universalist, humanitarian worldview. They despise all those ideologies such as nationalism and Communism that they perceive as dividing rather than unifying people. They stand for tolerance, for respecting differences between people—but they believe that distinctiveness pales in comparison with our common humanity.

While my parents resemble Holton and Sonnert's group of central European refugees in many of their most strongly held beliefs, some of their convictions result from their unique experiences. My mother is still indignant when she speaks of the wealthy ladies in Brussels who, however well intentioned and however instrumental in assuring her survival, treated the refugee children as objects of charity, as inferiors, and not as individual human beings who loved and longed, who ached and aspired. My father bristles when he thinks of the Swiss labor camps where he had to chop down enormous trees and move heavy rocks while living in poorly heated barracks, subsisting on substandard rations, with his one lifeline, communication to Cousin Bessie in America, cut off. My mother gets tears in her eyes when she describes how she was interrogated in the middle of the night by Swiss officials who shone a blinding light in her eyes while threatening her with *refoulement*—expulsion to France, into the hands of the Gestapo or their colleagues, the Vichy police—if she did not divulge her true birth date. Both my parents still get angry when they recall the countless humiliations they experienced as refugees: my mother had to deposit her meager earnings as a pediatric nurse into a blocked Swiss bank account and petition the authorities to release her own money so she could buy basic necessities; my father had to report to the police department weekly while attending university in Bern, as though he were a criminal on parole.

My parents burn with indignation at the way the world treated refugees in the thirties and forties. They have been vindicated by new international standards for behavior toward individuals persecuted by their home countries and threatened with death or loss of liberty. The nations of the world took the first step toward setting a new standard for responding to refugees when the UN General Assembly passed the Universal Declaration of Human Rights in December 1948, shortly after my parents married. "All human beings are born free and equal in dignity and rights. They are endowed with reason and conscience and should act towards one another in a spirit of brotherhood," proclaimed article 1 of the declaration. "Everyone has the right to life, liberty and security of person," said article 3. These universal rights and freedoms are due everyone, "without distinction of any kind, such as race, colour, sex, language, religion, political or other opinion." And, the declaration concluded, "everyone has the right to seek and to enjoy in other countries asylum from persecution."[12]

The sentiments expressed in the Declaration of Human Rights were noble, but it was only with the establishment of the Office of the United Nations High Commissioner for Refugees (UNHCR) in December 1950 that the UN began developing means for their implementation. Then, in July 1951, an international conference held in Geneva adopted the Convention Relating to the Status of Refugees. What this did, first and foremost, was to define a refugee as "a person with a well-founded fear of being persecuted for reasons of race, religion, nationality, membership of a particular social group or political opinion."[13] Refugees were to be accorded rights within the nations where they found asylum—rights that had been denied refugees by the Swiss. My parents had not been allowed to gather in groups of more than five people; they had not been granted access to public high school education; and they had not been able to hold jobs except with special permission. The convention, by contrast, asserted that refugees cannot be treated any differently from citizens "as regards the right to engage in wage earning employment." They are to be accorded the right to join "non-political and non-profit making associations" to the extent accorded foreign nationals generally. And signatories "shall accord refugees the same treatment as is accorded to nationals with respect to elementary education" as well as access to further schooling. Refugees are to be given freedom of movement within the host nation—unlike the situation encountered by my mother, who was not even permitted to go on vacation with the Brütsch family.

Most dramatic of all was the provision against expulsion of refugees. Adopting the term coined by the Swiss, Article 33 proclaimed: "No contracting state shall expel or return ('refouler') a refugee in any manner whatsoever to the frontiers of territories where his life or freedom would be threatened on account of his race, religion, nationality, membership of a particular social group or political opinion."[14]

Time and again while my mother was in the Swiss reception camp she was told that she would be taken to the border and turned over to the French police, who in turn would take her to the transit camp at Drancy and from there send her to Auschwitz—as happened to many refugees. Such threats were declared illegal under international law.

Other regulations were passed to provide additional protection in hopes of preventing a repeat performance by the nations of the world when faced with an influx of refugees. In 1954 the Convention Relating to the Status of Stateless Persons affirmed the rights of people who had been deprived of citizenship by their home country. In 1967 a "protocol" extended the time-limited provisions and geographical limitations of the Refugee Convention. In 1984 the UN Convention against Torture and Other Cruel, Inhuman or Degrading Treatment or Punishment banned inhumane interrogation techniques.[15] And finally, in 2001, on the fiftieth anniversary of the Refugee Convention, the signatories of either the original convention or the 1967 protocol reaffirmed their commitment to the "continuing relevance and resilience of this international regime of rights and principles, including at its core the principle of non-refoulement."[16]

The problem of refugees has not vanished, of course, with the establishment of a few conventions. The UNHCR has been woefully underfunded since its inception, relying largely on charitable donations to carry on its work. Its mandate does not include assistance for internally displaced persons, who may number as many as 25 million worldwide. Only 146 nations have ratified either the Refugee Convention or the 1967 protocol. But the Refugee Convention is an acknowledgment at the highest levels of jurisprudence and philosophy that the treatment my parents endured as refugees was profoundly wrong.

The Refugee Convention and the UNHCR were put to the test in Iraq after the U.S. invasion in 2003. More than 2 million Iraqis sought refuge in neighboring countries: as of mid-2007, Syria had taken in about 1.5 million, Jordan 750,000, and Egypt about 100,000. Lesser but still substantial numbers went to Lebanon, Iran, and Turkey.[17] As of early 2007 Iraq continued to hemorrhage 50,000 people each month, individuals who despair of any kind of meaningful existence, perhaps survival at all, in their homeland.[18]

The majority of the Iraqis leaving their country met the definition of a refugee spelled out in the 1951 UN Refugee Convention as someone who is outside his country and cannot return due to "well-founded fears of persecution due to race, religion, nationality, political opinion, or membership in a particular social group." But some countries to which the Iraqis have fled—including Syria and Jordan, the major destinations for the refugees—are not signatories of the Refugee Convention or the 1967 protocol. Syria and Jordan, though hospitable in many ways, have deliberately chosen to call the Iraqis "guests" rather than refugees.[19] Educational prospects for "guests" are limited: in both Jordan and Syria, no more than 10 percent of Iraqi refugee children attended school in 2006–7.[20] In Syria, Iraqis are not allowed to work.[21] Other countries have done little to help: Sweden has done more than any other country outside the Middle East, accepting 9,000 refugees. The United States took in only a few hundred in 2006.[22]

Some critics of the Refugee Convention claim that it is "outdated, unworkable, irrelevant and inflexible."[23] They argue that it adequately addresses neither the interests of host states nor of the refugees themselves. But while the convention may benefit from revision, and the UNHCR, which is charged with implementing it, clearly would benefit from more resources, the convention upholds those basic principles that were regularly violated during my parents' refugee experiences—the rights of non-*refoulement* and nondiscrimination.[24] For all its limitations, in its first fifty years of existence, the UNHCR has helped about 50 million people find food, shelter, or legal assistance and has won two Nobel Peace Prizes for its work.[25] What was at first intended as a temporary office dedicated solely to assisting World War II refugees has grown into a formidable organization that is active in more than one hundred countries, maintains a staff of more than six thousand, and helps millions of people each year.

~

When I asked my parents how they thought their experiences as refugees affected their sense of what matters most in life, they talked about the paramount importance of community. They remained firmly bonded to the other "children of La Hille," though the eighty-five who survived the war were dispersed across the globe. The majority are in the United States, with a substantial contingent in Israel and a few in Switzerland, France, England, and Argentina. My father stayed in touch with Peter Salz who, like him, had been one of the "mathematicians" in France. Peter immigrated to Israel and lived on Kibbutz Lehavoth Habashan, working as a high school math teacher. My parents visited Israel twice, and each time their visit to Peter was a high point of their trip. My mother remained in contact with Edith Moser, her closest friend in France and the sister of her first boyfriend. Edith lived in the San Francisco area and struggled with a difficult marriage. My mother was her confidante from afar, providing emotional support when she could until Edith died of lung cancer.

The children of La Hille held several reunions, most of them catalyzed and organized by the indefatigable Werner Rindsberg, who had been one of the few teenagers in the group to procure a visa and make his way to the United States during the war. He got out in 1942—before the traumatic incarceration in the camp of Le Vernet and the illegal escapes to Switzerland. Werner had made contact with my father in Switzerland while he was a soldier in the U.S. Army on furlough. But after he returned to the United States, he severed all his ties to the La Hille group. He had already changed his name to the American sounding Walter Reed; he embellished his new identity by telling his friends and later on his young children that he had been born in New York and his parents had died in a car accident.

Something happened to Walter/Werner after he retired from a successful business career. A vigorous, intellectually curious man at age seventy, he was in France to attend a friend's wedding and decided as an afterthought to visit Seyre and La Hille with his family, who by this time knew his true history. He learned from a local farmer that many of the children of La Hille had come back to visit. Sitting outside the gates of the castle, he read the book *La Filière,* describing some of the group's experiences and learned for the first time the details of what had happened to them after his departure in 1942.[26] He read with astonishment of the heroism of his first girlfriend, Ruth Schütz, in the Resistance. Very moved, Walter left his business card with the owner of the castle.

Several days later, two other former La Hillers happened to visit the château, discovered Walter's card, and contacted him, opening the floodgates of memory. Once Walter Reed began exploring his roots, there was no stopping him. He organized a reunion in Chicago in 1998, an expanded, more structured version of the get-together that had taken place in Israel in 1988, and another reunion in Toulouse in 2000. He traveled around the world to meet his old friends from La Hille, tracking them down principally in the United States and Israel, but also in France, Argentina, and Australia. He obtained documents relating to the role of the Secours Suisse aux Enfants from the Swiss Red Cross and found materials in the archives of the Leo Baeck Institute in New York and the United States Holocaust Memorial Museum in Washington, D.C. Walter came across the papers of Lily Felddegen, one of the members of the committee of women who had organized the original transport of German and Austrian Jewish children to Belgium and then, behind the scenes, had worked to get them into France. Mrs. Felddegen, like my Cousin Bessie, had kept all her correspondence with American officials, with refugee organizations, and with the children themselves, demonstrating her prodigious efforts to rescue the hundred children who had boarded trains in 1939 for what they thought would be a safe haven in Brussels. Now in his early eighties, Walter Reed is writing the history of the rescue effort in Belgium and France, an effort that began as a charity project, then turned into a passion, and ultimately evolved into something close to an obsession.

~

How do I think my parents' lives were changed by their experiences as refugees? What do I believe—having spent countless hours interviewing them and their friends, having pored over Hans's letters to Cousin Bessie, Ilse's poems written in France, and numerous books and essays, from *New York Times* articles on civil unrest in Sao Paulo in 1947 to the 2,500 pages of Richard Evans's three-volume work on the Third Reich? The values that I think were shaped in the crucible of Europe, the values they inculcated in me, are—ironically—the values at the core of traditional Judaism. For all their universalism, for all their disdain for religion and their steadfast insistence that I not receive any specifically Jewish education, despite the astonishment and perplexity with which they greeted the decision my husband and I made to send all three of our sons to Jewish day school, what they held most dear in the end are *tzedakah, gemilut chasadim,* and *tikkun olam.*

Tzedakah, usually translated as charity, really has quite a different flavor. Charity suggests doing good works out of magnanimity, a kind of noblesse oblige. *Tzedakah,* by contrast, is a word derived from the word for righteousness. Giving to the poor is an act of justice and fairness. In Jewish tradition, it is a fundamental obligation. *Gemilut chasadim,* or acts of loving-kindness, are characterized by the Talmud as of even greater merit than *tzedakah.* Anyone can be the recipient of acts of loving-kindness—rich, poor, young, old. And *tikkun olam,* or repairing the world, has come to be viewed as including both *tzedakah* and *gemilut chasadim.* Once a part of Judaism's mystical tradition, *tikkun olam* now refers to the social action mission embodied in the prophetic tradition. It is no accident, I think, that I have devoted my career as a physician to caring for the oldest and frailest of patients, some of the most vulnerable and neediest people in our health care system. It is not a coincidence that my husband and I are active members of a small, participatory congregation whose mantra is "community," or that I write about how older people (and probably all people) derive meaning in life from helping others, from service, not from fame or fortune.

Notes

Introduction

1. The text of Hitler's speech is available at the History Place, www.historyplace.com (accessed 8/17/09).

2. For a brief history of the British rescue project called Kindertransport, see the Kindertransport Association website, www.kindertransport.org/history/htm (accessed 8/19/09). With reference to children who were sent to Belgium and Holland, the term "Kindertransport" is used in a generic sense.

3. Helen Epstein beautifully documented the varying ways that parents broached the subject of their past in *Children of the Holocaust: Conversations with Sons and Daughters of Survivors* (New York: G. P. Putnam's Sons, 1979). A dramatic memoir by a woman whose parents created a new identity for themselves in which they deleted their Jewish past is Helen Fremont, *After Long Silence* (New York: Random House, 1999).

4. Lawrence Langer, *Holocaust Testimonies: The Ruins of Memory* (New Haven: Yale University Press, 1991).

5. Eva Hoffman *After Such Knowledge: Memory, History, and the Legacy of the Holocaust* (New York: Public Affairs, 2004).

6. Vera Friedländer, *Die Kinder von La Hille: Flucht und Rettung vor Deportation* (Berlin: Aufbau Taschenbuch Verlag, 2004). My translation.

7. Nir Rosen, "The Flight from Iraq," *New York Times Sunday Magazine,* May 13, 2007.

8. Office of the United Nations High Commissioner for Refugees, *The State of the World's Refugees: Human Displacement in the New Millennium* (New York: Oxford University Press, 2006).

9. The text of both the 1951 convention and the 1967 protocol, which extends the time period and geographic boundaries covered by the original convention, can be found at www.unhcr.org (accessed 8/17/09).

10. Erika Feller, "Asylum, Migration, and Refugee Protection: Realities, Myths, and the Promise of Things to Come," *International Journal of Refugee Law* 18 (2006): 509–36.

Chapter 1

1. From the diary of Edith Goldapper, quoted in Vera Friedländer, *Die Kinder von La Hille* (Berlin: Aufbau Taschenbuch Verlag, 2004), 12. My translation.

2. The recollections of Inge Joseph as cited in Inge Bleier and David Gumpert, *Inge: A Girl's Journey through Nazi Europe* (Grand Rapids, Mich.: William Eerdmans, 2004), 24.

3. W. Michael Blumenthal, *The Invisible Wall: Germans and Jews—A Personal Exploration* (Washington, D.C.: Counterpoint, 1998), 375.

4. Mark Harris and Deborah Oppenheimer, *Into the Arms of Strangers: Stories of the Kindertransport* (New York: Bloomsbury Publishing, 2000), 100.

5. Michel Carmona, *Haussmann: His Life and Times, and the Making of Modern Paris* (New York: Ivan Dee, 2003).

6. Clemens Heitmann, "Die Stettin-Frage: Die KPD, die Sowjetunion, und die Deutsch-Polnische Grenze 1945," *Zeitschrift für Ostmittleuropa Forschung* 51 (2002): 25–63.

7. Winston Churchill gave his iron curtain speech on March 5, 1946, when he received an honorary degree at Westminster College in Fulton, Mo., www.historyguide.org/europe/churchill.html (accessed 1/11/09).

8. The 1925 census of German Jews was reprinted in *American Jewish Year Book of 1930–1931,* ed. Henry Schneiderman (Philadelphia: Pennsylvania Jewish Publication Society, 1931), 252–57.

9. Donald Niewyck, *The Jews in Weimar Germany* (Baton Rouge: Louisiana State University Press, 1980), 13.

10. Marion Kaplan, "As Germans and as Jews in Imperial Germany," in *Jewish Daily Life in Germany, 1618–1945,* ed. Marion Kaplan (New York: Oxford University Press, 2005), 186.

11. Ibid., 211.

12. Marion Kaplan, "Redefining Judaism in Imperial Germany: Practices, Mentalities, and Community," *Jewish Social Studies* 9, no. 1 (2002): 11.

13. Richard Evans, *The Coming of the Third Reich* (New York: Penguin, 2004), 110.

14. Peter Gay, *My German Question: Growing Up in Nazi Berlin* (New Haven: Yale University Press, 1998), 61.

15. Martin Gilbert, *Kristallnacht: Prelude to Destruction* (New York: HarperCollins, 2006), 38.

16. Kaplan, "As Germans and as Jews," 195.

17. Kaplan, "Redefining Judaism," 17.

18. Ibid., 6.

Chapter 2

1. Martin Gilbert, *Kristallnacht: Prelude to Destruction* (New York: HarperCollins, 2006), 50.

2. Marion Kaplan, *Between Dignity and Despair: Jewish Life in Nazi Germany* (New York: Oxford University Press, 1998), 125.

3. Gilbert, *Kristallnacht,* 141.

4. *The Encyclopedia of Jewish Life before and during the Holocaust,* ed. Shmuel Spector (New York: New York University Press), 949.

5. Avraham Altman and Irene Eber, "Flight to Shanghai, 1938–1940: The Larger Setting," *Yad-Vashem Studies* 28 (2000):51–86.

6. Gilbert, *Kristallnacht,* 168.

7. Richard Evans, *The Third Reich in Power, 1933–1939* (New York: Penguin, 2005), 601.

8. Saul Friedländer, *Nazi Germany and the Jews: The Years of Persecution, 1933–1939* (New York: HarperCollins, 1997), 75.

9. Richard Evans, *The Coming of the Third Reich* (New York: Penguin, 2004), 106.

10. Ibid., 66.

11. Hans's estimate was based on the observation that Jews generally made up 1 percent of the population in small towns. *Encyclopedia of Jewish Life* states there were 158 Jews in Osterode in 1930 (949).

12. Trude Maurer, "From Everyday Life to a State of Emergency: Jews in Weimar and Nazi Germany," in *Jewish Daily Life in Germany, 1618–1948,* ed. Marion Kaplan (New York: Oxford University Press, 2005), 272–373.

13. Evans, *Coming of the Third Reich,* 66.

14. Ibid., 123–27.

15. Kaplan, *Between Dignity and Despair,* 22.

16. Evans, *Coming of the Third Reich,* 384.

17. Ibid., 390.

18. Kaplan, *Between Dignity and Despair,* 11.

19. W. Michael Blumenthal, *The Invisible Wall: Germans and Jews—A Personal History* (Washington, D.C.: Counterpoint, 1998), 341.

20. Kaplan, *Between Dignity and Despair,* 96.

21. Victor Klemperer, *I Will Bear Witness: A Diary of the Nazi Years, 1933–1941* (New York: Modern Library Paperback Edition, 1999), 195.

22. Trude Maurer, "From Everyday Life," 336.

23. Kaplan, *Between Dignity and Despair,* 95.

24. Lucy Dawidowicz, *The War against the Jews, 1933–1945* (New York: Holt, Rinehart, and Winston, 1975), 91.

25. Kaplan, *Between Dignity and Despair,* 38.

26. Klemperer, *I Will Bear Witness,* 190.

27. Kaplan, *Between Dignity and Despair,* 143.

28. Ibid., 102.

29. Peter Gay, *My German Question: Growing Up in Nazi Berlin* (New Haven: Yale University Press, 1988), 49.

30. Klemperer, *I Will Bear Witness,* 272.

31. Kaplan, *Between Dignity and Despair,* 38.

32. Evans, *The Third Reich in Power,* 486.

33. Gay, *My German Question,* 83.

34. Winston Churchill, *The Gathering Storm* (Boston: Houghton Mifflin, 1948).

Chapter 3

1. Peter Gay, *My German Question: Growing Up in Nazi Berlin* (New Haven: Yale University Press, 1988), 62–63.

2. Ruth Schuetz Usrad, "Entrapped Adolescence," typescript, translated from the Hebrew by Walter Reed.

3. The home page of the Royal Racing Club de Bruxelles is www.rrcb.be (accessed 8/18/09).

4. Vera Friedlaender, *Die Kinder von La Hille: Flucht und Rettung vor Deportation* (Berlin: Aufbau Taschenbuch Verlag, 2004), 18. My translation.

5. Ibid.

6. Sarah Ogilvie and Scott Miller, *Refuge Denied: The* St. Louis *Passengers and the Holocaust* (Madison: University of Wisconsin Press, 2006).

7. Martin Gilbert, *The Second World War: A Complete History,* rev. ed. (New York: Owl Books, 2004), 9.

8. Richard Evans, *The Third Reich in Power, 1933–1939* (New York: Penguin, 2005), 712.

9. Lucy Dawidowicz, *War against the Jews, 1933–1945* (New York: Holt, Rinehart, and Winston, 1975), 493.

10. "Brussels Is Raided: 400 Reported Killed—Troops Cross Border at Four Points," *New York Times,* May 10, 1940.

11. Evans, *Third Reich in Power,* 658.

12. Walter Reed, "Madame Felddegen's Children," *Passages, the Magazine of HIAS, the Hebrew Immigrant Aid Society* 5 (2006): 16–19.

13. Inge Bleier and David Gumpert, *Inge: A Girl's Journey through Nazi Europe* (Grand Rapids, Mich.: William Eerdmans, 2004), 64.

14. Gilbert, *Second World War,* 70

15. Paul Belien, "Belgian Authorities Destroy Holocaust Records," *Brussels Journal* 22 (2006):32.

16. Nora Levin, *The Holocaust: The Destruction of European Jewry, 1933–1945* (New York: Schocken Books, 1973), 421.

17. Ibid.

Chapter 4

1. Vera Friedländer, *Die Kinder von La Hille: Flucht und Rettung vor Deportation* (Berlin: Aufbau Taschenbuch Verlag, 2004), 44. My translation.

2. Ruth Schuetz Usrad, "Entrapped Adolescence," typescript, translated from the Hebrew by Walter Reed.

3. Inge Bleier and David Gumpert, *Inge: A Girl's Journey through Nazi Europe* (Grand Rapids, Mich.: William Eerdmans, 2004), 70.

4. Ibid., 72.

5. Ibid., 263.

6. First broadcast as prime minister, the Churchill Centre, www.winstonchurchill.org (accessed 5/31/07).

7. Martin Kitchen, *Between the Wars: A Political History* (New York: Longman Group, 1988).

8. Nora Levin, *The Holocaust: The Destruction of European Jewry, 1933–1945* (New York: Schocken Books, 1973), 423.

9. Ibid., 427.

10. Ibid., 430–31.

11. Documents obtained from the Swiss Red Cross by Walter Reed.

12. Irene Frank's unpublished memoir, courtesy of Walter Reed, reports that Ilse, "a charming and always happy girl" screamed when she read the card. Inge Joseph's recollection is that she fainted. Ilse remembers only that the card was in French rather than in German.

13. Memo from Long Breckinridge to the staff of the U.S. State Department, June 26, 1940. Quoted by the Jewish Virtual Library, www.jewishvirtuallibrary.org (accessed 7/14/09).

14. Bleier and Gumpert, *Inge*, 93–95.

15. Michael and Erica Royston, History and Biography Project, "Let Their Lives Speak," Summer 2005, www.swiss-quakers.ch/Documents/Let their lives speak.pdf (accessed 7/14/09).

16. Walter Reed, "Madame Felddegen's Children," *Passages, the Magazine of HIAS, the Hebrew Immigrant Aid Society* 5 (2006):16–19.

17. Letter from Maurice Dubois to Lily Felddegen, Felddegen Archive, courtesy of Walter Reed, now housed at the United States Holocaust Memorial Museum.

Chapter 5

1. Ruth Schuetz Usrad, "Entrapped Adolescence," typescript, translated from the Hebrew by Walter Reed.

2. Ibid.

3. Susan Zuccotti, *The Holocaust, the French, and the Jews* (New York: Basic Books, 1993).

4. Serge Klarsfeld, *French Children of the Holocaust: A Memorial* (New York: New York University Press, 1996).

5. Deborah Dwork and Robert Jan Van Pelt, *Flight from the Reich: Refugee Jews, 1933–1946* (New York: Norton, 2009).

6. Martin Gilbert, *The Second World War: A Complete History*, rev. ed. (New York: Owl Books, 2004), 197.

7. From Churchill's telegram to Eden after Pearl Harbor, cited in Gilbert, *Second World War*, 278.

8. Ibid., 268.

9. Ibid., 274–75.

10. Saul Friedländer, *The Years of Extermination: Nazi Germany and the Jews, 1939–1945* (New York: HarperCollins, 2007), 317.

11. Gilbert, *Second World War*, 296.

12. Victoria Raveis, Karolynn Siegel, and Daniel Kraus, "Children's Psychologi-

cal Distress following the Death of a Parent," *Journal of Youth and Adolescence* 28 (1999):165–80.

13. Nora Levin, *The Holocaust: The Destruction of European Jewry, 1933–1945* (New York: Schocken Books, 1973), 447.

14. *The French Talk to the French,* BBC Archives. August 25, 1942. The transcription refers to a roundup in the area occupied by the Nazis, so it may not have been clear that it would extend to the "free zone" as well.

15. Arthur Koestler, *The Scum of the Earth* (New York: McMillan, 1941), 17.

16. Ibid., 94.

17. Ibid., 98.

18. Inge Bleier and David Gumpert, *Inge: A Girl's Journey through Nazi Europe* (Grand Rapids, Mich.: William Eerdmans, 2004), 166.

19. Anne-Marie Im Hof-Piguet, *La Filière en France Occupée, 1942–1944* (Yverdon-les-Bains: Édition de la Thiele, 1985), 74.

20. The dramatic departure from Paris of virtually the entire population as the Nazis neared Paris is related by Hanna Diamond in *Fleeing Hitler: France, 1940* (New York: Oxford University Press, 2007). A fictional account is provided in the recently discovered novel by Irène Nemirovsky, *Suite Francaise* (New York: Alfred Knopf, 2006).

21. Vera Friedländer, *Die Kinder von La Hille: Flucht und Rettung vor Deportation* (Berlin: Aufbau Taschenbuch Verlag, 2004), 116. My translation.

22. Levin, *The Holocaust,* 445–47.

23. Ibid., 448. Pétain added that it was a matter of "internal concern."

24. Independent Commission of Experts, Switzerland—Second World War, *Switzerland and Refugees in the Nazi Era* (Bern: BBL/EDMZ, 1999), 104.

25. Ibid.

Chapter 6

1. This story by Gogol has been surprisingly popular to movie directors, beginning with silent movies and continuing through multiple talking versions.

2. Chazznut Online, Kathryn Cole, "Joseph Schmidt, Opera and Synagogue," www.chazzanut.com/schmidt.html (accessed 8/19/09).

3. Independent Commission of Experts, Switzerland—Second World War, *Switzerland and Refugees in the Nazi Era* (Bern: BBL/EDMZ, 1999), 155.

4. Ibid., 156.

5. Ibid., 158.

6. Ibid.

7. Ibid., 159.

8. Inge Bleier and David Gumpert, *Inge: A Girl's Journey through Nazi Europe* (Grand Rapids, Mich.: William Eerdmans, 2004), 179–81.

9. Vera Friedländer, *Die Kinder von La Hille: Flucht und Rettung vor Deportation* (Berlin: Aufbau Taschenbuch Verlag, 2004), 258–59. My translation.

10. Martin Gilbert, *The Second World War: A Complete History,* rev. ed. (New York: Owl Books, 2004), 381.

11. Jonathan Petropoulos, "Co-Opting Nazi Germany: Neutrality in Europe during World War II," *Dimension: A Journal of Holocaust Studies* 11 (1997): 15–21.

12. Simon Erlanger, "The Politics of 'Transmigration': Why Jewish Refugees Had to Leave Switzerland from 1944 to 1954," *Jewish Political Studies Review* 18 (2006): 71–85.

13. Independent Commission, *Switzerland and Refugees,* 114.

14. The report of the Independent Commission of Experts indicates that between 1939 and 1945, a total of 19,495 Jews found refuge in Switzerland and 20,000 were turned away.

Chapter 7

1. Marion Kaplan, *Between Dignity and Despair: Jewish Life in Nazi Germany* (New York: Oxford University Press, 1998), 153–54.

2. Internally displaced persons need protection from their own government and thus fall outside the UNHCR purview. The organization estimated that as of 2004 there were 25 million such individuals worldwide. Office of the United Nations High Commissioner for Refugees, *The State of the World's Refugees: Human Displacement in the New Millennium* (New York: Oxford University Press, 2006).

3. Richard Evans, *The Third Reich in Power, 1933–1939* (New York: Penguin, 2005), 608.

4. "Transport of Jews in Stettin Reported," *New York Times,* February 14, 1940.

5. Kaplan, *Between Dignity and Despair,* 150.

6. Ibid., 153.

7. William L. Shirer, *Berlin Diary: The Journal of a Foreign Correspondent, 1934–1941* (New York: Knopf, 1941), 486.

8. Ibid., 580.

9. Ibid., 500.

10. Maurer and Kaplan both see this as a turning point in the Nazi strategy of dehumanization.

11. Daniel Silver, *Refuge in Hell: How Berlin's Jewish Hospital Outlasted the Nazis* (Boston: Houghton Mifflin, 2003), 59.

12. Victor Klemperer, *I Will Bear Witness: A Diary of the Nazi Years, 1933–1941* (New York: Modern Library Paperback Edition, 1999), 2:12.

13. Ibid., 21.

14. Silver, *Refuge in Hell,* 9.

15. The example of health care workers who may have allowed some patients a merciful death is from the Jewish Hospital in Hamburg.

16. Kaplan, *Between Dignity and Despair,* 183.

17. Klemperer, *Witness,* vol. 2, summarized thirty-one new bans in his entry of June 2, 1942.

18. Ibid., 50.

19. Ibid., 63.

20. The International Tracing Service (an agency operating under the auspices of the International Committee of the Red Cross to preserve records documenting the

fate of the victims of Nazi persecution) provided photocopies of documents showing that Minna Lonky, born January 4, 1885, in Filehne, Poland, and living at Rheinstrasse 35, Berlin during the war, was deported to Lublin on June 2, 1942.

21. Klemperer, *Witness,* 2:105.

22. Central Database of Shoah Victims' Names (www.yadvashem.org) lists as its source the *Gedenkbuch Berlins der jüdischer Opfer des Nationalsozialismus,* Freie Universität Berlin, Zentralinstitut für sozialwissenschaftliche Forschung, Edition Hentrich, Berlin, 1995.

23. Gertrude Schneider, *Journey into Terror: Story of the Riga Ghetto,* new and expanded ed. (Westport, Conn.: Praeger Publishers, 2001).

24. Josef Katz, *One Who Came Back: The Diary of a Jewish Survivor* (Madison: University of Wisconsin Press, 2006), 49. Katz was sent to Riga in the summer of 1942 and reports that there was a selection at the train station, with 90 percent of the arrivals sent to the forest to be murdered and the remainder sent to the Riga ghetto.

25. Robert Kempner, "Die Ermordung von 35,000 Berliner Juden: Der Judenmordprozess Schreibt Geschichte," in *Gegenwart im Rückblick: Festgabe fuer die Jüdische Gemeinde zu Berlin 25 Jahre nach dem Neubeginn,* ed. Herbert Strauss and Kurt Grossmann (Heidelberg: Lothar Stiehm Verlag, 1970), 203.

Chapter 8

1. Martin Gilbert, *The Second World War: A Complete History,* rev. ed. (New York: Owl, 2004), 447.

2. Ibid., 448.

3. Raymond Daniell, "Eisenhower Acts, Montgomery Leads," *New York Times,* June 6, 1944.

4. Livia Rothkirchen, *The Jews of Bohemia and Moravia: Facing the Holocaust* (Omaha: University of Nebraska Press, 2005), 130–37.

5. Gilbert, *Second World War,* 559.

6. The train left Berlin on August 15 and arrived at the train station of Riga-Skirotava on August 18. The mean age of the "passengers" was forty-six and there were 57 children under age ten on board. All except one woman who had training as a nurse were taken to the forests of Rumbula and Bikernieki and shot (Alfred Gottwaldt and Diana Schulle, *Die "Judendeportationen" aus dem Deutschen Reich, 1941–1945: Eine Kommentierte Chronologie* [Wiesbaden: Marix Verlag, 2005], 255.)

7. Central Database of Shoah Victims' Names, www.yadvashem.org (accessed 8/18/09).

8. Hans Garfunkel to Alex Frank, February 15, 1946. Reprinted in Vera Friedländer, *Die Kinder von La Hille: Flucht und Rettung vor Deportation* (Berlin: Aufbau Taschenbuch Verlag, 2004), 263. My translation.

9. Editorial, *New York Times,* April 13, 1945.

10. *New York Times,* "Summary of News of the War and German Surrender," May 18, 1945.

11. Letter from Hans to Alex Frank, August 31, 1945, reprinted in Friedländer, *Die Kinder von La Hille,* 264. My translation.

Chapter 9

1. Ernst Heppner, *Shanghai Refuge: A Memoir of the World War II Jewish Ghetto* (Lincoln: University of Nebraska Press, 1995), 37.

2. Peter Vamos, "Home Afar: The Life of Central European Jewish Refugees in Shanghai during World War II," *Pacific Rim Report* no. 23 (2000).

3. W. Michael Blumenthal, *The Invisible Wall: Germans and Jews—A Personal Exploration* (Washington, D.C.: Counterpoint, 1998), 375.

4. Ernest Hauser, "Shadow over Shanghai," *New York Times,* April 23, 1939.

5. Heppner, *Shanghai Refuge,* 41.

6. David Kranzler, *Japanese, Nazis, and Jews: The Jewish Refugee Community of Shanghai, 1938–1945* (New York: Yeshiva University Press, 1976), 127.

7. Ibid., 131, reports this Heim opened on April 30, 1939, and that it included a scarlet fever isolation ward.

8. Kranzler discusses the health and sanitary conditions in Shanghai. He reports that when the typhoons came, the Chaoufoong Road became "a flowing river over two feet deep" (*Japanese, Nazis, and Jews,* 297).

9. Hallett Abend, "Shanghai: A Center of Soaring Crime," *New York Times,* March 13, 1939.

10. Hauser, "Shadow over Shanghai," 107.

11. Daily life is picturesquely described by Stella Dong in *Shanghai: The Rise and Fall of a Decadent City, 1842–1949* (New York: William Morrow, 2000), 225–59.

12. Blumenthal, *Invisible Wall,* 379.

13. Cable from the Shanghai Municipal Council to the American Joint Distribution Committee, sent on December 27, 1938. Quoted in James Ross, *Escape to Shanghai: A Jewish Community in China* (New York: Free Press, 1994), 52.

14. Kranzler, *Japanese, Nazis, and Jews,* 274.

15. Ibid., 91–99.

16. Heppner, *Shanghai Refuge,* 44.

17. Ross, *Escape to Shanghai,* 183.

18. Kranzler, *Japanese, Nazis, and Jews,* 45–65.

19. For a discussion of David Sassoon, see Kranzler, *Japanese, Nazis, and Jews,* 46–47.

20. Adapted from a description of Sir Victor by Dong, *Shanghai: Rise and Fall,* 220.

21. Chiara Betta, "A Forgotten Baghdadi Jewish Tycoon: Silas Hardoon in Shanghai, 1874–1931," *Nehardea Magazine* 4 (2003) www.babylonjewry.org.il (accessed 8/19/09).

22. Dong, *Shanghai: Rise and Fall,* 222.

23. Wei-Peh Ti, "A Peek Backwards into the Jewish Community of Shanghai," *Journal of the Hong Kong Branch of the Royal Asiatic Society* 32 (1992): 149–63.

24. Morris Harris and James White, "Shanghai Internationalism Ends: Writers Reveal Enemy Method," *New York Times,* July 28, 1942.

25. Bernard Wasserstein, *Secret War in Shanghai* (Boston: Houghton Mifflin, 1991), 91.

26. Kranzler, *Japanese, Nazis, and Jews,* 490.

27. Ross, *Shanghai Refuge,* 97–99.

28. Kano Ghoya is described in Kranzler, *Japanese, Nazis, and Jews,* as having a "psychotic personality"; he referred to himself as the "King of the Jews" (498).

29. Brooks Atkinson, "Shanghai Gripped by Soaring Prices," *New York Times,* February 16, 1944.

30. Dong, *Shanghai: Rise and Fall,* 278.

31. Ross, *Shanghai Refuge,* 218–19.

32. Ibid., 216.

33. Dong, *Shanghai: Rise and Fall,* 279.

34. Ross, *Shanghai Refuge,* 260.

Chapter 10

1. Daniel Smith, "Shock and Disbelief," *Atlantic* 287 (2001): 79–90.

2. For an interesting window on Swiss psychiatry, see G. Palmai and B. Blackwell, "The Burghölzli Centenary," *Medical History* 10 (1966): 257–65.

3. Institute of Medicine Report, *Posttraumatic Stress Disorder: Diagnosis and Treatment* (Washington, D.C.: National Academies Press, 2006).

4. Eric Dean, *Shook over Hell: Post-Traumatic Stress, Vietnam, and the Civil War* (Cambridge, Mass.: Harvard University Press, 1999).

5. Pierre Janet, *The Major Symptoms of Hysteria: Fifteen Lectures Given in the Medical School of Harvard University* (New York: MacMillan, 1920).

6. W. Viaweg, D. A. Julius, A. Fernandez, et al., "Posttraumatic Stress Disorder: Clinical Features, Pathophysiology, and Treatment," *American Journal of Medicine* 119 (2006): 383–90.

7. Anna Ornstein, "Survival and Recovery: Psychoanalytic Reflections," *Harvard Review of Psychiatry* 9 (2001): 10–22.

8. Judith Herman, *Trauma and Recovery* (New York: Basic Books, 1992).

9. Marion Kaplan, *Between Dignity and Despair: Jewish Life in Nazi Germany* (New York: Oxford University Press, 1998), 88, reports that the regime "advised, bribed, and threatened Aryans to divorce Jewish spouses."

10. Simon Erlanger, "The Politics of Transmigration: Why Jewish Refugees Had to Leave Switzerland," *Jewish Political Studies Review* 18 (2006): 71–85.

11. Ibid.

12. Tony Judt, *Postwar: A History of Europe since 1945* (New York: Penguin, 2005), 23.

13. Howard Sachar, *A History of the Jews in America* (New York: Knopf, 1992), 554.

14. According to Tony Judt, there were 6,795,000 refugees in the DP camps in western Europe at the end of 1946. They included 2 million Frenchmen, 1.6 million Poles, 700,000 Czechs, 300,000 Dutch, and 300,000 Belgians *(Postwar,* 28).

15. Sachar, *History of the Jews,* 555.

16. President Truman sent Earl Harrison, the U.S. representative on the Intergovernmental Committee on Refugees, to look into the conditions facing displaced persons in Germany. As a result of Harrison's report, Truman sent a letter to General Eisenhower on August 31, 1945, requesting more humane policies toward the Jews, www.jewishvirtuallibrary.org (accessed 8/19/09).

17. Sachar, *History of the Jews,* 556.

18. Jan Gross, *Fear: Anti-Semitism in Poland after Auschwitz—An Essay in Historical Interpretation* (Princeton, N.J.: Princeton University Press, 2006).

19. Sachar, *History of the Jews,* 559.

20. Ibid., 560–62.

Chapter 11

1. Robert Levine, *Father of the Poor? Vargas and His Era* (New York: Cambridge University Press, 1998).

2. "Good Wishes for Hitler; President Vargas of Brazil Sends May Day Message," *New York Times,* May 10, 1941.

3. Jeffrey Lesser, *Welcoming the Undesirables: Brazil and the Jewish Question* (Berkeley: University of California Press, 1999), 51.

4. Ibid., 68–74.

5. Ibid., 108.

6. Herbert Strauss, "Jewish Emigration from Germany: Nazi Policies and Jewish Responses," Leo Baeck Institute Year Book 25 (1980): 326.

7. Lesser, *Welcoming the Undesirables,* 135.

8. Strauss, "Jewish Emigration from Germany," 326.

9. Robert Levine, *The History of Brazil* (Westport, Conn.: Greenwood Press, 1999).

10. Lesser, *Welcoming the Undesirables,* 15–16.

11. Jeffrey Lesser, "The Immigration and Integration of Polish Jews in Brazil, 1924–1934," *Americas* 51 (1994): 173–91.

12. Lesser, *Welcoming the Undesirables.*

13. Thomas Skidmore, *Brazil: Five Centuries of Change* (New York: Oxford University Press, 1999), 114.

14. Stefan Zweig, *Brazil: Land of the Future* (New York: Viking Press, 1941), 10.

15. Ibid., 142.

16. Stefan Zweig, *The World of Yesterday: An Autobiography* (New York: Viking Press, 1943), 437. The suicide note, dated February 23, 1942, reads: "Before parting from life of my own free will and in my right mind, I am impelled to fulfill a last obligation to give heartfelt thanks to this wonderful land of Brazil which afforded me and my work such kind and hospitable repose. My love for this country increased from day to day, and no where else would I have preferred to build up a new existence, the world of my own language having disappeared for me and my spiritual home, Europe, having destroyed itself."

17. Skidmore, *Brazil,* 129.

18. Ibid., 130.

19. "Balloting Ignored by Third of Brazil," *New York Times,* January 21, 1947.

20. *New York Times,* "Sao Paulo Calm Again," August 23, 1947.

21. Frank Garcia, "Dip in Coffee Price Frightens Brazil," *New York Times,* April 12, 1947.

22. The lecturer, Samuel Putnam, published his observations in "Literary Notes from Rio" in the *New York Times Book Review,* October 6, 1946, 9.

23. Letter from Hans Garfunkel to Alex Frank, dated July 14, 1947. Included in Vera Friedländer, *Die Kinder von la Hille: Flucht und Rettung vor Deportation* (Berlin: Aufbau Taschenbuch Verlag, 2004), 274. My translation.

Chapter 12

1. Stephen Miller, "Herbert A. Strauss, 86, Historian, Scholar of Refugee Intellectuals," *New York Sun,* March 15, 2005.

2. *American Speeches: Political Oratory from Abraham Lincoln to Bill Clinton,* ed. Ted Widmer (New York: Library of America, 2006), 472–75.

3. Steven Lowenstein, *Frankfurt on the Hudson: The German-Jewish Community of Washington Heights, 1933–1983: Its Structure and Culture* (Detroit: Wayne State University Press), 1980.

4. Ibid., 66.

5. Ibid., 90.

6. Harold Callender, "Clashes in France Near Insurrection: Strike Bill Voted," *New York Times,* December 4, 1947.

7. "Strike Ties Up De Grasse," *New York Times,* December 9, 1947.

8. "The Struggle in France," editorial, *New York Times,* December 2, 1947.

9. "Jews' Ship Halted Close to Palestine," *New York Times,* December 23, 1947.

10. "2 Refugee Craft Seized by British," *New York Times,* October 3, 1947.

11. Sam Pope, "Small Ship Lands 200 in Palestine," *New York Times,* November 17, 1947.

12. "$250,000,000 Sought for Jewish Relief," *New York Times,* January 2, 1948.

13. Gertrude Samuels, "Children Who Have Known No Childhood," *New York Times,* March 9, 1942.

14. Beth Cohen, *Case Closed: Holocaust Survivors in Postwar America* (New Brunswick, N.J.: Rutgers University Press, 2007), 116.

15. Kathleen McLaughlin, "Convictions Due on SS Men Today," *New York Times,* April 9, 1948.

16. Kathleen McLaughlin, "14 Officers of SS Sentenced to Die," *New York Times,* April 10, 1948.

17. "The Einsatzgruppen Case," Military Tribunal II: Case 9, www.nizkor.com (accessed 8/19/09).

18. "State of Israel: Burned and Bombed," *New York Times,* May 16, 1948.

19. "The Partition of Palestine," *New York Times,* November 30, 1947.

Epilogue

1. Beth Cohen, *Case Closed: Holocaust Survivors in Postwar America* (New Brunswick, N.J.: Rutgers University Press, 2007), 139.

2. Gertrude Samuels, "DPs in America: 'We Have Become Alive,'" *New York Times Magazine,* March 28, 1948.

3. Maurice Davies and Samuel Koenig, "Adjustment of Refugees to American Life," *American Academy of Political and Social Science* 262 (1949): 159–65.

4. Gerald Holton and Gerhard Sonnert, "What Happened to the Austrian Refugee Children in America? A Report from Research Project 'Second Wave'" presented at the International Symposium, Austria and National Socialism: Implications for Scientific Humanistic Scholarship, June 5–6, 2003, at the University of Vienna; available online at www.physics.harvard.edu (accessed 8/19/09).

5. Gerhard Sonnert and Gerald Holton, *What Happened to the Children Who Fled Nazi Persecution* (New York: Palgrave Macmillan, 2006).

6. Ibid., 3.

7. Ibid., 75.

8. Ibid, 78–80.

9. Ibid., 85.

10. Ibid., 92.

11. Ibid., 111.

12. Universal Declaration of Human Rights, adopted by the UN General Assembly, December 10, 1948, www.un.org (accessed 8/19/09).

13. UNHCR, the UN Refugee Agency, "Convention Relating to the Status of Refugees," www.unhcr.org (accessed 8/17/09).

14. Ibid.

15. Nehemiah Robinson, *Convention Relating to the Status of Stateless Persons: Its History and Interpretation* (New York: Institute of Jewish Affairs, 1952).

16. UNHCR, the UN Refugee Agency, Declaration of States Parties to the 1951 Convention and/or Its 1967 Protocol Relating to the Status of Refugees, Geneva, Switzerland, December 12–13, 2001, www.unhcr.org (accessed 8/9/09).

17. Hassan Fattah, "Meeting on Aiding 2 Million Iraqi Refugees Highlights Divisions," *New York Times,* July 27, 2007.

18. Nir Rosen, "The Flight from Iraq," *New York Times Magazine,* May 13, 2007.

19. Lyse Doucet, "Mideast Facing Iraq Refugee Crisis: Jordan and Syria are Home to Millions Fleeing Relentless Violence at Home," *Toronto Star,* April 2, 2007.

20. Refugees International, "Iraqi Refugees: Time for the UN System to Fully Engage," July 27, 2007, www.refugeesinternational.org (accessed 8/19/09).

21. Ashraf al-Khalidi, Sophia Hoffmann, and Victor Tanner, "Iraqi Refugees in the Syrian Arab Republic: A Field-Based Snapshot," Brookings Institution—University of Bern Project on Internal Displacement, June 11, 2007, www.brookings.edu (accessed 1/11/10).

22. Doucet, "Mideast Facing Iraq Refugee Crisis."

23. Office of the United Nations High Commissioner for Refugees, *The State of the World's Refugees: Human Displacement in the New Millennium* (New York: Oxford University Press, 2006).

24. Erika Feller, "Asylum, Migration, and Refugee Protection: Realities, Myths, and the Promise of Things to Come," *International Journal of Refugee Law* 18 (2006): 509–36.

25. UNHCR Basic Facts, www.unhcr.org (accessed 8/19/09).

26. Anne-Marie Im Hof-Piguet, *La Filière en France Occupée, 1942–1945* (Yverdon-les-Bains: Édition de la Thule, 1985).

A Note on Sources

Literature on the period 1933 to 1945, which has ballooned into mammoth proportions, includes comprehensive histories, excursions into narrow historical realms, and assorted memoirs. For me, the first two volumes in Richard Evans's trilogy, *The Coming of the Third Reich* (New York: Penguin, 2001) and *The Third Reich in Power, 1933–1939* (New York: Penguin, 2005), were the most useful general history books. The final volume, *The Third Reich at War* (New York: Penguin, 2009), was published after I had completed this book. Evans's books are extremely well written, providing the big picture of all the major events he discusses and vignettes describing the experience of ordinary people, including German citizens, Jews, and soldiers. Also outstanding was the two-volume work by Saul Friedländer that focuses exclusively on the Jewish experience: *Nazi Germany and the Jews: The Years of Persecution, 1933–1939* (New York: HarperCollins, 1997) and *The Years of Extermination: Nazi Germany and the Jews, 1939–1945* (New York: HarperCollins, 2009). Martin Gilbert's *The Second World War: A Complete History* (New York: Holt, 2004), with its chronological rather than thematic focus, was a helpful reference, allowing me to pinpoint just what else was going on at any given moment in my parents' saga.

To understand what life was like for Jews in Germany under the Nazis, by far the most useful social history was Marion Kaplan's *Between Dignity and Despair: Jewish Life in Nazi Germany* (New York: Oxford University Press, 1998). For details on the Jewish experience before the Nazis came to power, I found the collection of essays edited by Kaplan extremely valuable: *Jewish Daily Life in Germany, 1618–1945* (New York: Oxford University Press, 2005). There are numerous memoirs from the Nazi period, but Victor Klemperer's *I Will Bear Witness: A Diary of the Nazi Years,* vols. 1 and 2 (New York: Random House, 1999) is one of the only continuous contemporaneously written accounts. Peter Gay's *My German Question: Growing up in Nazi Berlin* (New Haven: Yale University Press, 1988) provided insight on what it was like for a

Jewish teenager in Berlin as seen through the lens of a historian of modern history.

Life in France has had several chroniclers. Most useful to me were Susan Zuccotti, *The Holocaust, the French, and the Jews* (New York: Basic Books, 1993), and the relevant sections from Deborah Dwork's *Children with a Star: Jewish Youth in Nazi Europe* (New Haven: Yale University Press, 1991).

The role of the Swiss during the war has not been comprehensively addressed except by the Independent Commission of Experts, Switzerland—Second World War. The two reports of the commission, which have been translated into English and are available online (www.uek.ch/en.index/htm), are surprisingly readable: *Switzerland and Refugees in the Nazi Era* (1999) and *Switzerland, National Socialism, and the Second World War* (2002). The sole English language book about the experiences of another child who was at the Château de La Hille is *Inge: A Girl's Journey through Nazi Europe* by Inge Bleier and her nephew David Gumpert (Grand Rapids, Mich.: William Eerdmans, 2004). Although a compelling narrative that overlaps with the story told in *Once They Had a Country,* it is not always a reliable source. A highly readable discussion of post-traumatic stress disorder outside the war arena is Judith Herman's *Trauma and Recovery* (New York: Basic Books, 1992).

A good history of Brazil in the 1930s and 1940s is Robert Levine's *Father of the Poor? Vargas and His Era* (New York: Cambridge University Press, 1998). For a discussion of the Jewish refugee community in Brazil, the work of Jeffrey Lesser is key, particularly, *Welcoming the Undesirables: Brazil and the Jewish Question* (Berkeley: University of California Press, 1994). Stefan Zweig's largely forgotten book *Brazil: Land of the Future* (New York: Viking Press, 1941) provided an important view of Brazil from the perspective of a European Jewish refugee.

For a personal account of the Jewish experience in Shanghai during the war, I drew on Ernest Heppner, *Shanghai Refuge: A Memoir of the World War II Jewish Ghetto* (Lincoln: University of Nebraska Press, 1995). More comprehensive is David Kranzler's *Japanese, Nazis, and Jews: The Jewish Refugee Community of Shanghai, 1938–1945* (New York: Yeshiva University Press, 1976). For more of the Chinese context, I referred to the popular history by Stella Dong, *Shanghai: The Rise and Fall of a Decadent City, 1842–1949* (New York: William Morrow, 2000).

The role of the United States in receiving Jewish immigrants after the war is described in Howard Sachar's *History of the Jews in America* (New York: Knopf, 1992). A scholarly work that seeks to refute the widely held view that it was easy for European Jewish refugees to integrate into American society in the late 1940s is Beth Cohen's *Closed: Holocaust Survivors in Postwar America*

(New Brunswick, N.J.: Rutgers University Press, 2007). As the only study of how those refugees who left Europe as children fared, Gerhard Sonnert and Gerald Holton's *What Happened to the Children Who Fled Nazi Persecution* (New York: Pallgrave and MacMillan, 2006) is a jewel.

To put the refugee experience of my parents in a larger framework, I found Deborah Dwork and Robert Jan Van Pelt's *Flight from the Reich: Refugee Jews, 1933–1946* (New York: Norton, 2009) instructive. A good overview of the plight of refugees throughout the world today is the Office of the United Nations High Commissioner for Refugees, *The State of the World's Refugees: Human Displacement in the New Millennium* (New York: Oxford University Press, 2006).

This work draws heavily on letters sent from my father, Hans Garfunkel, to his cousin Bessie Silverman in Chicago, as well as a smaller number of letters and telegrams from Hans's parents in Berlin to him, his brother, Günther, and others. The majority of these letters are now part of the United States Holocaust Memorial Museum Archive in Washington, D.C., as are letters and postcards sent to my mother, Ilse Wulff Garfunkel, from her parents in Shanghai. Additional letters are part of a private collection. This book also draws heavily on documents pertaining to my parents that are part of the Schweizerisches Bundesarchiv (dossier no. 07748—Ilse Wulff, and dossier no. 07157—Hans Wolfgang Garfunkel). The archive includes petitions written by Hans and Ilse to the Swiss Department of Justice and Police, psychiatric evaluations, and arrest reports, among other wonderfully illuminating materials.

Index